NTC's
Dictionary
of
COMMON
MISTAKES
in
SPANISH

John Pride

Printed on recyclable paper

NTC Publishing Group
Lincolnwood, Illinois USA

1996 Printing

Introduction

The Purpose of the Book

The purpose of *NTC's Dictionary of Common Mistakes in Spanish* is to provide English-speaking learners of Spanish with a reference guide to those words and phrases which can so easily cause difficulties and confusion. It is quick and easy to use, and will enable learners to select the appropriate Spanish terms for the situations they find themselves in.

For ease of use and access, the entries in the book are presented in alphabetical order in English, just like a dictionary. But the words and phrases chosen for inclusion are those that are most likely to cause learners problems in everyday situations. The examples are carefully selected to alert learners to common errors, anglicisms, and false cognates. Personal, social, and business terms are all included so that the basic needs of learners of all kinds are met. Idioms are difficult to contend with in another language, and there is a wide range of idiomatic Spanish included to help learners cope with English concepts which are difficult to translate into another language. There are also some brief notes to draw attention to essential grammar rules. It should be noted that examples involving the word "you" are rendered by the *tú* form in Spanish, except where the phrase would normally be used to a stranger, or is of a very formal nature; in such cases the *usted* form is used.

NTC's Dictionary of Common Mistakes in Spanish can be used for individual study or in the classroom. It will be useful for learners at all levels of proficiency and in particular for those who are planning a trip to a Spanish-speaking country.

Latin American Spanish

Just as there are differences between the English of the USA, Canada, Britain, Australia, and the other English-speaking countries, there are also differences in the Spanish spoken in Spain and the various countries of North, Central, and South America. This has been taken fully into account in this book. The abbreviation *[LA]* following an entry indicates that the word is used throughout most or all of Spanish America, but not in Spain. Terms which are country-specific are likewise indicated.
(See the list of abbreviations on page vi.)

How to Use This Book

For browsing

Pick out the words and phrases you particularly want or need to use. Mark them in some suitable way so that you can find them easily.

You will probably find as you go through the book that you have been using expressions that are not authentically Spanish. You should pay special attention to these. After some entries there is a line or two introduced by the warning symbol Ø. This symbol indicates words that look very similar in both English and Spanish but have quite different meanings. They are the real *amigos falsos* (false friends). As an example, *el suceso* means "happening" and not "success;" "success" is *el éxito* which does not mean "exit."

For practice

As an English speaker, it is much easier for you to read or understand Spanish than to express yourself clearly in that language. There are words you recognize when you see or hear them, but are not part of your working, spoken vocabulary. It is often possible to guess unknown words from the context. However, when you want to speak Spanish, there is no substitute for knowledge; guessing won't do. By using the wrong word or phrase, not only might you be totally misunderstood, but you might even insult the person you are talking to!

A regular study plan will help you make excellent use of this text. Start with the entries you have marked for special attention, or pick a section you particularly want to learn. Repeat the Spanish aloud until you master it. A few days later, return to it, cover the Spanish side and see if you can recall the key phrases. You will find your fluency will improve with practice. The more regular and systematic your practice, the more successful the results.

For quick reference

If you are looking for a common word or expression, turn to this book before going to a standard bilingual dictionary. There is a good chance you will find what you need here. All the entries are presented in context, in both Spanish and English, to help you make the right choice and steer you away from errors. When you need to look up an English word in an English-Spanish dictionary, make sure you check the options available. If you are unsure about your choice, check in the Spanish-English section to make certain you pick the right word. In this way you can avoid major blunders such as: *Compró un tapón para la lámpara.* The word for an "electrical plug" is *un enchufe; tapón* refers to the plug you use in the bathtub or wash basin.

If you consult a Spanish dictionary or alphabetical vocabulary published before 1994, you will find that *ch* and *ll* are listed as separate letters of the alphabet, coming between *c* and *d*, and *l* and *m* respectively. This is now no longer the case.

For choosing the right word

Quite often the same English word may be translated into Spanish in a number of different ways, depending on context. In this book you will find a range of possibilities and clear examples to illustrate the various uses. For example, under the entry for the word *time*, you will find seven subheadings that will guide you to the correct choice. Examples of usage include:

"Have a good time!" *(¡Que lo pases bien!);* "What time is it?" *(¿Qué hora es?);* "from time to time" *(de vez en cuando);* "a long time ago" *(hace mucho tiempo);* "at the time of the Incas" *(en la época de los incas);* "at this time of the year" *(en esta estación del año).*

For identifying the part of speech

When you look up a word it is useful to know what part of speech it is. Be aware of English words that may be two different parts of speech.

Some examples:

help (verb) "to help somebody" *ayudar a alguien*
help (noun) "I need your help." *Necesito tu ayuda.*
half (adjective) "half a dozen eggs" *media docena de huevos*
half (noun) "I paid half of the cost." *Pagué la mitad del coste.*
hard (adjective) "This bread is hard." *Este pan es duro.*
hard (adverb) "She works hard." *Trabaja mucho.*
long (adjective) "It's a long trip." *Es un viaje largo.*
long (verb) "I long to go back to Chicago." *Anhelo volver a Chicago.*

When you look up a verb it is sometimes necessary to know if it is transitive (can take an object) or intransitive (cannot take an object). Examples:

move *(verb trans)* "They moved the piano." *Movieron el piano.*
move *(verb intrans)* "He moved to Lima." *Se trasladó a Lima.*

A note about prepositions

Prepositions are often used very differently in English and Spanish. For example, depending on context, "for" could be translated as *para, por,* or *de.* If you are not sure, pause for a moment to check your choice. Every preposition entry in this dictionary gives a broad selection of phrases illustrating Spanish usage, for example: "at home" *(en casa);* "at two o'clock" *(a las dos);* "at night" *(de noche);* "by hand" *(a mano);* "by airmail" *(por avión).*

Take it everywhere you go!

Take *NTC's Dictionary of Common Mistakes in Spanish* with you wherever you go — to class, the beach, the office. Consult it often to review phrases that you want to remember when speaking or writing. And of course, make sure you have it with you when you visit a Spanish-speaking country. Don't pack it! Keep it in your hand luggage!

Abbreviations

adj	adjective	masc	masculine
adv	adverb	masc pl	masculine plural
art	article	masc sing	masculine singular
conj	conjunction	n	noun
dem	demonstrative	pl	plural
excl	exclamation	prep	preposition
fam	familiar	pron	pronoun
fem	feminine	sing	singular
fem pl	feminine plural	v	verb
fem sing	feminine singular	v intrans	verb intransitive
fig	figurative	v trans	verb transitive
inter	interrogative		

Parts of speech

Please note that the part of speech indicated for each entry is for the English word. The Spanish equivalent will not necessarily be the same part of speech as the English.

Abbreviations used in the examples

sb   somebody
sth   something

Ø   warning symbol

Abbreviations used for the Spanish-speaking countries and areas

Arg	Argentina	Gua	Guatemala
Bol	Bolivia	LA	Latin America
Car	Caribbean	Mex	Mexico
Chi	Chile	Per	Peru
Col	Colombia	Sp	Spain
Ecu	Ecuador	Uru	Uruguay
ES	El Salvador	Ven	Venezuela

A

a *n*
[the letter a]

la a *[Note: all letters take the feminine article]*

a/an *art*
a(n)
a pencil/a house
a housewife/an axe

un *[masculine]* una *[feminine]*
un lápiz/una casa
un ama de casa/un hacha *[Note: **Un** is used in place of **una** before feminine nouns beginning with a stressed **a** or **ha.**]*

rate
The car was traveling at 80 kilometers an hour.
Gas costs one dollar a gallon here.
How much a kilo are the oranges?
It will cost five dollars a meter.
He visits his mother twice a week.
She used to earn 1000 pesos a week.

El carro iba a 80 kilómetros por hora.
Aquí la gasolina cuesta un dólar por galón.
¿Cuánto cuestan por kilo las naranjas?
Costará cinco dólares por metro.
Visita a su madre dos veces a la/por semana.
Ganaba mil pesos por semana.

with nationality, profession, religion
Are you an American?
His wife is Canadian.

She is a lawyer.
She is a brilliant lawyer.

Are they Christians or Jews?
Is he a Catholic or a Protestant?

¿Eres norteamericano(a)?
Su esposa es canadiense. *[Note: no article]*
Es abogada. *[Note: no article]*
Es una abogada brillante. *[Note:use of article when noun is modified.]*
¿Son cristianos o judíos?
¿Es católico o protestante? *[Note:no article]*

omitted
Does he have a car?
They don't have a house.
I'll wait half an hour.

¿Tiene carro?
No tienen casa.
Esperaré media hora.

ability *n*
[skill]
He doesn't have the ability to do it.
[general ability]
My son has a lot of ability.
to the best of one's ability
I did it to the best of my ability.
to have the ability to do sth

la habilidad/la capacidad
No tiene la habilidad de hacerlo.
el talento
Mi hijo tiene mucho talento.
lo mejor que se pueda/sepa
Lo hice lo mejor que pudiera/supiera.
ser capaz de hacer algo

able *adj*
[capable]

capaz

1

She is a very able person.

[skillful]
He's an able worker.
to be able to (do sth)
My uncle is unable to walk; he has broken his leg.

Are you able to speak Russian?

Is he able to do that alone?

about *prep*
relating to
They informed me about the accident.
Can you tell me something about the Incas?
I have a book about Mexican history.
What's that film about?
It's about a shipwreck.
What about your bill?

What's it all about?

verb + about
to ask about

They asked about your father.
We asked about the war.
to hear about
I've heard a lot about your horses.
to talk about
We were talking about music.
to walk about
They walked about the town.

on the point of
I am about to write to him.
We were just about to leave.

approximately *[see around]*

above *adv*
above
the apartment above
above all *[especially]*
see above *[in text]*

above *prep*
above
The bathroom is above the kitchen.
We are 500 meters above sea level.

Tiene mucho talento./Es una persona de mucho talento./Es muy capaz.
hábil
Es un obrero hábil.
poder/saber/ser capaz de
Mi tío no puede caminar; se ha roto la pierna. *[Note: **Poder** is used to denote physical ability.]*
¿Sabes hablar ruso? *[Note: **Saber** is used to denote having the 'know-how' to do something.]*
¿Es capaz de hacer eso solo?

de/acerca de/sobre/con respecto a
Me informaron sobre el accidente.

¿Puedes decirme algo acerca de los incas?
Tengo un libro sobre la historia de México.
¿De qué trata esa película?
Trata de un naufragio.
¿Y tu cuenta?/¿Con respecto a tu cuenta?
¿De qué se trata?/¿Qué pasa?

hacer preguntas sobre/pedir informes sobre
Preguntaron sobre tu padre.
Hicimos preguntas sobre la guerra.
oír hablar de
He oído hablar mucho de tus caballos.
hablar de
Hablábamos de la música.
pasearse por/andar por
Se pasearon por la ciudad.

Estoy a punto de escribirle.
Estábamos para salir.

arriba/encima/por encima
el apartamento de arriba
sobre todo
véase más arriba

encima de/sobre
El cuarto de baño está encima de la cocina.
Estamos a quinientos metros sobre el nivel del mar.

It's above me. *[fig.]* · No lo entiendo.

academic *adj*
the academic year · el año escolar *[school]*/el año académico *[University]*
That's an academic question. · Es una cuestión puramente teórica.

accent *n*
He speaks Spanish with a Mexican accent. · Habla castellano con acento mexicano.
You don't have an accent. · No tienes acento./Hablas sin acento.
a written accent · un acento gráfico

accidentally *adv*
[by chance] · por casualidad
We met by chance at the café. · Nos encontramos por casualidad en el café.
[unintentionally] · sin querer
She broke it accidentally. · Lo rompió sin querer.

account *n*
a bank account · una cuenta bancaria/de banco
[bill/invoice] · una cuenta/factura
[report] · una cuenta/un relato/un informe
to take sth into account · tener algo en cuenta
to be of no account · ser de poca importancia
on account of · por/a causa de/por motivo de
on that account · por eso
on no account · de ninguna manera
Ø **el cuento** means "story."

ache *n & v*
I have a headache. · Tengo dolor de cabeza.
I have a stomachache. · Tengo dolor de estómago.
I have a toothache. · Tengo dolor de muelas.
I ache all over. · Tengo dolores por todas partes.
My head/stomach aches. · Me duele la cabeza/el estómago.
That noise makes my head ache. · Ese ruido me da dolor de cabeza.
[see also hurt]

acknowledge *v*
[to admit, recognize] · admitir/reconocer
I acknowledge you are right. · Admito que tienes razón.
[to greet sb] · saludar a alguien
She acknowledged us in the street · Nos saludó en la calle.
[correspondence] · acusar
I acknowledge receipt of your letter. · Acuso recibo de su carta. *[Note: formal usage hence the usted form of the adjective]*
Ø **acusar** also means "to accuse."

across *prep*
[from one side to another] · a través de/al través de
They went across the bridge. · Fueron a través del puente.
to go across the street · cruzar/atravesar la calle
They ran across the street. · Cruzaron la calle corriendo.

She walked across the square.	Cruzó la plaza a pie.
We drove across the bridge.	Cruzamos el puente en carro.
[on the other side]	al otro lado de/del otro lado de
The park is across the street.	El parque está enfrente.
right across (the street) from her apartment	en el otro lado de la calle/ enfrente de su apartamento
the café across the street	el café del otro lado de la calle

act *n*

[action, deed]	un acto
[in the theater]	un acto
a play in three acts	una comedia en tres actos
[legal act, law]	una acta

actually *adv*

[the fact is]	es que
Actually, she's away.	Es que está fuera.
[really, in fact]	realmente/en realidad/en efecto
Actually they are nurses.	En realidad son enfermeras.
What I actually said was...	Lo que dije concretamente fue...
Did you actually hit him?	¿Lo pegaste realmente?

Ø **actualmente** means "at present."

add *v*

to add *[in general]*	añadir
You must add water.	Debes añadir agua.
Value Added Tax (VAT)	Impuesto de Valor Añadido (IVA)
to add up	sumar
He added up the bill.	Sumó la cuenta.
It doesn't add up to much.	Es poca cosa.

addict *n*/ addicted *adj*

an addict (fanatic)	un(a) partidario(a)/un(a) entusiasta
a tennis addict	un(a) entusiasta del tenis
a drug addict	un(a) toxicómano(a)
to be addicted to drugs	ser toxicómano(a)
to be addicted to gambling	ser aficionado(a) al juego

addition *n*

in addition	además
In addition, they're strangers.	Además, son forasteros.
In addition to the apartment he has a house in the country	Además del apartamento tiene una casa en el campo.

Ø **en adición** is not Spanish.

additional *adj*

They need additional workers.	Necesitan más obreros.
an additional *[extra]* week	una semana suplementaria
an additional charge	un suplemento

admire *v*

to admire	admirar

Ø **admirar** more often means "to amaze."

admission n

Free admission	Entrada gratis
No admission	Se prohíbe la entrada.
There's a charge for admission.	Hay que pagar la entrada.
[to a school/a club]	el ingreso
[acknowledgment]	una confesión
It's an admission of guilt.	Es una confesión de culpabilidad.

admit v

to own up to	reconocer, confesar
to admit a mistake	confesar un error
I must admit that I'm guilty.	Debo confesar que soy culpable.
He admitted the robbery.	Se confesó culpable del robo.

to let in

to let in	dejar entrar
Let them in!	¡Déjalos entrar!
to be admitted to a university/ a club	ingresar(se) en una universidad/ una sociedad

advantage n

advantage [general & in tennis]	una ventaja
to take advantage of sb	abusar de alguien
to take advantage of the conditions to ...	aprovecharse de las condiciones para...

advertise v

to advertise a product	anunciar/dar publicidad a un producto
to advertise in the paper	poner un anuncio en el periódico
to advertise for	buscar por medio de anuncios

Ø **advertir** means "to advise," "to inform."

advertisement n

an advertisement	un anuncio
classified ads	los anuncios
a TV ad [a commercial]	una emisión publicitaria

Ø **una advertencia** means "a warning."

advice n

advice	el consejo
a piece of advice	un consejo
to ask sb for advice	pedir consejos a alguien
to take sb's advice	seguir los consejos de alguien
to take legal/medical advice	consultar a un abogado/médico
[report, information]	un informe/una noticia/un aviso

Ø **aviso** means "warning," "announcement."

advise v

to advise sb to do sth	aconsejar a uno hacer algo
[to inform]	avisar/informar
to advise/warn	advertir
Keep me advised!	¡Tenme al corriente/al tanto!

affair n

a love affair	una aventura amorosa
one's affairs	sus asuntos personales

affluent

I explained the Nicaragua affair to them.	Les expliqué lo de Nicaragua.

affluent adj
We live in an affluent society.
an affluent family

Ø **un afluente** means "a tributary."

Vivimos en una sociedad opulenta.
una familia acaudalada

afford v
[money]
I can't afford it/that.

She can afford to buy it.
We can't afford a new car.

I can't afford to go.
Can you afford to wait?
You cannot afford to miss this chance.

tener bastante dinero/con que
No tengo bastante dinero.
No puedo permitírmelo.
Tiene bastante dinero para comprarlo.
No tenemos con que comprar un carro nuevo.
No me puedo permitir el lujo de ir.
¿Puedes esperar?
No puedes desperdiciar esta oportunidad.

afraid adj
to be afraid of
to be afraid of sb
He is afraid of his father.
to be afraid of sth
My daughter is afraid of lightning.
Don't be afraid!

tener miedo a alguien
Tiene miedo a su padre.
tener miedo de algo
Mi hija tiene miedo de los relámpagos.
¡No tengas miedo!/¡No temas!

to be afraid to
to be afraid to do sth
She is afraid to go in.
to be afraid that ...
I'm afraid (that) you'll get hurt.
I'm afraid of getting hurt.

temer/tener miedo de
Teme entrar./Tiene miedo de entrar.
temer que [+ subjunctive]
Temo que vayas a hacerte daño.
Temo hacerme daño. [Note: The infinitive is used if both verbs have the same subject.]

to regret
I'm afraid the manager is out.
I'm afraid I cannot go.

Lo siento, pero el gerente no está.
Lo siento, no puedo ir.

after adv
after(wards)
Afterwards they went home.
I'll do it afterwards.
soon after

después/más tarde
Después volvieron a casa.
Lo haré más tarde.
poco después

after prep & conj
after

I saw her after the game.
I read the paper after my wife had gone to bed.
They arrived at the station after the train had left.

después de [prep]/después de que [conj]
La vi después del partido.
Leí el diario después de que mi esposa se había acostado.
Llegaron a la estación después de que había salido el tren/después de la salida del tren. [Note: The noun form is preferred.]

6

I'll do it after he's paid me.	Lo haré después de que me haya pagado. [Note: **Después de que** takes the present subjunctive when future time is involved.]
She loaned me the magazine after reading it/she had read it.	Me prestó la revista después de leerla. [Note: The infinitive is used when the subject of both verbs is the same.]

afternoon n
Good afternoon
[see also **evening**]

Buenas tardes

again adv

once more	una vez más/otra vez/de nuevo
Do it again.	Hazlo una vez más.
I've lost my gloves again.	He perdido mis guantes otra vez.
He's absent again.	Está ausente de nuevo.
in a negative	no... más
He won't do it again.	No lo hará más.
never again	nunca más
verb + again	
to do sth again	volver a hacer algo
to go out again	volver a salir
to go up/down again	volver a subir/bajar
She went in again.	Volvió a entrar.

agenda n

[things to do]	el programa
[for a meeting]	el orden del día

Ø **la agenda** means "appointment book" or "diary."

aggravated adj
to be aggravated at sb/sth   estar irritado(a) con alguien/por algo

Ø **agravar** means "to make worse;" **agraviar** "to wrong."

ago adv

a long time ago	hace mucho tiempo
a short time ago	hace poco tiempo
many years ago	hace muchos años
a few minutes ago	hace unos minutos
He was born two days ago.	Nació hace dos días.
How long ago did she die?	¿Hace cuánto tiempo murió?

agree v

to be in agreement	estar de acuerdo/estar conforme
Do you agree?	¿Estás de acuerdo?/¿De acuerdo?/ ¿Conforme?
No, I don't agree (with you).	No, no estoy de acuerdo (contigo).
I agree with the others.	Estoy de acuerdo con los otros.
He doesn't agree.	No está de acuerdo.
to come to an agreement	ponerse de acuerdo/convenirse
They have agreed on the price.	Se han puesto de acuerdo sobre el precio.

ahead

Did he agree on the details?	¿Se convino en los detalles?
to consent	consentir en/quedar en
He agreed to sell the house.	Consintió en vender la casa.
Did they agree to come with us?	¿Quedaron en acompañarnos?
in grammar	
In Spanish, the adjective agrees with the noun.	En castellano, el adjetivo concuerda con el sustantivo.
of food	
Garlic doesn't agree with me.	El ajo no me sienta bien.

ahead adv

Go ahead!	¡Adelante!
Go straight ahead!	¡Va todo seguido(a)/derecho(a)!
to get ahead of sb	adelantarse a alguien
to get ahead	adelantar/progresar
to be ahead [sport]	ir ganando/llevar ventaja
The USA are ahead by 2-1.	Los Estados Unidos van ganando por 2 a 1.

all adj

	todo/toda/todos/todas
He does it all the time.	Lo hace todo el tiempo.
All the people attended.	Toda la gente asistió.
She read all (of) the books.	Leyó todos los libros. [Note: "Of" is not translated.]
I've seen all (of) the films.	He visto todas las películas.

all pron

	todo/toda/todos/todas
That's all.	Es todo.
They are all awake.	Todos están despiertos.
All of you must take part.	Todos deben participar. [Note: "Of" is not translated.]
We must all help.	Todos debemos ayudar.
Repeat all together.	Repitan todos juntos.
all (that)	todo lo que
All that he brought is on the table.	Todo lo que trajo está en la mesa.
Do all (that) you can.	Haz todo lo que puedas. [Note: Subjunctive used after **todo lo que** when what is referred to is indefinite.]

all right [see okay]

allow v

to permit	permitir/dejar a alguien hacer algo
to allow sb to do sth	No puedo permitirte entrar.
I cannot allow you to go in.	¡Permite que te ayude! [Note: The subjunctive is used.]
Allow me!	
Parking is not allowed.	Prohibido aparcar./Se prohíbe aparcar.
Bicycles not allowed.	Bicicletas prohibidas.
Is smoking allowed here?	¿Se puede fumar por aquí?

to allocate

I must allow an hour to reach the airport.	Debo dejar una hora para llegar al aeropuerto.

How much shall I allow per person?

almost adv
Lunch is almost ready.
She almost died/fell.

alone adj
[on one's own]
Are you alone?
[the only one]
I'm not alone in thinking so.
We stand alone.

along prep
along
along the river
The road runs along the river.
all along the beach/the street
Let's walk along the beach.

also adv
He also went to the concert.
I bought shirts and also shoes.

in addition
Also, I have a meeting.

although conj
although
She went out, although it was
  snowing.
I'll buy it although it
  will cost me a lot of money.

alumni/alumnae n
[graduates of a school]

A.M.
It's/At five A.M.

amaze v
to amaze
Their enthusiasm amazed me.

to be amazed at sth

I was amazed at her wealth.

America n
[general]

¿Cuánto dejo por persona?

La comida está casi preparada.
Por poco se muere/se cae.

solo(a)
¿Estás solo(a)?
el único/la única
No soy el único/la única en pensarlo.
Somos únicos(as).

por/a lo largo de
a lo largo del río
La carretera sigue el río/va a lo largo del río.
todo lo largo de la playa/la calle
Vamos por la playa.

Él también fue al concierto.
Compré camisas y zapatos también.

además
Además, tengo una reunión.

aunque
Salió aunque estaba nevando.

Lo compraré aunque me cueste
  mucho.
[Note: **Aunque** is followed by the
subjunctive when the English meaning
is "even if" or "even though," or when
the statement is contrary to
fact.]

los graduados/las graduadas

Son las/A las cinco de la mañana.

admirar/asombrar
Su entusiasmo me asombró./Me
  admiró su entusiasmo.
estar/quedarse asombrado(a) de/con
  algo/admirarse de algo
Me quedé asombrado(a) de/con su
  riqueza/Me admiré de su riqueza.

América

9

America *[USA]*

(los) Estados Unidos (de América)

American *n & adj*
[general]
American *[from the USA]*

americano(a)
norteamericano(a), estadounidense
[Note: Latin Americans are sensitive to the use of "America" and "American" to refer just to the USA.]

and *conj*
and
bread and butter
you and I
father and son
Teresa and Isabel

y/e
pan y mantequilla
tú y yo
padre e hijo
Teresa e Isabel *[Note:The e form is used before a word beginning with i or hi except where the next letter is a vowel, e.g., nieve y hielo "snow and ice."]*

angry *adj*
to be angry
to be angry about sth
I am angry about the decision.
to be angry at/with sb/sth

They are angry with you.
to get angry

Don't get angry!

estar enojado(a)/enfadado(a)
estar enojado(a)/enfadado(a) por algo
Estoy enojado(a) por la decisión.
estar enojado(a)/enfadado(a) con alguien/algo
Están enfadados contigo.
enojarse *[LA]*/enfadarse/ponerse furioso(a)
¡No te enojes!/¡No te enfades!/No te pongas furioso(a)/enojado(a)/ enfadado(a)

announcer *n*
radio/TV announcer

el locutor/la locutora
el anunciador/la anunciadora *[Mex]*

another *adj*
additional
I would like another cup of coffee.
We need another two players.
without another word

otro(a)/más
Quisiera otra taza de café.
Necesitamos dos jugadores más.
sin decir palabra

different
They want another car; they
    don't like this one.

otro(a)/distinto(a)
Quieren otro carro; no les gusta
    éste.

[Note otro and otra are never used with un and una.]

another (one) *pron*
additional
She's lost her map; she needs
    another (one).

otro(a)/uno(a) más
Ha perdido su mapa; necesita otro.

different
I don't like this film. I'm
    going to watch another one.

otro(a)
No me gusta esta película. Voy a
    mirar otra.

answer *v*
to answer sb
to answer a letter

contestar/responder a alguien
contestar/responder a una carta

to answer to the description	corresponder a la descripción
to answer a charge	defenderse a una acusación
to answer for sth	responder de algo
You will answer for his behavior.	Responderás de su conducta.
to answer for sb	responder por alguien
I'll answer for my grandson.	Responderé por mi nieto.
to answer s.o. back	replicarle a alguien
Don't answer me back!	¡No me repliques!/¡No seas respondón(ona)!

antique n

[an object]	una antigüedad
[a piece of furniture]	un mueble de época
an antique shop	un anticuario/una tienda de antigüedades
[old relic]	una antigualla
Their TV set is an antique.	Su televisor es una antigualla.
an antique dealer	un anticuario/un comerciante en antigüedades

Ø **una antigüedad** also means "antiquity."
Ø **antiguo(a)** means "ancient," "old."

anxious adj
worried

Is he anxious about the exam?	inquieto(a)/preocupado(a)
	¿Se inquieta por el examen?

eager

anxious to help	deseoso(a)
They're anxious to see you.	deseoso(a) de ayudar
	Tienen ganas de verte.

any adj
whatever, whichever

You can take any train.	cualquier
Any taxi driver will take you.	Puedes tomar cualquier tren.
Buy any hat you like.	Te llevará cualquier taxista.
	Compra cualquier sombrero que te guste. [Note: subjunctive after **cualquier** when the reference is to any object or person, no matter who or what.]

in a question

Is there any fruit?	¿Hay fruta?
Are there any cookies?	¿Hay galletas? [Note: Spanish rarely uses a word for "any" in such questions.]

after a negative

He doesn't have any money.	ningún/ninguna
	No tiene dinero. [Note: "Any" is often not translated in such sentences.]
I don't have any brothers.	No tengo ningún hermano. [Note: singular]
	No tengo hermanos.

any pron
any (one) at all

What brand of coffee do you want? - Any one will do.	cualquiera
	¿Qué marca de café quieres? - Me bastará cualquiera.
You can have any one you like.	Puedes tener cualquiera que te guste. [Note: subjunctive after

anybody/anyone

cualquiera when the reference is to any object no matter which one.]

any (some)

alguno(a)/algunos(as)
ninguno(a)/ninguno(s)

Do you want ice-cream? - No, I
don't want any.

¿Quieres helado? - No, no quiero
ninguno. *[Note: the **ninguno** forms
are used after the negative **no**.]*

We have no more stamps. Do
you have any?

No nos quedan estampillas. ¿Tienes
algunas?

anybody/anyone *pron*
anyone you like
Anybody will tell you.
Anybody else would have helped.
Tell anyone you meet.

cualquiera
Cualquiera te lo dirá.
Cualquier otro hubiera ayudado.
Díselo a cualquiera con quien
encuentres. *[Note: subjunctive after
cualquiera when the reference is to any
person, no matter who.]*

in the negative
I didn't speak to anybody.
Don't tell anybody!

nadie
No hablé con nadie.
¡No se lo digas a nadie!

in a question
Is there anyone there?
Did you see anyone?
Do you know anybody who speaks
Portuguese?

alguien
¿Hay alguien?
¿Viste a alguien?
¿Conoces a alguien que hable
portugués? *[Note: subjunctive
after **alguien** when the reference is to any
person, no matter who.]*

anyhow/anyway *adv*
at any rate

de todos modos/de todas formas/con
todo

[in spite of everything]
They are coming anyway.
It was raining but I played
golf anyway.
[haphazardly]
He keeps his accounts anyway.

sin embargo/a pesar de todo
Vienen a pesar de todo.
Estaba lloviendo, sin embargo jugué
al golf.
de cualquier modo
Lleva las cuentas de cualquier
modo.

anyone *[see anybody]*

anything *pron*
anything you like
You can buy anything.
They give her anything she
wants.

cualquier cosa/todo lo que
Puedes comprar cualquier cosa.
Le dan todo lo que quiera. *[Note:
subjunctive after **todo lo que** when
the reference is something indefinite or
non-specific.]*

something
She is going to buy something
for her children.
I have something to do.

algo/alguna cosa
Va a comprar algo para sus hijos.

Tengo algo que hacer.

in the negative

nada

12

We couldn't find anything.
Marta hasn't anything to read.

No encontramos nada.
Marta no tiene nada que leer.

in a question
Did they find anything?
Anything else? *[in a store, restaurant, etc.]*

algo
¿Encontraron algo?
¿Algo más?

any time *adv*
[whenever]
You can phone me any time.

cuandoquiera/en cualquier momento
Puedes llamarme cuando quieras/
en cualquier momento.

anyway *[see anyhow]*
anywhere *adv*
wherever

We can go anywhere.
You can buy them anywhere.

a cualquier parte/en cualquier
parte/dondequiera/en todas partes
Podemos ir a cualquier parte.
Puedes comprarlos dondequiera.

in a question
Did you go anywhere?
Did you see them anywhere?

a/en alguna parte
¿Fuiste a alguna parte?
¿Los viste en alguna parte?

in a negative
They didn't go anywhere.
I couldn't find it anywhere.

a/en ninguna parte
No fueron a ninguna parte.
No lo encontré en ninguna parte.

apartment *n*

el apartamento/el departamento
[Mex, Chi], el piso *[Sp]*

apologize *v*
to apologize for
They apologized for the noise.

disculparse de/pedir perdón por
Se disculparon del ruido./Pidieron
perdón por el ruido.

I apologize for not writing sooner.
to apologize to sb

Me disculpo de no haber escrito antes.
disculparse con alguien/pedir
perdón a alguien

I apologized to the clients.

Me disculpé con los clientes./Pedí
perdón a los clientes.

[for absence]
He apologized for his absence.

presentar sus excusas
Presentó sus excusas.

apology *n*
an apology
to make an apology

una disculpa/una excusa
disculparse/presentar sus excusas

Ø **la apología** means "apologia."

apparent *adj*
apparent

evidente

Ø **aparente** means "suitable."

appear *v*
to seem, look
She appeared tired.
It appears that...

parecer
Pareció cansada.
Resulta/Parece que...

to come into view

aparecer/presentarse

13

appearance

He appeared in the distance.	Apareció a lo lejos.
She appeared on the balcony.	Se presentó en el balcón.

Ø **aparear** means "to pair, match, mate."

appearance *n*

[looks]	la apariencia/el aspecto
to have a/be of good appearance	tener buen aspecto
His appearance amazed me.	Su aspecto me admiró.
[act of appearing]	la aparición
The appearance of the horses startled her.	La aparición de los caballos la sobresaltó.
to make an appearance	aparecer/presentarse/dejarse ver
to make a personal appearance	aparecer en persona
to keep up appearances	guardar/salvar las apariencias

appetizers *n*

[snacks served before a meal with drinks	los aperitivos/las botanas *[Mex]/* los bocadillos *[Per]/*los pasapalos *[Ven]/*las bocas*[ES]/* las tapas *[Sp]*
[first course of a meal]	los entremeses

application *n*

[most senses]	la aplicación
for external application (use) only *[medical]*	solamente para uso externo
a job application	una solicitud para un puesto
to make an application for	solicitar
I'm going to put in an application.	Voy a presentarme.
to fill out an application	rellenar un formulario de solicitud.

apply *v*

to apply for a job	solicitar un puesto/presentarse a un puesto
to apply for a passport	solicitar un pasaporte
to apply to a university	presentarse a una universidad
to apply to sb for sth	dirigirse a alguien para algo
He applied to the secretary for the details.	Se dirigió al secretario para los detalles.
[to concern]	tener que ver con/ser aplicable a/ referirse a
This does not apply to me.	Esto no tiene nada que ver conmigo.

appoint *v*

to appoint *[to a position/an office]*	nombrar
She was appointed president.	La nombraron a ella presidenta.
I appointed him to the position.	Lo nombré a él para el puesto.
at the appointed time	a la hora fijada/señalada

Ø **apuntar** means "to write down," "to make notes," and also "to aim/point at."

appointment *n*

[date, engagement]	una cita/un compromiso
We made an appointment.	Nos dimos una cita.
to make an appointment with sb	citarse con alguien
Do you have an appointment?	¿Tiene usted hora?
I have an appointment with the doctor at five.	El médico me dio hora para las cinco.

by appointment (only)   sólo por hora citada
[position, job]   un puesto/un empleo

Ø **el apunte** means "note" (taken in class).

appreciate v
to be grateful for   agradecer
I appreciate your help.   Te agradezco tu ayuda.

in a business letter
We would appreciate a prompt   Les estaríamos muy agradecidos
  reply.   por una respuesta inmediata.

to like sth   entender/saber apreciar
She doesn't appreciate poetry.   No entiende de poesía./
     No sabe apreciar la poesía.

to understand   comprender
We appreciate your problems.   Comprendemos tus problemas.

Ø **apreciar** also means "to esteem, estimate."

ardor n
ardor   el fervor/el entusiasmo/la pasión
to cool sb's ardor   enfriar la pasión de alguien

Ø **ardor** means "heat" or "burning sensation," e.g., **un ardor de estómago** "a burning sensation in the stomach."

area n
[surface extent]   la superficie (en metros cuadrados)
It has an area of 50 square   Tiene una superficie de 80
  miles.   kilómetros cuadrados.
[of a country]   una región
[of a town]   un barrio
[place, spot]   el área [masc]
a depressed/prohibited area   una zona deprimida/prohibida
postal area   el distrito postal
area of expertise   el campo
[see also field]

argument n
debate   una discusión/una disputa
to have an argument with sb   tener una discusión con alguien
I had a heated argument with   Tuve una discusión acalorada con
  the boss.   el jefe.
We had an argument.   Nos disputamos.

reason   el argumento
an argument for/against sth   un argumento en pro de/en contra de
     algo

Ø **el argumento** also means "plot" (of book/film).

arm n
[part of body]   un brazo
[sleeve]   una manga
[of record player]   un brazo
weapon   un arma [fem]
arms race   la carrera de armamentos
arms [heraldry]   las armas

armored

coat of arms	un escudo de armas

armored *adj*
armored	blindado(a)
an armored car	un vehículo blindado

around *adv & prep*
approximately

I have around a hundred books.	Tengo más o menos cien libros.
Around 10,000 people attended.	Asisitieron unas diez mil personas.
around fifty	unos cincuenta

time
a eso de
They came back around five.	Volvieron a eso de las cinco.

position
[movement within a place] — por
to walk around the garden	pasearse por el jardín
to walk around the house	andar por la casa

[surrounding] — alrededor de
the gardens around the hotel	los jardines alrededor del hotel
There were gardens all around the palace.	Había jardines alrededor del palacio.

[alongside] — al lado de
They were sitting around the swimming pool.	Estaban sentados al lado de la alberca.

[everywhere] — por todas partes
There were people all around.	Había gente por todas partes.

[around the corner] — a la vuelta de la esquina
It's around the corner.	Está a la vuelta de la esquina.

other expressions
to go around the world	dar la vuelta al mundo
Is Manuel around?	¿Está Manuel?
Are they are around?	¿Están por aquí?
When she's around her friends ...	Cuando está con sus amigas...

arrangements *n*
He made all the arrangements.	Lo arregló todo./Lo preparó todo./ Hizo todos los preparativos.
to make one's own arrangements	obrar por cuenta propia

musical arrangement — una adaptación

arrest *n & v*
They arrested him at home.	Lo detuvieron en casa.
They were arrested by the police.	Fueron detenidos(as) por la policía.
to be under arrest	estar detenido(a)
You're under arrest.	Queda usted detenido(a).

art *n*
art	el arte *[Note: masculine in the singular]*
fine arts	las bellas artes *[Note: feminine in the plural]*
an art museum	un museo de bellas artes
an art school	una escuela de arte
a work of art	una obra de arte

academic subjects
Faculty of Arts
a Bachelor of Arts

arts and crafts

as *conj & prep*
in comparisons
as ... as
as big as
as quickly as
as soon as
as long as *[see long]*
as much as *[see much]*
as many as *[see many]*
as if/as though
She looked as if she were ill.

time
She left as they were arriving.

because, since
As I don't speak Greek I can't
  read the sign.

manner
As often happens in New York.

As I was saying ...

concerning
As for me, I don't like it.

in the capacity of
As a lawyer, I do not agree.
He is working as a teacher.

disguised as/dressed as
I was dressed as a cowboy.

ask *v*
to ask for sth

to ask sb for sth
They asked him for money.
to ask sb to do sth

I asked her to open the door.
to ask a question

asleep *[see sleep]*

assist *v*
to assist sb
Can I assist you?

las Letras
la Facultad de Filosofía y Letras
un(a) Licenciado(a) en Filosofía y
  Letras
artes y oficios

tan... como
tan grande como
tan rápidamente como
lo más pronto posible

como si *[+ subjunctive]*
Parecía como si estuviera enferma.

como
Salió como llegaban.

como/ya que
Ya que no hablo griego no sé leer
  el letrero.

como/según
Como ocurre a menudo en Nueva
  York.
Como/Según decía yo...

en cuanto a/por lo que se refiere a
En cuanto a mí, no me gusta.

como
Como abogado, no estoy de acuerdo.
Trabaja como profesor. *[Note: no
  article]*

disfrazado(a)/de/vestido(a) de
Iba vestido de vaquero. *[Note: no
  article]*

pedir algo *[Note: "For" is not
  translated.]*
pedir algo a alguien
Le pidieron dinero.
pedir/rogar a alguien que haga algo
  [Note: subjunctive]
Le pedí/rogué que abriera la puerta.
preguntar/hacer una pregunta

ayudar a alguien
¿Puedo ayudarte?

Ø **asistir a** means "to be present at" or "to attend."

17

assume υ

to assume responsibility	asumir la responsabilidad/hacerse responsable
to assume [suppose]	suponer
I assume she's going.	Supongo que vaya. [Note: subjunctive]

at prep
position

at the office	en la oficina
at school	en el colegio [Note: use of article]
at the hairdresser's	en la peluquería
at the theater	en el teatro
at home	en casa
at Carmen's (house)	en casa de Carmen
at his uncle's (house)	en casa de su tío
at my/your house	en mi/tu casa
	en casa mía/tuya
at sea	en el mar
to be (sitting) at the table	estar sentado(a) a la mesa
to be (standing) at the door/window	estar en la puerta/ventana
to be at peace/at war	estar en paz/en guerra

time

at two o'clock	a las dos
at noon/midnight	a mediodía/a medianoche
at that time	en ese momento/en esa época
at the moment	en este momento
at times	de vez en cuando
two at a time	de dos en dos
at night	de noche/por la noche

with verbs

to be at work/at home	estar en el trabajo/en casa
to be angry at sb	estar enojado(a) con alguien
to be astonished at sb/sth	asombrarse de alguien/algo
to be good at (history)	ser hábil/fuerte en (la historia)
to be surprised at sb/sth	sorprenderse de alguien/algo
to laugh at sb/sth	reírse de alguien/algo
to look at sb/sth	mirar a alguien/mirar algo
He looked at the doctor.	Miró al médico.
We looked at the photos.	Miramos las fotos.
to rush at sb/sth	arremeter contra alguien/algo
to stare at sb/sth	mirar fijamente a alguien/mirar fijamente algo

attend υ
to be present at, go to regularly

	asistir
I attended the concert.	Asistí al concierto.
We have to attend a meeting.	Tenemos que asistir a una reunión.
She attends a history class on Thursdays.	Asiste a una clase de historia los jueves.
to attend a school/university/ church	ir a un colegio/una universidad/ una iglesia

to attend to

	atender
I must attend to the customer.	Tengo que atender al cliente.

attentive *adj*
[heedful]   atento(a)
[polite]   cortés(esa)/obsequioso(a)

attractive *adj*
[in general]   atractivo(a)
[interesting]   atrayente/interesante/sugestivo(a)
an interesting offer   una oferta interesante
[person]   atractivo(a)/mono(a)/guapo(a)
His sister is very attractive.   Su hermana es muy atractiva/mona/
                                           guapa.
What an attractive guy!   ¡Qué chico bien parecido/guapo!

audience *n*
[gathering]   el público
There was a large audience.   Hubo mucho público.
[in a theater]   el público/el auditorio
[at a sports event]   los espectadores
[on the radio]   los radioyentes
[on television]   los telespectadores

Ø **la audiencia** means "the audience" one has with a Head of State or the Pope.

available *adj*
people
I am not available tomorrow.   No estoy libre/Tengo compromiso mañana.
Is the senator available?   ¿Está libre el senador?

goods
Are these boots available in   ¿Estas botas existen en otros
  other colors/sizes?   colores/otras tallas?
That model is no longer available.   Ese modelo ya no está disponible.
Coffee was not available in   No se podía conseguir café en el
  the village.   pueblecito.
The swimming pool is available   La alberca está a la disposición de
  to everyone.   todos.

average *adj & n*
average   medio(a)
the average price   el precio medio
The thief is of average height.   El ladrón es de regular estatura/de
                                           estatura mediana.
on the average   por término medio
the average [numerical]   el promedio
The average age of the players   El promedio de edad de los
  is ...   jugadores es...
[typical]   típico
the average Mexican   el mexicano típico

avocado *n*
avocado   el aguacate/la palta [Arg, Chi, Uru]

away *adv*
They're away.   No están./Están fuera./Están ausentes.
She's away for a month.   Pasa un mes fuera.
The stadium is five kilometers   El estadio está a cinco
  away.   kilómetros (de aquí).

19

away

Our house is ten miles away from the border.	Nuestra casa está a diez millas de la frontera/dista diez millas de la frontera.
far away	lejos
The mountains are far away.	Las montañas están lejos.
to go away	irse/marcharse
Go away!	¡Vete!/¡Váyase/¡Váyanse!
to go away from	alejarse de
to get away [to leave]	salir/irse/marcharse
to get away [to escape]	escaparse

B

baby n & adj
[human]   un bebé/un nene/una nena
[animal]   una cría
[adjective]   infantil

bachelor n
[unmarried man]   un soltero
[university graduate]   un(a) licenciado(a)
to have a bachelor's degree   ser licenciado(a) en letras/
  in arts/law/science   derecho/ciencias

Ø **un bachiller** would be somebody holding a high school diploma.

back n
[part of human body]   la(s) espalda(s)
back to back   espalda con espalda
back to front   al revés
with one's back to   de espaldas a
She was sitting with her back   Estaba sentada de espaldas a la
  to the door.   puerta.
He turned his back on my son.   Volvió las espaldas a mi hijo.
[of an animal]   el lomo
[of a chair]   el respaldo
[of a check]   el dorso
[of a house]   la parte de atrás
The back is a ruin.   La parte de atrás es una ruina.
The garage is in back of the house.   El garaje está detrás de la casa.
I was in the back of the hall.   Estaba en el fondo de la sala.
back-up   el apoyo

back adj
back   trasero(a)/de atrás
the back seat [of a car]   el asiento de atrás/el asiento trasero
the back tires   las llantas de atrás
Sit in the back row!   ¡Siéntate en la última fila!
back tooth   una muela

back adv
verb + back
to answer back   replicar
to be back   estar de vuelta
to come back/go back (home)   volver/regresar (a casa)
to fly back   volver en avión
to get back (home)   regresar/volver a casa
to get sth back   recuperar/recobrar algo
to give back   devolver
to pay back   reembolsar
to phone back   volver a telefonear
to run back   volver corriendo
to walk back   volver a pie

21

background

background *n*

in the background	en el fondo
background music/noise	la música/el ruido de fondo
[training, experience]	la formación (profesional)
What is his background?	¿Cuál es su formación?/¿Qué formación tiene?

[social class]	el origen/los antecedentes
They are of Cuban background.	Son de origen cubano.
She comes from a working-class /middle-class background.	Sus antecedentes son de la clase obrera/de la clase media.
[information]	los antecedentes/la información previa
Do you have the background to the problem?	¿Tienes los antecedentes del problema?

bad *adj*

The weather is bad.	Hace mal tiempo. *[Note: **Malo** shortens to **mal** before masculine singular noun.]*
[wicked]	malo(a)
a bad man	un hombre malo
a bad accident/mistake	un accidente/error grave
a bad cold	un resfriado fuerte
He's bad at Spanish.	Es malo en castellano.
[sick]	malo(a)/enfermo(a)
I feel bad *[sick]*.	Me siento mal.
I feel bad about it.	Lo siento/lamento.
*[see also **feel**]*	
to be bad tempered	estar de mal humor
It's going from bad to worse.	Va de mal en peor.

badly *adv*

to dress badly	vestirse mal
badly written	mal escrito(a)
badly injured	gravemente herido(a)
I need/want it badly.	Lo necesito/deseo muchísimo.

bag *n*

[purse/handbag]	una cartera *[LA]*/una bolsa *[LA]*/un bolso
paper bag	una bolsa de papel
shopping bag	una bolsa de la compra
[sack]	un saco

Ø **La Bolsa** *[note the capital]* means "stock exchange;" **el bolsillo** means "pocket."

bake *v*

[bread/cake, etc.]	cocer al horno/hornear
She bakes her own bread/cakes.	Hornea su propio pan/sus propios pasteles.
[meat/fish]	asar
baked chicken	pollo asado
baked potatoes	papas al horno *[LA]*/patatas al horno *[Sp]*
baked beans	judías en salsa de tomate

balance n

[state]	el equilibrio
to lose one's balance	perder el equilibrio
[scales]	una balanza
[commerce]	el balance
a balance sheet	un balance
[statement of an account]	el balance/el estado de cuentas
[remainder]	el resto/el saldo
the balance of payments	el balance de pagos

balance v

to balance	mantener el equilibrio
to balance the budget	nivelar el presupuesto
to balance the books	hacer balance/cerrar los libros

Ø **balancearse** means "to swing."

ball n

[small, e.g., golf, tennis]	una pelota
[large, e.g., football]	un balón/una bola *[LA]*
snowball	una bola de nieve
[globe, sphere]	un globo/una esfera
[a dance]	un baile (de etiqueta)
to have a ball *[enjoy oneself]*	pasarlo en grande
ball game	un partido de béisbol
It's a whole new ball game.	Todo ha cambiado.

band n

[music]	una orquesta/banda
dance/jazz band	una orquesta de baile/de jazz
brass band	una banda/una charanga
military band	una banda/música militar
town band	una banda/música municipal
[a combo]	un conjunto/un grupo (de jazz)
[gang of people]	una gavilla/una pandilla/una cuadrilla
[strip of material]	una banda

bath n

bath *[bathtub]*	un baño/una bañera/una bañadera *[LA]*/una tina *[Mex]*
to have/take a bath	bañarse/tomar un baño

bathroom n

bathroom	un cuarto de baño
*[see also **toilet**]*	

battery n

[dry for radios, etc.]	una pila
I need a battery for my clock.	Necesito una pila para mi reloj.
[wet for cars, etc.]	una batería
The battery is dead.	La batería está descargada.

Ø **la batería** also means "a set of drums," "a hit/stroke" (in baseball) and, in Colombia, "a round of drinks."

be v

ser/estar

Ser is used to denote permanent
characteristics such as identity,
nationality:

They are Peruvians.	Son peruanos.
She is a very intelligent girl.	Es una chica muy inteligente.
It's a very beautiful house.	Es una casa muy hermosa.
I'm an engineer.	Soy ingeniero.
These shirts are (made of) silk.	Estas camisas son de seda.
My friends are from New York.	Mis amigos son de Nueva York.

Ser is also used with a past
participle to form the passive voice:

He was run over by a car. Fue atropellado por un carro.

Estar indicates position(permanent
and temporary),temporary states,
and with a past participle a state
resulting from an action:

My parents are in Chile.	Mis padres están en Chile.
Bogotá is in Colombia.	Bogotá está en Colombia.
Where is the police station?	¿Dónde está la comisaría?
Her husband is not very well.	Su esposo no está muy bien.
Their grandmother is ill.	Su abuela está enferma.
The doors were open.	Las puertas estaban abiertas.
He's sitting in the garden.	Está sentado en el jardín.

Estar is also used with a gerund
to form the continuous present
tense:

It's raining. Está lloviendo.

Ø You can say **Soy casado(a)** or **Estoy casado(a)** for "I am married."

because conj & prep
introducing clause porque
because he's ill porque está enfermo

because of + noun a causa de/debido a
because of the snow a causa de la nieve

become v

to become	llegar a ser
He became very famous.	Llegó a ser muy famoso.
[by one's own efforts]	hacerse
She became an accountant.	Se hizo contable.
[by promotion]	llegar a ser
I became a colonel.	Llegué a ser coronel.
[of emotions]	ponerse
They became violent.	Se pusieron violentos.
She's becoming pale.	Se pone pálida.
He became mad.	Se volvió loco.
[to be changed/transformed]	transformarse
The palace has become a hotel.	El palacio se ha transformado en hotel.

to become of ser de
What has become of his son? ¿Qué es de su hijo?
What will become of them? ¿Qué será de ellos?

bed *n*
[for sleeping in]   una cama
to go to bed   acostarse
to put a child to bed   acostar a un niño
[of river]   un cauce/un lecho

bedroom *n*   la recámara *[LA]*/el dormitorio/la
                                               alcoba/la habitación/ el cuarto de dormir

before *adv*
[time]   antes
a moment before   un momento antes
I saw him the day/night before.   Lo vi el día/la noche anterior.
the week/year before   la semana/el año anterior
Have you seen that film before?   ¿Has visto esa película alguna vez?
No, I've never seen it before.   No, no la he visto nunca.
Have you been to Mexico before?   ¿Has estado en México alguna vez?

before *conj*
before   antes de *[+ infinitive]*
                                               antes de que *[+ subjunctive]*
I'll do it before I go home.   Lo haré antes de volver a casa.
Do it before the boss gets back.   Hazlo antes de que vuelva el jefe.
                                               [Note: **Antes de** is used when the subject
                                               of both verbs is the same; **antes de
                                               que** is followed by the subjunctive
                                               when the subject of the verbs is
                                               different.]

before *prep*
time   antes de
before Christmas   antes de la Navidad
before midday   antes del mediodía

in front of
[place]   delante de
He was standing before the   Estaba delante del altar.
  altar.
[in the face of]   ante
before the enemy   ante el enemigo

begin *v*
to begin   comenzar/empezar
to begin to do sth   comenzar a/empezar a hacer algo
We began to sing.   Comenzamos a/Empezamos a cantar.
I began painting.   Comencé a/Empecé a pintar.
to begin by doing sth   comenzar/empezar + present
                                               participle
She began by saying that ...   Comenzó/Empezó diciendo que...
To begin with, I would like to say ...   Para empezar quisiera decir...

behind *adv & prep*
[adverb]   detrás/por detrás/atrás
[preposition]   detrás de
[see **back**]

believe v
[to think]
I believe he's sick.
I believe so./I don't believe so
[to have faith in]
Do you believe in God?
I don't believe in ghosts.

creer
Creo que está enfermo.
Creo que sí./Creo que no.
creer en
¿Crees en Dios?
No creo en los fantasmas.

belong v
possession
Who does this belong to?

It belongs to me/José.
Does this bag belong to you?
The house belongs to my uncle.

ser (de)/pertenecer
¿De quién es esto?/¿A quién pertenece
  esto?
Es mío/de José.
¿Este saco es tuyo?
La casa pertenece a mi tío.

membership
I belong to the Rotary Club.
We belong to the Liberal party.

Soy socio de la Sociedad Rotaria.
Somos miembros del partido Liberal.

below adv
below
Who lives in the apartment
  below?
See below. [in a text]

abajo/(por) debajo
¿Quién vive en el apartamento de
  abajo?
Véase más abajo.

below prep
[under]
The damage is below the
  waterline.
below average
The temperature was below
  normal.

bajo/debajo de
El daño está debajo de la línea de
  flotación.
por debajo de la media
La temperatura estaba inferior a la
  normal.

beside prep
[next to]
There was a table beside the bed.

al lado de/junto a
Había una mesita al lado de la cama.

besides adv & prep
[additionally/in addition to]
Besides, the train was late.
Besides his money he lost his
  credit cards.
[with a negative]
Nobody was hurt besides the
  driver.

además/además de
Además, el tren llegó con retraso.
Además de su dinero, perdió sus
  tarjetas de crédito.
excepto/fuera de
No fue herido nadie excepto el
  conductor.

best n
the best thing
to do one's best
[see also better/best]

lo mejor [invariable]
hacerlo lo mejor posible

bet v
to bet on a horse
I bet you 50 dollars I'll win.
You bet!

apostar a un caballo
Te apuesto 50 dólares a que gano.
¡Ya lo creo!

better/best *adj*

better	mejor/mejores
best	el/la mejor
	los/las mejores
the better camera	la mejor cámara (de las dos)
the best camera	la mejor cámara (de todas)
	[Note: **La mejor cámara** *can mean "the better camera" or "the best camera."]*
These are the better/best ones.	Éstas son las mejores.
Buy the best camera in the shop.	Compra la mejor cámara de la *tienda.* *[Note: After a superlative* **de** *is used to translate "in."]*

better/best *adv*

better	mejor
best	(lo) mejor
He speaks Spanish better than I.	Habla castellano mejor que yo.
His wife speaks Spanish the best.	Su mujer es la que habla mejor castellano.
much better than	mucho mejor que
better and better	cada vez mejor
It would be better not to say anything.	Más valdría no decir nada.
You had better/best wait for her.	Más vale que la esperes. *[Note: subjunctive after* **más vale que.**]*
The best thing you can do is to leave.	Lo mejor que puedas hacer es irte. *[Note: subjunctive after* **lo mejor.**]*

big *adj*

big	grande
My father is a big man.	Mi padre es un hombre grande.
They lived in a big house.	Vivían en una casa grande.
my big brother	mi hermano mayor
to get big	crecer

Ø **grande** can also mean "great;" in such cases it precedes the noun it describes and also shortens to **gran**: e.g., **El Presidente es un gran hombre.** "The President is a great man."

bill *n*

[invoice]	una factura
electricity bill	una factura/una cuenta de la electricidad
[restaurant, hotel, shops]	una cuenta
[banknote]	un billete
a thousand peso bill	un billete de cien pesos
bill *[on billboard]*	un cartel
Post no bills!	¡Prohibido fijar carteles!

billboard *n*

billboard	la cartelera

billion *n*

one billion	mil millones
1,000,000,000	1.000.000.000 *[Note Spanish punctuation]*

Ø **un billón** is US trillion.

birthday *n*
a birthday   un cumpleaños
birthday party   una fiesta de cumpleaños
[see also saint's day]

blame *v*
to blame   culpar/echar la culpa
to blame sb for sth   echar la culpa a alguien de algo
They blamed me for the mistake.   Me culparon del error.
to be to blame for sth   tener la culpa de algo
I am not to blame.   No tengo la culpa.
He is to blame for the row.   Tiene la culpa de la bronca.
Who is to blame?   ¿Quién tiene la culpa?
I'm not to blame; you are.   La culpa no es mía; es tuya.
And I don't blame them!   ¡Y los comprendo perfectamente!

blanket *n*
blanket   la cobija *[LA]*/la frazada
    [Arg, Chi, Uru]/la manta *[Sp]*

block *n*
[of stone]   un bloque
[of buildings]   una cuadra/una manzana *[Mex & Sp]*
It's two blocks away.   Queda a dos cuadras de aquí.

Ø **la manzana** also means "apple."

boil *v*
[liquid]   hervir
The water is boiling.   El agua está hirviendo.
[to cook]   cocer
to boil an egg   pasar un huevo por agua
boiled potatoes   papas *[LA]*/patatas cocidas al agua

bored *adj*
to be bored   estar aburrido(a)
to get bored   aburrirse
I'm bored with all this.   Estoy harto(a) de todo esto.
I was bored to death.   Me aburrí como una ostra.
You look bored.   Pareces aburrido(a).

boring *adj*
boring   aburrido(a)/pesado(a)
It was a very boring film   Fue una película muy aburrida.

Ø Note that **aburrido** means "bored" and "boring."

born *v*
to be born   nacer
Where were you born?   ¿Dónde naciste?
I was born in Quito.   Nací en Quito.

borrow *v*
to borrow sth from sb   pedir prestado algo a alguien
I borrowed a thousand dollars   Pedí prestado mil dólares a mi
   from my father.   padre.
May I borrow your pen?   ¿Me prestas tu pluma?

boss n
[general]   el jefe
[owner]   el amo/el patrón; el ama [fem]/la
     patrona
[manager]   el gerente

both adj
both   ambos(as)/los dos/las dos
He broke both legs.   Se rompió ambas piernas.
from both sides   por ambos lados
I had to fill out both forms.   Tuve que rellenar los dos formularios.

both pron
both   los dos/las dos/ambos(as)
Both of us are going to the game.   Los dos vamos al partido.
I intend to buy both of them.   Pienso comprar los dos.
They both arrived late.   Llegaron tarde las dos.

both ... and conj
I like both tea and coffee.   Me gusta tanto el té como el café.
Both my cousin and his wife are   Tanto mi primo y su esposa
   going to the meeting.   van a la reunión.
She likes both swimming and riding.   Le gusta tanto nadar como
     montar.

bother v
to bother sb   molestar a alguien
I'm sorry to bother you.   Siento molestarte.
[to be a nuisance]   fastidiar
The noise of the traffic   El ruido del tráfico nos fastidia
   bothers us every day.   todos los días.
[worry]   preocuparse
Don't bother about that.   No te preocupes por eso.

bottom n
at the bottom of [box, cup,   en el fondo de
   garden, river, sea]
at the bottom of the sea   en el fondo del mar
at the bottom of [hill, page,   al pie de
   stairs]
at the bottom of the stairs   al pie de la escalera

boyfriend n
her boyfriend   su novio
[a man friend]   un amigo

brain n
[mind, intelligence]   el cerebro
[anatomy]   el seso
brains [cooked]   los sesos
brain dead   clínicamente muerto(a)

break n
a break [rest]   un descanso
to take a break   descansar
the class break   el recreo

[interruption]	una interrupción
without a break	sin descansar/interrupción

break away υ
[to withdraw]	separarse
[to escape]	escaparse

break down υ/**breakdown** n
to break down [machinery]	descomponerse [LA]/estropearse
to break down [vehicles]	descomponerse [LA]/quedarse parado/ averiarse
They have had a breakdown.	Se han quedado parados.
a breakdown	una pana [LA]/una descompostura [Mex]/una avería [Sp]

emotions
to break down [person]	perder el control
to break down [in tears]	romper a llorar
to have a nervous breakdown	sufrir un colapso nervioso

break off υ
to break off an engagement	romper un compromiso
to break off a branch	cortar una rama
[to interrupt]	interrumpirse
They've broken off the talks.	Se interrumpieron las conferencias.

bright adj
I like bright colors.	Me gustan los colores vivos.
a bright light	una luz clara
bright sunshine	un sol brillante
[clever, intelligent]	listo(a)/inteligente
His son is not very bright.	Su hijo no es muy listo/inteligente.
[cheerful]	alegre/animado(a)/optimista
It's a very bright room.	Es una habitación bien iluminada.

bring υ
to bring	traer
Bring the children.	Trae a los niños.
I'll bring the glasses.	Traigo los vasos.

brown adj
brown	marrón/castaño(a)/pardo(a)/café (color café)
My hair is brown./I have brown hair.	Tengo pelo castaño.
He always wore brown shoes.	Siempre llevaba zapatos marrones.
Do you like brown bread?	¿Te gusta el pan moreno?
[from the sun]	moreno(a)

brush n
hairbrush	un cepillo para el pelo
toothbrush	un cepillo de dientes
paintbrush	una brocha
artist's brush	un pincel

building *n*

a building	un edificio
[property]	un inmueble
[the process of building]	la construcción
building land	tierra *[fem]* para construcción
a building lot/plot/site	un solar
the building trade	la industria de la construcción

bulb *n*

[light bulb]	un foco *[Mex]*/una bombilla/una ampolleta *[Chi]*
[flower bulb]	un bulbo

bus *n*

a (city) bus	un autobús/un camión *[Mex]*/un colectivo *[Arg]*/un guagua *[Cub]*/un micro *[Chi & Per]*
a tour bus/coach	un autocar

business *n*

in general

	el comercio/los negocios *[Note: plural]*
a business man/woman	un hombre/una mujer de negocios
a business meeting	una reunión/sesión de negocios
a business trip	un viaje de negocios
to be on business	estar de negocios
to go away on business	irse de negocios
to do business with sb	comerciar con alguien
Business is good.	Los negocios marchan bien.

affair, matter

Mind your own business!	¡No es asunto tuyo!
	el asunto/la cuestión

a company

un comercio/una empresa/una casa

academic subject

business administration	la administración de empresas
business college/school	una escuela de comercio
business studies	estudios de la empresa/estudios empresariales

busy *adj*

general

	ocupado(a)
Are you busy?	¿Estás ocupado(a)?
I'm busy tonight.	No estoy libre esta noche.
	Tengo mucho que hacer esta noche.
She was busy with her studies.	Estaba ocupada en sus estudios.
They were busy reading.	Estaban ocupados leyendo/en leer.

telephone

The line is busy.	La línea está ocupada. *[LA]*/Están comunicando. *[Sp]*

places

	concurrido(a)
The street was very busy.	La calle estaba muy concurrida.

but *conj*

but	pero
[after a negative]	sino
He isn't in Colombia but in Ecuador.	No está en Colombia sino en Ecuador.

by

by *prep*

general, by means of

I paid by check.	Pagué por cheque.
Is this made by hand or by machine?	¿Está hecho a mano o a máquina?
I know her by name/sight.	La conozco de nombre/de vista.
to do sth all by oneself	hacer algo solo/hacer algo por sí

attributed to

de

He bought a painting by Goya.	Compró un cuadro de Goya.
Have you read any novels by Gabriel García Márquez?	¿Has leído unas novelas de Gabriel García Márquez?

manner

[means of transportation]
by bicycle/boat/bus/car/ motorcycle/plane/train

en
en bicicleta/barco/autobús/carro/ moto(cicleta)/avión/tren

[to send mail, goods]
We sent the goods by air/rail.

por
Enviamos los géneros por avión/ ferrocarril.

measurement

por

The box measures two feet long by six inches wide.

La caja mide dos pies de largo por seis pulgadas de ancho.

place

[near to]
He lives by the beach.

cerca de
Vive cerca de la playa.

[alongside]
by the sea/the lake/the river
to go/pass by
They went by the theater.
to come by *[to call, visit]*
Come by tonight.
Will you come by and pick me up?

a orillas
a orillas del mar/del lago/del río
pasar por delante
Pasaron por delante del teatro.
pasar (por casa)
Pasa por casa esta noche.
¿Quieres pasar a recogerme?

rate

por

It is sold by the kilogram/ liter/meter.
to pay by the hour/day/week

Se vende por kilo/litro/metro.

pagar por hora/día/semana

time

by day/by night
I like traveling by night.
You must finish it by this evening.
I must be in Madrid by the fifth of April.

de día/de noche
Me gusta viajar de noche.
Debes terminarlo para esta tarde.
Tengo que estar en Madrid antes del cinco de abril.

verb + by + gerund

He succeeded by working hard.

Tuvo éxito trabajando mucho.

past participle + by + noun
descriptive state [with estar]

to be covered by
to be surprised by
to be surrounded by
The house was surrounded by trees.

estar cubierto(a) de
estar sorprendido(a) de
estar rodeado(a) de
La casa estaba rodeada de árboles.

passive [with ser]

The house was surrounded by the police.
He was accompanied by his wife.

La casa fue rodeada por los policías.
Fue acompañado por su esposa.

C

cabin *n*

a (log) cabin   una cabaña (de madera)

Ø **la cabina** means "an aircraft cabin" or "cabin of a truck;" **una cabina telefónica/ de teléfono** is "a telephone booth."

call *v*

[to shout]	gritar
[to name]	llamar
[to telephone]	telefonear/llamar por teléfono
Who's calling? *[on telephone]*	¿De parte de quién?/¿Quién llama?

call *n*

telephone call	una llamada
long distance call	una llamada de larga distancia

camera *n*

a still camera	una máquina (fotográfica)
a movie/TV camera	una cámara

can *v*

[to be physically able to]	poder
He can't play tennis today. He has broken his arm.	No puede jugar al tenis hoy. Se ha roto el brazo.
Can I *[may I]* help?	¿Puedo ayudarte?
[to know how to]	saber
Can you swim?	¿Sabes nadar?
I can't play chess.	No sé jugar al ajedrez.
[see also **could**]	

can *n*

a can of tomatoes	un bote/una lata de jitomates
a can of beer	una lata de cerveza
a garbage can	un cubo para basuras/de la basura

cancel *v*

to cancel	cancelar/anular
to cancel a check	anular un cheque
I cancelled the meeting.	Anulé la reunión.

Ø **cancelar** is often used in Latin America to mean "to pay" (of bills, etc.).

car *n*

[an automobile]	un carro *[most of LA]*/un coche *[Sp, Arg & Uru]*/un automóvil

Ø **un autocar** is a "tour bus".

care *n & v*

to take care of, to look after *[people]*	cuidar de/atender
Their grandfather takes care of them.	Su abuelo cuida de ellos(as).

careful

Dr. Sosa is taking care of her.	El doctor Sosa la atiende/asiste.
Take care of yourself!	¡Cuídate bien!
I can take care of myself.	Sé cuidar a mí mismo(a).
[in store] Are you being taken care of?	¿Le atienden a usted?

[things]
guardar/tener cuidado de/ encargarse de

You must take care of your passport.
Debes guardar tu pasaporte.

She takes good care of her clothes.
Tiene gran cuidado de su ropa.

He'll take care of the arrangements.
Se encargará de los preparativos.

to be concerned about
querer/preocuparse de/tener interés en

He cares for her very much.
La quiere mucho.

They really care about peace.
Se preocupan mucho de la paz.

I don't care.
Me es igual./No me importa.

I couldn't care less.
Eso me trae sin cuidado./Me importa un pepino./Me importa todo un rábano.

Who cares?
¿A quién le importa?/¿Qué más da?/ ¿Quién se preocupa (por eso)?

to like, want something
querer/gustar

Would you care for a drink?
¿Te gustaría tomar algo?

Would you care to go to the movies?
¿Quieres ir al cine?

She doesn't care for garlic.
No le gusta el ajo.

to be careful
tener cuidado

Take care!
¡Atención!/¡Cuidado!/¡Ojo!

Take care not to lose it!
¡Ten cuidado, no lo pierdas!/ ¡Guárdate de no perderlo!

Handle with care.
Manéjese con cuidado.

in care of (c/o) *[on letter]*
en casa de

Mr. X care of Mrs. Y
El Sr. X en casa de la Sra. Y

anxiety, worry
un cuidado/una inquietud

I haven't a care in the world.
No tengo ninguna preocupación en la vida.

carefree
to be carefree
estar despreocupado(a)/libre de preocupaciones

careful *adj*
cautious
cuidadoso(a)/cauteloso(a)/prudente

a careful driver
un(a) conductor(a) prudente

Be careful what you say!
¡Ten cuidado con lo que dices!

painstaking
cuidadoso(a)/esmerado(a)/competente

a careful worker
un obrero cuidadoso/esmerado

carpet *n*
a carpet
una alfombra

Ø **una carpeta** is "a file" *[in which letters, etc. are kept]*.

cartoon *n*
[animated film]
los dibujos animados

[humorous drawing as in newspaper]
un dibujo cómico/un chiste/una caricatura

[comic strip]
una tira humorística/cómica

34

[comic book/paper] un libro de historietas *[Mex & Par]*/ una revista de historietas *[Arg]*/una comiquita *[Ven]*/un tebeo *[Sp]*
[art] un cartón

case *n*
[container] una caja
[suitcase] una valija *[LA]*/un veliz *[Mex]*/ una maleta *[Sp]*

[instance] un caso/un asunto
in this case en este caso
This is a strange case. Esto es un asunto raro.
[medical] un caso
in case of en caso de
in case they come por si vienen/en caso de que vengan
  *[Note: the subjunctive after **en caso de que**]*

just in case por si acaso
in any case en todo caso/por todas formas

cash *n*
[money] el dinero/la plata *[LA]*
[notes & coins] el dinero contante/el efectivo
I don't have any cash on me. No tengo dinero conmigo.
cash price el precio al contado
to pay cash pagar al contado/en efectivo
*[see also **money**]*

cash *v*
to cash a check cobrar un cheque
to cash a traveler's check cambiar un cheque de viajero

casserole *n*
[the container] la cacerola
[the food] la cazuela

Ø **la cacerola** is also the general word for "saucepan."

casual *adj*/**casually** *adv*
[fortuitous] fortuito(a)/casual/accidentado(a)
a casual meeting un encuentro fortuito/casual
[clothing] informal/de sport/corriente
to dress casually vestirse de sport
casual clothes la ropa de sport/el traje de calle
[off hand] despreocupado(a)
[of work] temporero(a)/eventual
a casual worker un jornalero/un temporero
casual earnings los ingresos ocasionales
*[see also **informal**]*

catch *v*
[in general] agarrar *[In Spain only: **coger**]*
to catch a ball agarrar/parar/atrapar una pelota
[animals] atrapar/entrampar un animal
I caught a salmon yesterday. Capturé/tomé un salmón ayer.
[transportation] tomar

I'll catch the train/bus.	Voy a tomar el tren/el autobús.
[a disease]	contagiarse de/contraer
She caught the flu.	Se contagió de/Contrajo la gripe.
I've caught a cold.	Me he resfriado/Me he acatarrado.
[to perceive]	comprender/oír
I didn't catch what he said.	No oí lo que dijo.

Ø The verb **coger**, which can cover almost all senses of "to catch," is in widespread use in Spain and in many Latin American countries, but should be avoided in Argentina, Paraguay, Uruguay, and parts of Mexico and Venezuela.

cave *n*

[natural]	la cueva
[man made]	la caverna

Ø **la cava** is the word used for Spanish sparkling wines made by the champagne method.

challenge *n*

a challenge	un reto/un desafío
[of job or opportunity]	un estímulo/un incentivo

chance *n*

fate, luck

	la casualidad/la suerte
by (sheer) chance	por (pura) casualidad

risk

	un riesgo
to take a chance	arriesgarse

possibility, probability

	la posibilidad/la probabilidad
The chances are that they will win the game.	Lo más probable es que ganen el partido. *[Note: subjunctive]*
I have a good chance of getting them.	Tengo buenas probabilidades de conseguirlos.
He hasn't got a chance.	No tiene posibilidad alguna.

opportunity

	la oportunidad/la ocasión
We have the chance of going to Peru.	Tenemos la ocasión de ir al Perú.
Give her a chance!	¡Dale la oportunidad!

Ø **chance** (m/f) may be encountered in Latin America meaning "chance/opportunity" *[an anglicism]* or "luck" *[a gallicism]*.

change *n*

[alteration/modification]	una modificación
[foreign exchange]	el cambio
[small change]	la moneda suelta/el suelto
[money returned]	el vuelto *[LA]*/la vuelta *[Sp]*
Keep the change!	¡Quédese con el vuelto/la vuelta! *[Note: **usted** form]*

change *v*

to change	cambiar
You haven't changed a bit!	¡No has cambiado en lo más mínimo!
[to exchange for]	cambiar por
You will have to change dollars for pesos.	Tendrás que cambiar dólares por pesos.
[clothes, mind, trains, etc.]	cambiarse de
to change one's clothes	cambiarse de ropa

I had to change my shoes.	Tuve que cambiarme de zapatos.
She's changed her mind.	Ha cambiado de opinión.
We change trains in Madrid.	Cambiamos de tren en Madrid.
[to change into]	transformarse en
It changed into a butterfly.	Se transformó en mariposa.

character n

[nature of sth/sb]	el carácter/el índole
[moral quality]	el carácter
a person of good character	una persona de buena reputación
He's a bad character.	Tiene mala fama/reputación.
[in film, story]	un personaje
[individual]	un tipo
He's an odd character.	Es un tipo raro.

charge n
responsibility

to be in charge of	estar encargado(a) de
the person in charge	el/la encargado(a)/la persona responsable
Who's in charge here?	¿Quién manda aquí?
to take charge of sth	encargarse de/hacerse cargo de

cost

admission charge	el precio de entrada
free of charge/no charge	gratis
There's no admission charge.	La entrada es gratis/gratuita.
an extra charge	un suplemento

charge v

How much do you charge?	¿Cuánto cobran ustedes?
The lawyer charged me $1000 for the advice.	El abogado me pidió/cobró mil dólares por el consejo.
You have charged me 1000 pesos too much.	Me has cobrado mil pesos de más.
to charge with a credit card	pagar con tarjeta de crédito
Charge it to my account.	Cárguemelo en mi cuenta.
Cash or charge?	¿Al contado o a crédito?

cheap adj

[inexpensive]	barato(a)
This tie was cheap.	Esta corbata fue barata.
[of travel tickets]	ecónomico(a)
He bought a cheap ticket to Mérida.	Sacó un boleto económico para Mérida.
cheaper [less expensive]	más barato(a)/menos caro(a)
It's just cheap junk.	No son más que baratijas.
a cheapskate	un(a) tacaño(a)

cheat v

to cheat at cards/in an exam	hacer trampas
to cheat sb	estafar/timar/defraudar a alguien
She cheated her brother out of the money.	Estafó el dinero a su hermano.
[be unfaithful]	engañar a/burlar de alguien
He cheated on his wife.	Engañó a su esposa.

check n

a bank check	un cheque

check

a traveler's check	un cheque de viajero
[in a restaurant]	una cuenta
[invoice]	una factura
Check! [in chess]	¡Jaque!
Check! [OK!]	¡Vale!

check v
to make sure

	chequear [LA]/comprobar/verificar
to check [information]	verificar
to check the date/the quality	verificar la fecha/la calidad
to check the accounts	chequear/verificar las cuentas
to check off [list]	marcar
to check a box [on a form]	marcar en un recuadro
[to count]	contar
to check on sb	investigar a alguien

traveling

to check passports/tickets [e.g., at an airport]	controlar los pasaportes/los boletos
to check in [flights/hotel]	registrarse
to check (in) [luggage]	facturar/chequear [LA] el equipaje
to check out	pagar la cuenta y marcharse
What time do you check out?	¿A qué hora te marchas?
to check one's coat	depositar/dejar el abrigo en el guardarropa

checker n

[in supermarket]	un(a) cajero(a)
[in cloakroom]	un(a) encargado(a) de guardarropa
checkers [game]	las damas

check-out n

| [at supermarket] | la caja |

checkup n

| [medical] | un reconocimiento general |
| I need a checkup. | Necesito un reconocimiento general. |

cigar/cigarette n

| cigar | un puro |
| cigarette | un cigarro/cigarrillo |

claim v

to claim	pretender
They claim to have done it.	Pretenden haberlo hecho.
She claims to be poor.	Pretende ser pobre.

Ø "to pretend" is translated by **fingir** or **imaginarse**.

class n
education

[a group of students]	una clase
the class of '85	la promoción de 1985
a classmate [in school]	un(a) compañero(a) de clase
to be classmates [in university]	estudiar juntos(as)
a former classmate	un(a) antiguo(a) compañero(a) de clase
a classroom	un aula [fem]/una clase/un salón de clases

[a course]	un curso
to take a class in Spanish	hacer un curso de lengua española
social class	la clase
the working/middle/upper class	la clase obrera/media/alta
class struggle/war	la lucha de clases

clerk [see worker]

climb v

to climb the stairs	subir (por) la escalera
I cannot climb those steps.	No puedo subir esos peldaños/esas gradas.
to climb a hill [a slope]	subir una cuesta/una colina
to climb a mountain	subir a/escalar una montaña
to climb a fence/tree/wall	trepar a una valla/un árbol/una tapia
to climb over a wall	franquear una tapia
to climb down	bajar por

close adj

[of relationships]	íntimo(a)
a close friend	un(a) amigo(a) íntimo(a)
a close family	una familia unida
The brothers are very close.	Los hermanos son muy unidos.
Juan and Pepe are very close (friends)	Juan y Pepe son muy amigos..
[of contests, etc.]	reñido(a)
a close election	una elección reñida

close prep & adv

He works close to the harbor.	Trabaja cerca del puerto.
The stadium is close by.	El estadio está muy cerca.
We're getting close to the airport.	Nos acercamos al aeropuerto.

closet n

[a cupboard]	un armario/un closet [Mex]
[for clothes]	un ropero

coat n

coat	un abrigo
coat of paint	una mano de pintura

coffee n

black coffee	un café negro [LA]/solo [Sp]
coffee with a little milk	un café cortado
coffee with milk	un café con leche
espresso coffee	un café exprés
coffee-colored	de color café
coffee pot	una cafetera

cold adj

It's (very) cold. [weather]	Hace (mucho) frío
I'm (very) cold.	Tengo (mucho) frío.
Your hands are cold.	Tienes las manos frías.
The water is (very) cold.	El agua está (muy) fría.

cold n

[temperature]	el frío
I can't stand the cold.	No puedo soportar el frío.

collect

[infection]	un resfriado/un constipado/un catarro
to have a cold	estar resfriado(a)/constipado(a)/
	acatarrado(a)
to catch a cold	acatarrarse/resfriarse

collect *v*
[as a collector]	coleccionar
I used to collect stamps.	Coleccionaba estampillas.
[to pick up sth]	recoger
They collected firewood.	Recogieron leña.
[to pick up/fetch sth]	ir a buscar algo/ir por
He went to collect the mail.	Fue a buscar/Fue por el correo.
to call collect *[telephone]*	llamar a cobro revertido
a collect call	una llamada a cobro revertido

college *n*
a college	una universidad
to go to/be in college	ir a/estar en la universidad

Ø **un colegio** can be an elementary or high school.

color *n*
What color is it?	¿De qué color es?
It's a blue/red color.	Es de color azul/rojo.
color film/photography/TV	una película/una fotografía/un
	televisor en colores

come *v*
to come	venir
(I'm) coming!	¡Voy!
Come on!	¡Vamos!
[to happen]	pasar
Come what may.	Pase lo que pase.

come + adverb
to come back (home)	regresar a casa/volver a casa
to come by *[house]*	pasar por casa
to come by *[obtain]*	conseguir/adquirir
to come down/up	bajar/subir
to come in/out	entrar/salir
to come up *[to happen]*	ocurrir/pasar/suceder
I'm sorry I'm late. Something came up.	Siento llegar tarde. Algo sucedió.

comfortable *adj*
of furniture
a comfortable bed	cómodo(a)
a comfortable armchair	una cama cómoda
	un sillón cómodo

of people
to be/feel comfortable	encontrarse a su gusto
to make oneself comfortable	acomodarse a su gusto
Make yourself comfortable!	¡Acomódate a tu gusto!/¡Ponte
	cómodo(a)!

of income
to be comfortably off	adecuado
	tener unos ingresos adecuados/una
	renta adecuada

40

commencement *n*
[beginning, start] — el comienzo/el principio
[graduation ceremony] — la ceremonia de entrega de diplomas

commute *n & v*
to commute — viajar diariamente/a diario al trabajo
to commute from the suburbs to downtown. — viajar desde las afueras hasta el centro.
the daily commute — el viaje diario
commute time — la duración del viaje diario
We have a half hour commute. — Tardamos media hora en hacer el viaje al trabajo.

Ø **conmutar** means "to commute a sentence" or "to commute a payment."

commuter *n*
commuter — un viajero(a) diario(a)/una persona que viaja diariamente al trabajo

There is no real equivalent in Spanish for "commuter."

company *n*
a business — un comercio/una empresa/una casa/una firma/una sociedad

people
[guests] — invitados
to have company — tener invitados/visita
I'm expecting company tonight. — Espero invitados/visita esta noche.
[military, theater] — una compañía
[ship's] — una tripulación
He's good company. — Es un compañero divertido.
to part company — separarse de

competition *n*
[contest] — un concurso
an international chess competition. — un concurso internacional de ajedrez
[in business] — la competencia
unfair competition — la competencia desleal

complain *v*
in general
to complain (about) — quejarse (de)
I can't complain! — ¡Yo no me quejo!
She's always complaining about something. — Siempre se queja de algo.

to make a formal complaint — formular/presentar una queja / formular una reclamación
You should complain to the police. — Deberías presentar una reclamación a la policía.
I complained to the manager about the noise. — Presenté una queja del ruido al gerente.

of health — presentar síntomas de/sufrir de
He's complaining about his throat. — Sufre de la garganta.

concentrate *v*
to concentrate (on) — concentrarse en/concentrar la atención en

41

concern

You must concentrate on your work	Debes concentrarte en tu trabajo.
to concentrate on doing sth	concentrarse para hacer algo
She's concentrating on solving the problem.	Se concentra para resolver el problema.
I can't concentrate.	No sé concentrarme.
He has trouble concentrating.	Lo encuentra difícil concentrarse.

concern υ
[to affect] — tener que ver con/interesar
That doesn't concern you. — Eso no tiene nada que ver contigo.
as far as I'm concerned — en cuanto a mí/por lo que a mí se refiere
[to be worried about] — inquietarse por/preocuparse de
We're concerned about him. — Nos trae preocupados(as).
to concern oneself with — interesarse por/ocuparse de

condominium n
a condominium — una copropiedad
a condominium apartment — un condominio *[LA]*/un apartamento en copropiedad

conductor n
orchestra conductor — un director de orquesta
a train conductor — un revisor
lightning conductor — un pararrayos

Ø **un conductor** means "a driver."

conference n
[assembly, meeting] — un congreso
a national conference — un congreso nacional
a conference center — un palacio de congresos

Ø **una conferencia** means "a lecture."

confidence n
[general] — la confianza
to have confidence in sb/sth — tener confianza en alguien/algo
I have every confidence in my colleagues. — Tengo entera confianza en mis colegas.

Ø **una confidencia** means "a personal secret/revelation."

confident adj
self-confident — seguro(a) de sí mismo(a)/lleno de confianza
She was very confident. — Estaba muy segura de sí misma.
They look very confident. — Parecen llenos(as) de confianza.

certain
to be confident of sth — estar seguro(a) de algo
I am confident you will win. — Estoy seguro(a) de que ganarás.

Ø **un confidente** means "a confidant" or "an informer."

conflict n
[clash, dispute] — un conflicto
a conflict of evidence — una contradicción de testimonios
a conflict of interests — una incompatabilidad
conflicting engagement — un compromiso
I have a conflict. — Ya tengo compromiso.

confuse v

[to mix up]
You are confusing Paraguay and Uruguay.
to confuse the issue

confundir (con)
Confundes el Paraguay con el Uruguay.
complicar la cuestión

confused adj

to be confused *[situation]*
to be confused *[person]*
He looks confused.
to get confused
I'm confused *[don't understand]*.

estar confuso(a)/desconcertante
estar perplejo(a)
Parece perplejo.
desorientarse
No lo comprendo bien.

confusing adj

It's confusing.
It's all very confusing.

Está confuso./No queda claro.
Todo ello es muy difícil de comprender.

connect v

[on phone]

poner a alguien (en comunicación) con

connection n

geographical
The connections between the town and the coast are bad.

la comunicación
Las comunicaciones entre el pueblo y la costa son malas.

relation
There's no connection between his company and mine.
I used to have good business connections with Ecuador.

la relación
No hay ningunia relación entre su firma y la mía.
Tenía buenas relaciones de negocios con Ecuador.

transit
There is a connection in Lima for Cuzco.
[connecting line in the metro]

la correspondencia/el enlace
Hay correspondencia en Lima para Cuzco.
la correspondencia

Ø **una conexión** means "an electrical or mechanical connection."

conservative adj

conservative
the conservative party

conservador(a)
el partido conservador

Ø **conservativo** usually means "preservative."

considerate adj

considerate
to be considerate towards sb
They were very considerate towards me.
That's very considerate of you.

considerado(a)/atento(a)
ser atento(a) con
Fueron muy atentos conmigo.

Es muy amable de tu parte.

consist v

to consist of
What does the collection consist of?
The meal consisted of five courses.

consistir en/constar de
¿En qué consiste la colección?
La comida constó de cinco platos.

contact v

to contact sb

ponerse en contacto con/comunicar con

I'll contact her tomorrow.	Me pondré en contacto con ella mañana.

contents n
the contents of the bag/bottle/safe	el contenido de la bolsa/de la botella/de la caja fuerte
[of book]	el índice de materias

controversial adj
controversial	controvertible/discutido(a)/discutible
a controversial speech	un discurso controvertible

convenient adj
practical
	práctico(a)
This system is not very convenient.	Este sistema no es muy práctico.

suitable
	conveniente/apropiado
It would be a convenient place for the factory.	Sería un sitio apropiado para la fábrica.
Friday is convenient for me.	El viernes me conviene.
When is it convenient for your clients?	¿Cuándo les conviene a tus clientes?
It's not convenient for the manager.	No es conveniente al gerente.

convention n
[a meeting]	una asamblea/un congreso/una convención
a convention center	una sala/un palacio de congresos/un centro de convenciones
[social convention/custom]	una convención

Ø **una convención** can also mean "agreement."

cook v
[in general]	cocinar/guisar
[by boiling]	cocer
Cook the meat slowly.	Cocina la carne a fuego lento./Que se cocine la carne a fuego lento.
I do the cooking at home	Soy yo el/la que hace la cocina/que prepara las comidas en casa.
[with name of a meal]	preparar
to cook lunch/dinner	preparar la comida/la cena
What's cooking? [slang]	¿Qué pasa?

copy n
[reproduction]	una copia
a photocopy	una copia/una fotocopia
[of a book]	un ejemplar
I've lost my copy of Don Quixote.	He perdido mi ejemplar de Don Quijote.
[of a journal]	un número
Is this the latest copy of "Time"?	¿Éste es el número más reciente de "Time"?

corner n
[in a room]	un rincón
She was sitting in the corner.	Estaba sentada en el rincón.
[outside, e.g., on the street]	una esquina
I'll wait for you on the corner.	Te esperaré en la esquina.
Let's meet in the café on the corner.	Vamos a reunirnos en el café de la esquina.

| [in soccer] | una esquina/un córner |
| to take a corner | sacar una esquina/un córner |

correct adj
[in general]	correcto(a)
[exact, right]	exacto(a)/justo(a)
the correct change	la moneda exacta/el suelto exacto
the correct time	la hora exacta
Correct!	¡Exacto!/¡Justo!
to be correct	tener razón

could v
past tense
[was/was not able to]
| I couldn't do it. | No podía hacerlo/No pude hacerlo. |
[did/did not know how to]
| I couldn't do it. | No sabía hacerlo. |

conditional
[would/would not be able to]
| I said I could do it tomorrow. | Dije que podría hacerlo mañana. |
[would/would not know how to]
| I told him you could do it. | Le dije que tu sabrías hacerlo. |

conditional perfect
[would/would not have been able to]
| I could have done it if I had tried. | Habría podido hacerlo si me hubiera esforzado. |

imperfect subjunctive
[would/would be able to after **si** "if"]
| I would do it if I could. [was able to] | Lo haría si pudiera. |
| I would do it if I could. | Lo haría si supiera. |
[knew how to]
[see also **can**]

country n
[nation]	la nación/el país
[motherland/fatherland]	la patria
[countryside]	el campo
[region]	la región/la tierra

couple n
a few
in a couple of minutos	unos pocos/unas pocas
just a couple of minutes	en unos pocos minutos
I'll be in Chile only a couple of weeks.	dos minutos nada más
	Estaré en Chile sólo un par de semanas.

a pair [of things]
| I've got a couple of things to tell you. | un par (de) |
| | Tengo un par de cosas que decirte. |

two people together
a married couple	una pareja
a young married couple	un matrimonio
	un matrimonio joven

course n
| course of action | una línea de conducta/acción |
| course of events | la marcha de los acontecimientos |

court

a class
to take a math course

un curso
hacer un curso de matemáticas

on a menu
the main course
the first course

un plato
el plato principal
el primer plato

sport
a golfcourse
a racecourse [horse-racing]

una cancha de golf [LA]/un campo de golf
un hipódromo

court n
[of law]
[in sport]
a tennis court
[royal court]

un tribunal
una cancha [LA]/una pista [Sp]
una cancha de tenis
una corte

cream n
[in general]
[on whipped cream]
strawberries and cream
a cream cake
suntan cream

la crema
la nata
fresas con nata
un pastel de nata
la crema de broncear/la bronceadora

credit n
to buy on credit
a credit card
to pay with a credit card
credits [cinema]

comprar a crédito/a plazos
una tarjeta de crédito
pagar con tarjeta de crédito
los títulos/rótulos de crédito

crowded adj
[in general]
The streets were crowded.
The bus was crowded.
[room]
The lecture room was crowded.

concurrido(a)/lleno(a) de gente
Las calles estaban concurridas.
El camión iba muy lleno.
apretado(a)/atestado(a)
El aula estaba apretada.

cry v
[to shout]
[to weep]

gritar
llorar

cup n
[drinking vessel]
[trophy]

una taza/un pocillo [Col]
una copa

Ø **una copa** also means "a wine glass."

curious adj
inquisitive
odd

curioso(a)
extraño(a)/raro(a)

cute adj
attractive
She's really cute.

lindo(a)/mono(a)/chulo(a) [Mex]
Es muy linda.

shrewd
What a cute (clever) guy!

astuto(a)/listo(a)
¡Qué tío tan listo!

D

dance *n*

a dance *[social event]*	un baile
a formal dance/a ball	un baile de etiqueta
to go dancing	ir a bailar/ir al baile
ballet dancing	el baile clásico
folk dancing	el baile tradicional
[ritual or tribal]	una danza
a dance hall	un salón de baile

dark *n*

the dark	las tinieblas/la oscuridad
She's afraid of the dark.	Tiene miedo de las tinieblas.

dark *adj*

It's dark.	Anochece/Se hace de noche.
It'll be dark at eight.	Anochecerá a las ocho.
Their kitchen is very dark.	Su cocina es muy oscura.
[of a color]	oscuro
His suit is dark blue.	Su traje es azul oscuro.

date *n*

the date *[calendar]* — la fecha

What's the date today? — ¿A cuántos estamos hoy?/¿Cuál es la fecha de hoy?

a personal or business date — una cita

a date *[romantic]*	una cita amorosa
to have a date	tener una cita
to make a date with sb	citarse con/darse cita con

the person invited — *[Note: There is no real equivalent in Spanish for "a date" referring to a person although it can sometimes be translated by el novio/la novia meaning "fiancé(e)" or "boyfriend"/"girlfriend".]*

his/her date — la chica/el chico con quien sale

date *v*

We're dating.	Salimos juntos.
Who are you dating?	¿Con quién sales?
Have you started dating?	¿Has comenzado a salir con chicos(as)?
to date a document	poner la fecha
to be up to date (with work)	estar al día
to be up to date (with the news)	estar al corriente
to bring sb up to date	poner a alguien al corriente
to bring sth up to date	poner algo al día

to date *adv*

to date — hasta la fecha

Ø **una data** means "an item *[in commerce]*;" **un dato** is "a fact" or "piece of information;" **los datos** means "data."

dated

dated [see *old-fashioned*]

day *n*

a day	el día [Note: *masculine*]
What day is it?	¿Qué día es?
the first day of the week	el primer día de la semana
I'll be back in three days.	Volveré dentro de tres días.
the day before	el día anterior
the day before yesterday	anteayer
the next day/the following day	el día siguiente/al día siguiente
the day after tomorrow	pasado mañana
all day	todo el día
every day	todos los días/cada día
by day	de día
a day off	un día libre/un día de descanso
this very day	hoy mismo
Mother's Day	el día de la madre
a work day	una jornada
They have a ten-hour work day.	Tienen una jornada de diez horas.
Have a good day!	¡Que le vaya bien!/¡Que tenga un buen día! [Note: **usted** forms]

[See also **today**]

deal *n*

a quantity

a good deal (of)	mucho(a)/muchísimo(a)
He has a good deal of money.	Tiene mucho dinero.
She sleeps a good deal.	Duerme mucho.
They have done a good deal of the work.	Han hecho gran parte del trabajo.

business

a business deal	un trato/un negocio/una transacción
It's a deal!	¡Trato hecho!

a bargain

Only 100 pesos! That's a really good deal.	¡Sólo cien pesos! Es una verdadera ganga.

an agreement

[political, diplomatic]	un convenio
[business]	un trato
to make a deal	hacer un trato
to close a deal	cerrar un trato

deal with *v*

[to see to arrangements, etc.]	ocuparse de
My wife dealt with the arrangements.	Mi esposa se ocupó de los preparativos.
[to behave towards sb]	portarse con/tratar
They dealt very fairly with you.	Se portaron muy bien contigo./Te trataron muy bien.
[to have business dealings with]	tratar con
He deals with big companies.	Trata con grandes empresas.
[to deal with sb]	encargarse de
I'll deal with him.	Me encargaré de él.
[to confront, to handle]	enfrentarse con

48

The policeman will deal with this situation.	El guardia se enfrentará con esta situación.

dear adj & noun

a dear friend (of mine)	un querido amigo mío/una querida amiga mía
She was very dear to us all.	Todos la queríamos mucho./Fue querida por todos nosotros.
my dear/my darling	querido mío/querida mía

in letters

Dear Sir/Dear Madam/Dear Sirs	Muy señor mío/Muy señora mía/Muy señores míos
[to a specific person not personally known to you]	Distinguido(a) señor(a)
Dear Mr. Mateos	Estimado señor Mateos
Dear Mrs./Miss Ruiz	Estimada señora/señorita Ruiz
[to a colleague]	Mi distinguido(a) colega
Dear Dr. Gómez	Estimado(a) Doctor(a) Gómez
[to a friend]	Mi querido(a) amigo(a)
Dear Peter	Mi querido Pedro/Querido amigo (Pedro)/Querido Pedro
Dear Mary	Mi querida María/Querida amiga (María)/Querida María

decision n

to make a decision	tomar una decisión [Note: not **hacer**]

definite adj

certain

	seguro(a)/cierto(a)
Is it definite they're coming?	¿Es seguro que vienen?

exact, clear

	claro(a)/concreto(a)/determinado(a)/ definitivo(a)
a definite date	una fecha determinada
a definite result	un resultado concreto/definitivo

grammar

the definite article	el artículo definido

definitely adj

[certainly]	desde luego/claro que sí

Ø **definitivamente** means "finally" or "once and for all."

degree n

university

	un título
to have/get a degree	sacar un título
to have a degree in arts/law	ser licenciado(a) en letras/derecho
to get a degree in science	licenciarse en ciencias
a bachelor's degree	una licenciatura
a doctorate (degree)	un doctorado

[Note: The degree system in universities in Spanish-speaking countries differs from that in the USA. There is no equivalent term for "a master's degree."]

temperature

	un grado
The boiling point of water is 212 degrees (Fahrenheit).	El punto de ebullición del agua es 100 grados (centígrados).

demand

Normal body temperature is
  98.6 degrees.
It was 86 degrees today.

La temperatura normal del cuerpo es
  37 grados.
Registraba 30 grados hoy.

demand *n*

The president has many demands
  on his time.
I have many demands on my time.
by popular demand
on demand
demands for (health) insurance

Los asuntos le tienen muy ocupado
  al presidente.
Los asuntos me tienen muy ocupado(a).
a petición del público
a petición
la urgente necesidad de seguro

demand *v*
to call for
The union demanded an increase.

reclamar
El sindicato reclamó un aumento.

to insist on, to require
I demanded an explanation from
  the manager.
She demands that you leave at
  once.

exigir
Le exigí una explicación al
  gerente.
Exige que te marches al instante.
  [Note: subjunctive]

∅ **demandar** means "to sue."

demonstration *n*
in general
She gave a demonstration of
  the new dishwasher.

una demostración
Hizo una demostración del
  lavaplatos nuevo.

a protest
to hold a demonstration
a violent demonstration

una manifestación
hacer una manifestación/manifestarse
un motín/un tumulto

den *n*
[animal's lair]
[study]

una guarida
un estudio

deny *v*
to deny
I don't deny it.

negar
No lo niego.

∅ **negarse** means "to refuse:" "He refused to pay." **Se negó a pagar.**

depart *v*
[people]
[trains, etc.]
We will depart at six.
The train departs at seven.

irse/marcharse/partir
salir
Nos iremos/marcharemos a las seis.
El tren sale a las siete.

department *n*
in a store
The household appliances
  department is in the basement.
a department store

el departamento
El departamento de
  electrodomésticos está en el sótano.
un gran almacén/grandes almacenes

in a business
the maintenance department
the accounting department

el departamento/el servicio
el servicio de conservación
el servicio de contabilidad

in a university	la sección
the Spanish department	la sección de español
in government	el ministerio
the State Department	el Departamento de Estado

deposit n
down payment

[on rent, hotel room]	una señal/un depósito
[on purchase]	un abono [LA]/un depósito/una señal
to pay/leave a deposit of $50	dejar una señal de 50 dólares
to put a deposit on an apartment	dar una entrada para un apartamento
to pay a deposit on sth	pagar el desembolso inicial

at a bank

to make a deposit	hacer un depósito/ingreso

depress v

to depress [mentally]	deprimir
to be depressed	estar deprimido(a)/desanimado(a)
to get depressed	deprimirse
I feel depressed.	Me siento deprimido(a).
This place depresses me.	Este lugar me deprime.
This is very depressing.	Esto es muy deprimente.

detour n

to make a detour	desviarse/hacer un rodeo
We made a detour via León.	Nos desviamos por León.
I made a detour because the road was blocked.	Hice un rodeo porque la carretera estaba cortada.
[rerouting of traffic]	una desviación

development n
event, happening

a sad development	un acontecimiento/un hecho
	un acontecimiento triste

progress, expansion

	el desarrollo
a development plan	un plan de desarrollo
a housing development	una urbanización
an industrial development	un complejo industrial
a high-rise development	una torre de apartamentos

discovery

	un descubrimiento
the latest developments in physics.	los últimos descubrimientos de la física

diary n

[a journal of personal experiences]	un diario
[appointment book]	una agenda/una libreta

Ø **diario** is the usual word for "a daily newspaper;" the adjective **diario(a)** means "daily."

direction n
in the direction of

	en (la) dirección a
in the opposite direction	en sentido contrario/opuesto
Is this the right direction for the hospital?	¿Es éste el camino al hospital?
You're going in the wrong direction.	Te has equivocado de camino.

51

director

She doesn't have much sense of direction.	Le falta sentido de orientación.
Could you give me directions to the university?	¿Cómo se va a la universidad, por favor?
directions for use	el modo de empleo/las instrucciones para el uso

Ø **dirección** also means "address," "management," and "steering" [of a car].

director n
all senses
	un director/una directora
the managing director	el director/la directora gerente
the board of directors	el consejo de administración/la junta directiva

disappoint v
to disappoint	decepcionar/desilusionar
The book disappointed me.	El libro me decepcionó.
The actors disappointed us.	Los actores nos decepcionaron.
You have really disappointed her.	La has decepcionado mucho.
It was a disappointing result.	Fue un resultado decepcionante.
I'm very disappointed to learn that you are leaving.	Siento mucho saber que te marchas.

disappointment n
What a disappointment!	¡Qué decepción!

Ø "deception" and "to deceive" are rendered in Spanish by **el engaño** and **engañar** respectively.

discuss v/discussion n
to discuss	discutir/hablar de/estudiar/tratar de
We must discuss it.	Debemos estudiarlo.
discussion	una discusión/una conversación

Ø **discutir** and **discusión** more often than not mean "to argue" and "argument."

dish n
a serving dish	una fuente
a bowl	un plato hondo
a course/dish on a menu	un plato
a set of dishes	la vajilla
to do/wash the dishes	lavar los platos/la vajilla
a dishwasher	un lavaplatos

dispute [see argument]

disturb v
to bother, interrupt sb	molestar a alguien
I'm sorry to disturb you.	Siento molestarte.
Please do not disturb.	Se ruega no molesten. [Note: subjunctive]
Do not disturb!	¡No se moleste!
Don't disturb yourself!	¡No te molestes!/¡No se moleste!

to upset sb
	inquietar/perturbar a alguien
I am very disturbed by your comments.	Tus observaciones me inquietan mucho.

52

divorce n & v
to divorce/to get a divorce from sb	divorciarse de alguien
He/She is divorced.	Está divorciado(a)
They are divorced.	Están divorciados.
Both women are divorced.	Las dos mujeres están divorciadas.
I divorced my husband.	Divorcié a/Me divorcié de mi marido.
He got a divorce ten days ago.	Se divorció hace diez días.
We got divorced last year.	Nos divorciamos el año pasado.
You should ask for a divorce.	Deberías pedir el divorcio. [Note: "the" divorce]

do v
for emphasis

	[Note: **hacer** is not used for this]
I do want them to come.	Quiero mucho que vengan.
Will John come? I do hope so.	¿Vendrá Juan? Espero que sí.
If the team does win ...	Si en realidad/en efecto gana el equipo...

to have finished

	haber acabado/terminado
Are they done?	¿Han terminado/acabado?

in a question, a negative

	[Note: **hacer** is not used]
Do you want to go out?	¿Quieres salir?
Don't you know me?	¿No me conoces?
Did you visit the museum?	¿Visitaste el museo?

to do without

	pasarse sin/prescindir de
She can't do without the car.	No puede pasarse sin el coche.
They can't do without him.	No pueden prescindir de él.

to have to do with

	tener que ver con
I want to have nothing to do with you.	No quiero tener nada que ver contigo.
It's (got) nothing to do with it.	No tiene nada que ver con ello.

to fare

How is he doing?	¿Cómo le va?/¿Qué tal le va?

to be suitable

Will this shirt do?	¿Qué te parece esta camisa?
Yes, that one will do.	Sí, me quedo con ésa.

domestic adj
of the home

domestic work	las faenas domésticas/de casa
domestic life	la vida de familia

national

domestic affairs	los asuntos interiores
a domestic flight	un vuelo nacional/interior

dormitory n
a student dormitory	una residencia

Ø **un dormitorio** is a "bedroom."

double adj
a double bed	una cama de matrimonio
a double room	una habitación doble/para dos

down *adv & prep*

The theater is down the street.   El teatro está un poco más abajo de la calle.

Her office is down below.   Su oficina está abajo.
down the street   calle abajo

verb + down
to come/go down   bajar
She hasn't come down yet.   Todavía no ha bajado.
I went down the street.   Bajé la calle.
They ran down the street.   Bajaron la calle corriendo.
to get down from [to get off]   apearse de/bajar de
He got down from the train.   Se apeó del tren./Bajó del tren.
to take/bring sth down   bajar
Take the suitcases down, please   Haga el favor de bajar las maletas.
to fall down   caer/caerse al suelo
to lay/put sth down (on)   poner/deponer algo (en)
to lie down   acostarse/echarse

downstairs *adv*
to come/go downstairs   bajar la escalera
The dog sleeps downstairs.   El perro duerme abajo.

downtown *n*
downtown   el centro de la ciudad
to go downtown   ir al centro

dozen *n*
a dozen eggs   una docena de huevos

dress *n*
[in general]   el vestido
[clothes]   la ropa
casual dress   la ropa de sport
formal or evening dress   el traje formal [LA]/el traje de etiqueta [men]/el traje de noche [women]

They were all in evening dress.   Todos estaban/iban vestidos de etiqueta
street or business clothes   el traje de calle

dress *v*
to dress/get dressed   vestirse
to dress up [for an occasion]   vestirse de etiqueta
to dress well   vestirse con gusto
to dress up as   disfrazarse de
to be dressed in   estar/ir vestido(a) de

drink *n*
a drink   una bebida
a drink [alcoholic]   una copa
to have a drink   tomar una bebida
to have a drink [alcoholic]   tomar una copa/echar un trago
a before-dinner drink   un aperitivo/un cóctel
an after-dinner drink   un licor

drive v
to drive a car   manejar [LA]/conducir/guiar un coche
Can you drive?   ¿Sabes manejar?
to drive to work   ir al trabajo en coche [Note: When "to drive"
                                          just means "to go by car" use **ir en
                                          coche**.]
Shall we drive or walk?   ¿Vamos en coche o a pie?
to drive sb home   llevar a alguien a casa

drop v
to drop sth   dejar caer [deliberately]
                                        caerse [accidentally]
I dropped the glass.   Se me cayó el vaso.
to drop out of school   abandonar sus estudios

drugs n
prescription drugs   los medicamentos
[narcotics]   las drogas/los narcóticos
to take drugs   drogarse
drug addiction   la toxicomanía
a drug addict/user   un toxicómano/un drogadicto
drug traffic   el tráfico de narcóticos
a drug trafficker   un traficante en drogas

drugstore n
a drugstore   una farmacia

Ø **una droguería** is a store where cleaning products for the home are sold; you will not find medicine here.

due adj
time due
The invoice is due for payment   La factura es pagadera ahora mismo.
  right now.
When is the train due?   ¿Cuándo debe llegar el tren?
He is due to be in New York   Tiene que estar en Nueva York
  tomorrow.   mañana.

due to
due to [because of] the fog   debido a/por causa de la niebla
due to [thanks to] my sister   gracias a mi hermana

E

each *adj*
each man/each woman   cada hombre/cada mujer
each day/each night   cada día/cada noche
each time   cada vez
[Note: **Cada** *is invariable.]*
[See also **every**.*]*

each *pron*
each (one)   cada uno/cada una
Each of my sons will come.   Cada uno de mis hijos vendrá.
He gave us each 100 dollars.   Nos dio a cada uno cien dólares./
     Nos dio cien dólares por persona.
each (one) of us/them   cada uno(a) de nosotros(as)/ellos(as)
They're worth 500 pesos each.   Valen quinientos pesos cada uno(a).
To each his own.   A cada cual lo suyo.

each other/one another *pron*
each one/one another   nos/se *[Note:* **el uno el otro/la una**
     la otra/los unos los otros/las unas las
     otras *may be added for clarity.]*
We've never written each other.   No nos hemos escrito nunca.
They don't help each other.   No se ayudan (el uno al otro).
They should talk to one another.   Deberían hablarse (unos a otros).
We were sitting across from   Estábamos sentados el uno enfrente
   each other.   del otro.

ear *n*
the ear *[external]*   la oreja
the ear *[internal/sense of hearing]*   el oído
She has an earache.   Tiene dolor de oídos./Le duele el oído.
I have a good ear for music.   Tengo buen oído para la música.
My daughter has no ear for   Mi hija no tiene oído para los
   languages.   idiomas.
to play by ear *[music]*   tocar de oído
to play it by ear   improvisar sobre la marcha
ear of corn   una mazorca

early *adj & adv*
for a set time   temprano/con tiempo/de anticipación
He always arrives early at the   Siempre llega temprano a la
   office.   oficina.
The train left ten minutes   El tren salió con diez minutos de
   early.   anticipación.
You must reserve your tickets   Debes reservar tus boletos con
   early.   tiempo.

in a time period
I got up early.   Me levanté temprano.
as early as possible   lo más pronto posible/cuanto antes
the early morning   la madrugada
early in the morning   de madrugada/muy de mañana

at an early date *[letters]*	en fecha próxima
He/She's an early riser.	Es madrugador(a).
to take the early flight	tomar el primer vuelo del día
in the early eighties	al principio de los (años) ochenta
He's in his early thirties.	Tiene poco más de treinta años.

earth *n*
[planet]	la Tierra
[soil]	el suelo/la tierra

easy *adj*
easy	fácil/sencillo(a)
Take it easy!	¡Tranquilo!
an easy chair	un sillón

eat *v*
to eat out	comer fuera/en un restaurante
to eat up	comerse
to eat away *[metal]*	desgastar
to eat into *[fig]*	consumir
with name of a meal	*[Note: Do not use **comer** with the name of a meal.]*
to eat breakfast	desayunar/tomar el desayuno
to eat lunch	almorzar/tomar el almuerzo/tomar la comida
to eat dinner	cenar/tomar la cena

Ø **comida** can also be used to mean "dinner;" this usage can vary from country to country so it is best to follow the local practice.

edge *n*
[of a cliff]	el borde
[of the water]	la orilla
[of a cutting tool]	el filo/el corte
[of a page]	el margen
to have the edge on sb	llevar ventaja a alguien
My nerves are on edge.	Tengo los nervios de punta.
the edge of town	las afueras

editor *n*
newspaper editor	el editor/la editora *[LA]*
	el director/la directora *[Sp]*
text editor	el redactor/la redactora

Ø In Spain **editor** means "publisher."

educated *adj*
Where were you educated?	¿Dónde cursaste tus estudios?
I was educated at the University of Madrid.	Cursé mis estudios en la Universidad de Madrid.
a well-educated person	una persona culta
He's very well educated.	Es muy culto.

Ø **bien educado(a)** means "well-bred," "well-mannered;" **mal educado(a)** means "badly behaved," "rude."

education *n*
[in general]	la educación
[instruction in a school]	la enseñanza

educational

[vocational training]	la formación
primary/secondary education	la enseñanza primaria/secundaria
further education	la enseñanza superior/los estudios universitarios

educational *adj*

educational background	la formación
an educational film	una película instructiva
educational policy	la política educativa
educational television	la televisión educativa
educational texts [for schools]	los libros escolares

Ø **educacional** is an anglicism for "educational" which will sometimes be heard.

effective *adj*
come into operation — en vigor

effective from 1 May	en vigor a partir del primero de mayo
The curfew became effective at eleven o'clock.	El toque de queda entró en vigor a las once.

efficient [of things] — eficaz
Her medication is very effective	Su medicina es muy eficaz.

efficient [of people] — capaz/eficiente/competente
She's a very effective worker.	Es una trabajadora muy capaz.

effort *n*

effort	un esfuerzo
[an attempt]	un intento

either (one) *adj & pron*

either (one)	cualquier... de los/las dos
	cualquiera de los/las dos
	uno u otro
Either one (will do).	Cualquiera de los dos me servirá./ Cualquiera de los dos valdría./No me importa cualquiera.
Either car will do.	Cualquier coche (de los dos) me servirá.
Which color do you prefer? – I'll take either.	¿Qué color prefieres? – Llevaré cualquiera/uno u otro.

in the negative — no... ninguno/ni... ni
I don't want either of them.	No quiero ninguno de los dos.
She doesn't like either.	No le gusta ni el uno ni el otro.

either ... or *conj*
either ... or	o... o
I'll go either to Mexico or to Colombia.	Iré o a México o a Colombia.
You could either go to the game or watch it on TV.	Podrías o ir al partido o mirarlo en la televisión.

in the negative
She doesn't like wine or beer.	No le gusta ni el vino ni la cerveza.
They're not going either.	No van tampoco.

elective *n*

an elective course	un curso facultativo
an elective subject	una asignatura facultativa

elevator n
an elevator — un elevador [LA]/un ascensor [Sp]

else adv
something else — algo más/otra cosa
nothing else/not ... anything else — nada más [+ no with verb]
We don't need anything else. — No necesitamos nada más.
everything else — todo lo demás
somebody else — otro(a)/otra persona
nobody else/not ... anybody else. — nadie más
Nobody else can do it. — Nadie más (que tú/él, etc.) sabe hacerlo.
He didn't see anybody else. — No vio a nadie más.
everybody else — todos los demás/todos los otros
somewhere else [with motion] — a (cualquier) otro sitio/otra parte
somewhere else [position] — en (cualquier) otro sitio/otra parte
nowhere else [with motion] — a ningún otro sitio/a ninguna otra parte
nowhere else [position] — en ningún otro sitio/en ninguna otra parte
What else?/Anything else? [in a store or café, etc.] — ¿Algo más?
What else could I do? — ¿Qué más podría hacer?
Who else is coming? — ¿Quién más viene?
or else ... — si no...

embarrass v
to embarrass — apenar [LA]/avergonzar/desconcertar/turbar/azarar
to embarrass [deliberately] — poner en un aprieto
to be/feel embarrassed — apenarse [LA]/avergonzarse
— sentirse confuso(a)/azarado(a)/avergonzado(a)/molesto(a)/violento(a)
She looked embarrassed. — Parecía confusa.
I'm really embarrassed about it. — Me siento algo avergonzado(a) por eso.
It was an embarrassing situation. — Fue una situación violenta.
We were embarrassed by his behavior. — Su comportamiento nos desconcertó.

Ø **embarazar** means "to hinder," "to obstruct," or "to make pregnant;" **embarazada** means "pregnant," not "embarrassed."

emotional adv
of a person
[warm-hearted] — emocional
[taking things too hard] — sentimental
[over-emotional] — demasiado sensible
— exagerado(a)/exaltado(a)

relating to the emotions — emocional
an emotional experience/shock/state — una experiencia/una conmoción/un estado emocional

emphasis n/**emphasize** v
to accent — acentuar
In Spanish you put the accent on the next-to-the-last syllable. — En castellano se acentúa la penúltima sílaba.

to stress the importance — enfatizar
The guide emphasized the importance of not going into that area. — El guía enfatizó la importancia de no pasar por ese barrio.

He emphasized that we should
arrive on time.

Enfatizó que deberíamos llegar a
tiempo.

enclose *v*/enclosure *n*

to enclose something
enclosed
Please find enclosed ...
I enclose a check for 50 dollars.

adjuntar algo/remitir algo adjunto
adjunto(a)
Le mandamos adjunto(a)...
Remito un cheque de cincuenta dólares.

end *n*

opposite of beginning
the end of the century/the
 film/the paragraph/the week
at the end of the month

el fin
el fin del siglo/de la película/del
 párrafo/de la semana
a finales del mes

of a time or place
at the end of the corridor
at the other end of the street

el final
al final del pasillo
al otro extremo de la calle

other
from one end to another
a candle end
the end of a table
To what end?
to no end
You'll never hear the end of it.

de un extremo al otro
un cabo de vela
el extremo de una mesa
¿Con qué propósito?
en vano
No te dejarán olvidarlo nunca.

end *v*

to end [in general]
This word ends with a "t."
She ended by saying ...

terminar/acabar
Esta palabra termina en "t."
Terminó diciendo...

energetic *adj*

an energetic person

una persona enérgica

Ø **energético(a)** is an anglicism, often used in Latin America.

engaged *adj*/engagement *n*

to be engaged [to be married]
They got engaged yesterday.
She got engaged to a Peruvian.
to announce one's engagement

estar prometido(a)
Se prometieron ayer.
Se prometió con un peruano.
darse palabra de casamiento

business/social occasion
She has an engagement tonight.
You have an engagement at six.

Tiene un compromiso esta noche.
Tienes una cita a las seis.

engine *n*

[of a car]
[of a train]
a jet engine

el motor
la máquina/la locomotora
un motor de reacción

enjoy *v*

to possess
She enjoys good health.

disfrutar de/gozar de
Disfruta de buena salud.

to take pleasure in
I enjoyed the film.
Do you enjoy reading?

gustar/disfrutar con
Me gustó la película.
¿Te gusta leer?

He enjoys classical music. — Disfruta con la música clásica.
They enjoyed their vacation. — Se divirtieron en las vacaciones.

to enjoy oneself — divertirse/pasarlo bien
He enjoyed himself in the country. — Se divirtió en el campo.
I didn't enjoy myself in Chile. — No lo pasé bien en Chile.

enough *adj & adv*
You don't eat enough. — No comes bastante.
I don't have enough time. — No tengo suficiente tiempo.
He didn't have enough money. — No tenía suficiente dinero.
They are rich enough to pay for it. — Son bastante ricos para pagarlo.
It's good enough. — Está bien.
I've had enough. *[I'm fed up.]* — Estoy harto(a).
That's enough! — ¡Basta ya!
oddly enough — por extraño que parezca

enroll *v*
to enroll in a club — inscribirse en una sociedad
to enroll in a course — matricularse para un curso

entertain *v*
to hospitality, meals, etc. — agasajar/invitar
They entertained her at the Palace. — La agasajaron en el Palacio.

to amuse — divertir/entretener
He entertained the children. — Divirtió/Entretuvo a los niños.

entree *n*
the entree *[main course]* — el plato principal

errand *n*
an errand — un encargo/un recado/una diligencia *[Arg]*

escape *n*
[in general] — una fuga/una huída
[of gas] — un escape

escape *v*
[to make one's escape] — escaparse
He escaped from jail. — Se escapó de la cárcel.
[to avoid] — evitar/librarse de
to escape danger — librarse del peligro
They narrowly escaped death. — Por poco evitaron la muerte.

establish *v*
[proof] — demostrar
[facts] — constatar
[fame] — consolidar

estimate *n & v*
to assess — calcular
I estimate that it will cost too much. — Calculo que va a costar demasiado.

for work to be done — presupuestar/hacer un presupuesto
an estimate — un presupuesto

He estimated for the building materials.	Hizo un presupuesto del material de construcción.

Ø **estimar** means "to esteem," "to respect."

even *adj*

flat, level, smooth	llano(a)/liso(a)
an even piece of land	un terreno llano
an even surface	una superficie lisa
uniform	uniforme/regular
at an even pace	a paso uniforme/regular
equal	igual
The teams are even.	Los equipos son iguales.
opposite of odd	par
odd or even numbers	números pares o impares

even *adv*

even	aun/hasta/incluso
Even the President attended.	Hasta el Presidente asistió.
even at night	aun de noche
Everybody left, even the teachers.	Todos salieron, incluso los profesores.
even so	aun así
even on Saturdays	incluso los sábados
even if/even though	aunque *[+ subjunctive]*
	si bien que *[+ indicative]*
I wouldn't help them even if I could.	No los ayudaría aunque pudiera.
Even though he bought a ticket he didn't go to the concert.	Si bien que sacó una entrada no asistió al concierto.
Even though it is easy he won't do it.	Aunque sea fácil no quiere hacerlo.
not even	ni siquiera
She didn't even read the instructions.	Ni siquiera leyó las instrucciones.

evening *n*

the evening	la tarde
at seven o'clock in the evening	a las siete de la tarde
this evening/yesterday evening /tomorrow evening	esta tarde/ayer por la tarde/ mañana por la tarde
every evening	todas las tardes
all evening/the whole evening	toda la tarde
I always go out in the evening.	Siempre salgo por las tardes.
She's going out in the evening.	Sale por la tarde.
Good evening!	¡Buenas tardes!
during the evening	durante la tarde
a musical evening	una velada

Ø In the Spanish-speaking world the day is essentially divided into three: morning/before lunch (**la mañana**), between lunch and darkness falling (**la tarde**) which corresponds to our afternoon and early evening, and night (**la noche**).

event *n*

an event/a happening	un suceso/un acontecimiento

Ø **suceso** can also mean "accident" or "crime;" "success" is translated by **el éxito**.

eventful adj
eventful   memorable

eventually adv
[in time]   finalmente/al fin y al cabo/eventualmente
                                               [LA]
to do sth eventually   acabar por hacerlo
He'll do it eventually.   Lo hará con el tiempo/a la larga.

Ø **eventualmente** also means "by chance."

ever adv
Have you ever been to Peru?   ¿Has ido alguna vez al Perú?
forever   para siempre/por siempre

every adj
every   cada/todos los/todas las
every tourist   cada turista/todos los turistas
every Sunday   todos los domingos
every other day   cada dos días
every ten minutes   cada diez minutos
every half hour   cada media hora
every one   cada uno(a)
every one of them   todos ellos/todas ellas
every one of us   todos nosotros/todas nosotras

everybody/everyone pron
everybody   todo el mundo/todos
Everybody will be there.   Estará todo el mundo. [Note: singular
                                               verb]/Estarán todos.

everything pron
everything   todo
We sold everything.   Lo vendimos todo.
Everything's fine.   Todo va/está bien.
to do everything   hacer de todo
everything that   todo lo que
everything (that's) good   todo lo bueno
everything (that) you want   todo lo que quieras [Note: subjunctive]
I'll do everything I can.   Haré todo lo que pueda.

everywhere adv
everywhere in Mexico   en todas partes de México
There are tourists everywhere.   Hay turistas en todas partes.
We went everywhere in Spain.   Fuimos a todas partes de España.
She looked everywhere.   Buscó por todas partes.
everywhere they go   dondequiera que vayan

evidence n
[proof]   las pruebas
[signs]   los indicios
to give evidence   prestar declaración

evil adj
[of person]   malo(a)/malvado(a)
[of things]   malo(a)/pernicioso(a)

63

exam *n*
in school
a final exam
an oral exam
to take an exam
to pass an exam

to fail an exam
You have failed.

medical exam
He had a physical exam.

un examen
un examen de fin de curso
un examen oral
hacer un examen/presentarse a un examen
aprobar/ser aprobado(a) en un
    examen *[Note: not **pasar**]*
suspender un examen *[Note: not **faltar**]*
Te han suspendido.

un reconocimiento médico
Le dieron un reconocimiento médico.

examine *v*
[in general]
[in jurisprudence]

examinar
interrogar

exchange *n & v*
I'd like to exchange this
  shirt for a larger size.
The exchange rate of the
  dollar has gone up.
foreign exchange
Stock Exchange
telephone exchange
[of ideas]
in exchange for

Quisiera cambiar esta camisa por
  una talla más grande.
Ha subido el tipo de cambio del
  dólar.
las divisas
la Bolsa
la central telefónica
un intercambio
a cambio de

excited *adj*
enthusiastic
to be excited
to be excited about

I'm very excited about my new car.
She was very excited about my
  news.

estar emocionado(a)
emocionarse por
entusiasmarse con/por
Me entusiasmo con mi coche nuevo.
Se quedó muy entusiasmada por mis
  noticias./Mis noticias le hicieron mucha
  ilusión.

over-excited
The children were over-excited.
Don't get too excited!

Los niños estaban nerviosas.
¡No te emociones tanto!/No te excites!

looking forward to
We're getting excited about
  our trip to Brazil.
She was getting excited about
  the holidays.

Esperamos con ansia nuestro viaje
  al Brasil.
Esperaba con mucha ilusión las
  vacaciones.

exciting *adj*
exciting

emocionante

excuse *v*
to interrupt
Excuse me. Could you please ...

Perdón, señor/señora/señorita.
  ¿Podría usted... ?
Perdone usted, señor/señora/
  señorita. ¿Podría... ?

to apologize
Excuse me (for disturbing you)

Discúlpame por haberte molestado.
Discúlpeme por haberle molestado.
Me disculpo por molestarte/molestarle.
Te/le pido perdón por molestarte/
  molestarle.

to seek permission
*[on leaving table, getting
  off crowded bus/metro,
  pushing through crowd, etc.]*

Con (su) permiso.

to justify
He cannot excuse his conduct.

justificar
No puede justificar su conducta.

to excuse sb from doing sth
I excused them from attending.

dispensar/eximir a alguien de hacer algo
Les dispensé de asisitir.

executive *n*
executive

un ejecutivo/una ejecutiva

exercise *n*
a written exercise
to do (physical) exercises

exercise book

un ejercicio escrito
hacer ejercicios/hacer gimnasia/
  practicar la gimnasia
un cuaderno

exercise *v*
to exercise *[physically]*
to exercise the dog
to exercise rights/duties

hacer ejercicio físico/entrenarse
sacar el perro de paseo
ejercer derechos/obligaciones

exhaust *n*
an exhaust
exhaust fumes

un (tubo de) escape
los gases de combustible

exhaust *v*
to exhaust
The work exhausted me.

agotar
El trabajo me agotó.

exhibition *n*
[a show of art, etc.]
[an exhibition of sports]
to make an exhibition of oneself

una exposición
una exhibición
ponerse en ridículo

exit *n*
the exit

la salida

Ø **el éxito** means "success."

expect *v*
to await
I am expecting him shortly.
My wife is expecting a baby.

esperar
Lo espero dentro de poco.
Mi esposa espera un niño.

to anticipate sth
They didn't expect that.
We expect to see them soon.
He is expecting us to come.

esperar
No lo esperaban.
Esperamos verlos pronto.
Espera que vengamos. *[Note: subjunctive]*

expense

That is to be expected.	Es de esperar.
As was to be expected.	Como era de esperar./Como podía esperarse.

to plan to — contar con/tener la intención de
They expect to leave tomorrow.	Cuentan con salir mañana.
When do you expect to return?	¿Cuándo tienes la intención de volver?

to think likely
I expect so.	Supongo que sí.
I don't expect so.	Supongo que no.

expense *n*
expense	un gasto
at my expense	a costa mía/a mi costa
expense account	una cuenta de gastos de representación
to go to any expense	hacer todo lo posible
to meet expenses	hacer frente a los gastos

experience *n*
an experience	una experiencia
to learn by experience	aprender por la experiencia

experience *v*
to experience pleasure	experimentar placer
to experience pain/grief	sufrir dolor
to experience a loss	sufrir una pérdida
to experience difficulty	tener dificultad

experiment *n*
to do an experiment	hacer experimentos/pruebas
They do experiments on rabbits.	Hacen experimentos con conejos.

expire *v*
[to die]	morir/expirar
[contract]	vencer
[passport, driver's license]	caducar

express *adj*
special delivery — urgente
express mail	el correo urgente
an express package/letter	un paquete/una carta urgente

of transport
an express train	un rápido/un expreso

extend *v*
to extend [in general]	extender
[to enlarge]	ampliar
[to lengthen]	alargar
[to prolong]	alargar
to extend a visa	prorrogar una visa [LA]/un visado
to extend an invitation	invitar

extent *n*
extent	una extensión
[limit]	un límite

to a certain extent	hasta cierto punto
to a greater or lesser extent	en mayor o menor grado
to a large extent	en gran parte
to what extent?	¿hasta qué punto?

extra *adj*
[additional]   adicional
I need an extra blanket.   Necesito una cobija adicional.
[to spare]   de más/de sobra
some extra towels   unas toallas de sobra
two extra towels   dos toallas más
an extra charge   un recargo
[a supplement on a ticket]   un suplemento
an extra payment   un pago extraordinario

Ø **extra** can often mean "of superior quality."

extravagant *adj*
in spending   pródigo(a)/despilfarrador(a)
He's an extravagant person.   Es una persona pródiga.

exaggerated
She has extravagant ideas.   Tiene ideas extravagantes.
These prices are extravagent.   Estos precios son exorbitantes.

F

fabric *n*
[cloth]   el tejido/la tela

Ø **la fábrica** means "factory" and also "fabric" or "framework" [of a building].

fabricate *v*
[to make]   fabricar/labrar
to fabricate a story   forjar una historia
[documents, evidence, etc.] falsificar

face *n*
[of a person]   la cara/el rostro
[countenance]   el semblante
[of a clock]   la esfera/el cuadrante
to make faces   hacer muecas/gestos
to wear a long face   poner mala cara
face value   el valor nominal
to keep a straight face contener la risa
to tell sb to his/her face decir a uno a rajatablas

face *v*
The library faces the river. La biblioteca da al río.
My room faces south.   Mi cuarto da al sur.
They were (sitting) facing Estaban (sentados) uno frente al
  each other.   otro./Estaban (sentadas) una
                     frente a la otra.
to face (up) to a problem afrontar/arrostrar/hacer frente a
                     un problema
Let's face it.   Hay que reconocerlo.
She can't face it.   No tiene la resolución para afrontarlo.
to face the music   dar la cara/afrontar las consecuencias
[to put a new surface on] revestir

facility *n*
a facility for music/math/ una facilidad para la música/las
  languages, etc.   matemáticas/los idiomas, etc.
a sports facility   unas instalaciones deportivas
transportation facilities los medios de comunicación

fact *n*
in general   el hecho/la realidad
[data/information]   los datos
The fact of the matter is (that) La verdad es (que)

in fact (emphasizing) en efecto/efectivamente
I often go to see him; in Voy a verlo frecuentemente; en
  fact, I went to see him   efecto fui a verlo hoy.
  today.

in fact (on the contrary) en realidad/de hecho
They claim to be experts, but Pretenden ser peritos, pero en
  in fact they know very little. realidad/de hecho saben muy poco.

faculty *n*
[*school or university staff*]   el profesorado

Ø **la facultad** is a "school" or "college" in a Spanish-speaking university, e.g., **la facultad de derecho** "law school."

fade *v*
[*color*]   desteñirse/descolorarse
[*flower*]   marchitarse
[*light*]   apagarse
to fade away   desvanecerse
to fade in   aparecer progresivamente
to fade out   desaparecer progresivamente

fail *v*
to fail an exam   ser reprobado(a) [*LA*]/suspendido(a) en un examen [*Note: not* **faltar**]

[*brakes, harvest, memory*]   fallar
The brakes failed.   Fallaron los frenos.
to fail sb   fallar a alguien
not to fail to do sth   no dejar de hacer algo
I won't fail to tell him.   No dejaré de decírselo.
[*of plans, events, etc.*]   fracasar
The film/plan failed.   La película/El proyecto fracasó.

fair *adj*
[*in appearance*]   hermoso(a)
[*of hair*]   rubio(a)
[*just*]   justo(a)
[*of weather*]   bueno
The weather is fair.   Hace buen tiempo.
[*of price*]   razonable
fair play   el juego limpio

fall *v*
to fall   caer/caerse
[*prices, temperature*]   bajar
[*date, night, silence*]   caer
Night fell.   Cayó la noche/Anocheció/Se hizo de noche.
to fall down [*person*]   caerse
to fall down [*building*]   hundirse/derrumbarse/venirse abajo
to fall down the stairs   caer rodando por la escalera
to fall for sb   enamorarse de alguien
to fall through [*plans, etc.*]   fracasar

false *adj*
[*mistaken, wrong*]   falso(a)/erróneo(a)
[*of teeth, hair, jewels*]   postizo(a)
a false bottom   un doble fondo
a false ceiling   un cielo raso
false imprisonment   la detención ilegal
a false start   una salida nula
a false step   un paso en falso

familiar *adj*
well known   bien conocido/familiar
That's a familiar situation.   Es una situación bien conocida.

fan

They look familiar.	Me parece que los conozco.
His voice is familiar.	Me parece que conozco la voz.
a familiar story	un cuento de todos los días
That sounds familiar.	Eso me suena.
to be on familiar terms with sb	tener confianza con alguien

to be familiar with sth

[a place]	conocer
I'm not familiar with Puebla.	No conozco Puebla.
[facts/information]	estar enterado(a) de
She's not familiar with the facts.	No está enterada de los datos.

Ø **familiar** is also used as an adjective meaning "family,", e.g., **asuntos familiares** "family matters."

fan *n*

[a cooling device]	un abanico *[manual]*/un ventilador *[mechanical]*
[admirer of a star]	un(a) admirador(a)
[supporters of a team]	las hinchadas *[LA]*/los (las) hinchas/los (las) aficionados(as)
He's a supporter of Santa Fe.	Es hincha del Santa Fe.
[an enthusiast, a "buff"]	un(a) aficionado(a)/un(a) entusiasta
I'm a boxing/baseball fan.	Soy aficionado(a) del boxeo/béisbol.

far *adv*

far away/far	lejos
It's not far from the station.	No está lejos de la estación.
Is it far (from here)?	¿Está lejos?/¿Dista mucho (de aquí)?
It's too far to walk.	Está demasiado lejos para caminar/ir a pie.
Keep going as far as the park.	Sigue/Siga hasta el parque.
How far is it to San Juan?	¿Cuánto hay de aquí a San Juan?
We went as far as the bank.	Fuimos hasta el banco.
as far as I can tell	que yo sepa
She's by far the best.	Es con mucho la mejor.

farm *n*

a farm	una granja/una finca *[LA]*/una estancia *[LA]*/una hacienda/un cortijo/una quinta *[LA]*/un rancho *[Mex]*
cattle farm	una hacienda [LA]/un rancho *[LA]*/una estancia *[Arg]*
farmhouse	un cortijo/una alquería/una casa de labranza/una casa de hacienda *[LA]*

fast *adj*

[quick]	rápido(a)/ligero(a)
a fast train	un tren rápido
to be fast *[of a clock]*	adelantar
My watch is ten minutes fast.	Mi reloj adelanta diez minutos/está diez minutos adelantado.
fast colors	los colores sólidos

fast *adv*

[rapid]	de prisa/rápidamente
He speaks fast.	Habla de prisa.
She was going very fast.	Ella iba muy de prisa/con mucha velocidad.

Not so fast!	¡Un momento!

fast *v*

to fast	ayunar

fat *adj*

of a person

to get/grow fat	gordo(a)/grueso(a)
	engordar

of food

It was too fat.	que tiene mucha grasa/grasiento(a)
	Tenía demasiada grasa.

fat *n*

for cooking

[lard]	la manteca de cerdo/el lardo
[suet]	el sebo

in meat

There's a lot of fat in this pork.	la grasa
	Hay mucha grasa en este cerdo./ Este cerdo tiene mucha grasa.

faucet *n*

a faucet	un grifo/una llave/un caño [Per]

fault *n*

a weakness

He has his faults.	un defecto
	Tiene sus defectos.

blame

Whose fault is it?	la culpa
It's not my fault.	¿Quién tiene la culpa?
	No es culpa mía.

geological

a fault	una falla

error

faults in spelling	errores de ortografía

Ø **falta** means "a fault" [in tennis], "a mistake," or "a lack."

fault *v*

to fault, find fault with	criticar
You cannot fault her taste.	No puedes criticar su gusto.

favorite *adj & n*

favorite	preferido(a)/favorito(a)
the favorite	el preferido/la preferida
This is my favorite opera.	Ésta es mi ópera preferida.
This song is my favorite.	Ésta es la canción que más me gusta.
She is her mother's favorite.	Es la hija predilecta de su madre.

fed up *adj*

to be fed up (with sth)	estar harto(a) (de algo)
We're fed up with traveling.	Estamos hartos(as) de viajar.

feel *v intrans*

health

How do you feel?	sentirse
I don't feel very well.	¿Cómo te sientes?
	No me siento muy bien.

feel

My wife feels sick.	Mi esposa se siente enferma.
[see also **sick**]	

physical state

Do you feel hot/cold?	¿Tienes calor/frío?
The children feel thirsty.	Los niños tienen sed.

inclination

to feel like doing sth	tener ganas de
Do you feel like going?	¿Tienes ganas de ir?

emotional

I feel bad that ...	Siento que.../Me da lástima que.../ Lamento que...
I feel bad that her father is ill.	Siento que su padre esté enfermo. [Note: subjunctive]
He feels bad that he upset you.	Le da lástima que te desconcertó.
to feel good that ...	estar contento(a)/satisfecho(a) [+ subjunctive]
He feels good (that) you are better.	Está contento de que estés mejor.
They feel good about the new house.	Están satisfechos(as) de la casa nueva.

feel v trans

to touch

The doctor felt my ribs.	La médica me palpó las costillas.
to feel sb's pulse	tomar el pulso a alguien

to be aware of

I felt that somebody was in the room.	Sentí que alguien estaba en el cuarto.

to experience

They are feeling the effects of the earthquake.	Sienten los efectos/Se resienten de los efectos del terremoto.
to feel affection/pity for	sentir cariño/compasión por
to feel regret	sentirlo/sentir pesar
I feel no interest in your affairs.	No me interesan tus asuntos.

to have the impression (that)

He feels they are talking about him.	Tiene la impresión de que hablan de él.

to believe

She feels I am too old.	Cree que soy demasiado viejo(a).
I feel you are lying.	Estoy convencido(a) de que mientes.

fender n

[bumper]	un parachoques
[mudguard]	un guardabarros/un guardafango/una aleta

fertile adj

[soil]	fértil
[biologically]	fecundo(a)

few adj

in number

Few people came.	Vino poca gente.

The town has few stores.	El pueblo tiene pocas tiendas.
some, several	unos(as)/algunos(as)/unos(as) pocos(as)/unos(as) cuantos(as)
The town has a few bookstores.	El pueblo tiene unas cuantas librerías.

fewer *adj*
fewer ... (than)	menos... (que/de)
There are fewer tourists this year.	Hay menos turistas este año.
There are fewer tourists than last year.	Hay menos turistas que el año pasado.
I have fewer books than you.	Tengo menos libros que tú.
I have fewer books than you think.	Tengo menos libros de lo que piensas.
She has fewer than fifty.	Tiene menos de cincuenta.
the fewer the better	cuantos(as) menos mejor

fewest *adj*
the fewest	los(las) menos/el menor número de
This area has the fewest tourists.	Esta región tiene el menor número de turistas.

field *n*
[an open space]	un campo
[a soccer field]	una cancha[LA]/un campo de fútbol
a field of interest [a speciality]	un campo/un terreno de actividad
It's not my field.	No es mi terreno.
[magnetic, electric, accoustic]	un campo

fierce *adj*
[animal]	feroz/fiero(a)
[person]	cruel/violento(a)
[weather]	horroroso(a)

fight *n & v*
to fight physically
	luchar/pelear/batirse con
to have a fight with sb	batirse con alguien
I had a fight with him.	Me batí con él./Peleé con él.
They were fighting in the street.	Peleaban/Se batían en la calle.

to quarrel
	disputar/reñir
to have a fight with sb	reñir con alguien
We had a fight.	Reñimos.

to fight against
	luchar contra
to fight against drugs	luchar contra las drogas
the fight against poverty	la lucha contra la pobreza

figure *n*
[a number]	un número/una cifra
to keep/lose one's figure	guardar/perder la línea
to have a good figure	tener buen tipo/tener un tipo estupendo/tener buen físico [LA]

fill *v*
to fill a glass	llenar un vaso
to fill out a form	rellenar un formulario/completar un formulario [Arg]

to fill up with gas	echar gasolina (al coche)
Fill her up!	¡Llénelo!
to fill a vacancy	cubrir un puesto
to fill a tooth	empastar una muela
to fill a crack	llenar una hendedura
to fill an order	despachar un pedido

film n & v

[cinema, photographic]	la película/el film/el filme
roll of film	un rollo/un carrete de fotografías
film star	un astro de cine [man]/una estrella de cine [woman]
film industry	la industria cinematográfica
silent film	una película muda
[thin layer]	una capa
[mist, smoke, etc.]	un velo
to film	filmar/rodar

final adj & n

[last]	último(a)/final
the final exam	el examen del fin de curso
the final [in sports]	la final
the final chapter	el último capítulo

finally adv

[at last]	al fin/por fin/finalmente
They have finally done it.	Por fin lo han hecho.

financial aid n

[in general]	la ayuda económica/financiera
[a grant]	una beca
[a loan in general]	un préstamo
[a commercial loan]	un empréstito

find v

to find [general]	encontrar
Have you found the keys?	¿Has encontrado las llaves?
No, I can't find them.	No, no las encuentro.
[to go and find]	ir a buscar
I'm going to find something to read.	Voy a buscar algo que leer.
[to surprise]	sorprender
I found him spying on us.	Lo sorprendí espiándonos.
[to establish]	comprobar
It has been found that ...	Se ha comprobado que...

fine adj

a fine meal	una comida excelente
a fine garden	un jardín hermoso
a fine dress	un vestido elegante
a fine afternoon [occasion]	una tarde agradable
a fine day [weather]	un buen día

finish v

to finish	acabar/terminar
She finished by bursting into tears.	Acabó por echarse a llorar.
I have finished writing.	He terminado de escribir.

fire n

a fire	un fuego/un incendio
to make/light a fire	encender un fuego
to be sitting by the fire	estar sentado(a) al lado de la chimenea
to be on fire	estar ardiendo/en llamas
to catch fire	encenderse
to set fire to	pegar fuego a/incendiar
to put out a fire	apagar un fuego
the fire department	los bomberos/el cuerpo de bomberos
fireworks	los fuegos artificiales

fire v

to fire at [with a gun]	tirar a/hacer fuego a
to open fire	abrir fuego
Fire!	¡Fuego!
[to dismiss sb]	despedir a/echar a alguien

first adj

first	primero(a)
the first time	la primera vez
the first row	la primera fila
the first chapter	el primer capítulo [Note: **primero** shortens to **primer** before a noun]
the first six months	los seis primeros meses [Note word order]
the first of March	el primero de marzo
Charles I (the first)	Carlos Iº (primero) [Note: no article]

first adv

(at) first/first of all	en primer lugar/ante todo/primero
first and foremost	antes que nada/ante todo
head first	de cabeza
ladies first	las señoras primero
My family comes first.	Mi familia es lo primero.
We first went there last month.	Fuimos allí por primera vez el mes pasado.
[before]	antes/primero
You must see me first.	Tienen que verme primero.

first pron

the first	el primero/la primera
They were the first to arrive.	Llegaron primeros.

fish n & v

a fish [alive in the water]	un pez
a fish [food]	un pescado
to fish	pescar
to go fishing	ir a pescar/ir de pesca
fishing	la pesca

fix v

[to repair sth]	reparar algo
to fix a meal	preparar una comida
to fix [arrangements, etc.]	arreglar

Ø **fijar** has numerous meanings, e.g., "to fix," "to secure," "to stick down," "to focus," etc.

flat *n*
a flat *[tire]*

una ponchadura *[LA]*/un pinchazo *[Sp]*/una llanta baja

flavor *n*
taste
This coffee has a bitter flavor.

el gusto/el sabor
Este café tiene un sabor amargo.

flavoring
I want an ice-cream with a chocolate flavor.
This cake has an orange flavor.

Quiero un helado con sabor a chocolate.
Este pastel tiene sabor a naranja.

flight attendant
flight attendant/stewardess

la aeromoza *[LA]*/la azafata *[Sp]*

floor *n*
the floor *[beneath one's feet]*
on the floor
dance floor
floor show

el piso *[LA]*/el suelo *[Sp]*
en el suelo
una pista (de baile)
atracciones (en la pista de baile)/un espectáculo de caberet

[of ocean]
floor level *[storey]*

el fondo
el piso/la planta *[Note: Numbering in Spanish-speaking countries is different from U.S.]*

the first floor
the second floor
the top floor
His office is on the 50th floor.

la planta baja
la planta primera/el primer piso
el piso alto
Su oficina está en el piso cincuenta.

flu *n*
flu

la gripe/el trancazo *[Sp]*

fly *v*
of planes, birds
The plane was flying from Los Angeles to Caracas.

volar
El avión volaba desde Los Angeles hasta Caracas.

passengers
She flew to New York yesterday.
I prefer flying to driving.

ir en avión
Fue en avión a Nueva York ayer.
Prefiero ir en avión que en coche.

food *n*
general
They lacked healthy food.
[for animals]
food poisoning

el alimento/la comida
Les faltaba el alimento sano.
el pasto
la intoxicación alimenticia

to eat
I want some food.
I enjoy my food.
to give food to sb
She has to give the workers their food.
It is forbidden to give food to the animals.

Quiero algo que comer.
Me gusta comer.
dar de comer a alguien
Tiene que dar de comer a los obreros.
Se prohíbe dar de comer a los animales.

edibles

I keep the food in the food cupboard.

You must keep the frozen food in the freezer.

Do they sell food?

What do you think of the price of food?

los comestibles

Guardo los comestibles en la despensa.

Debes guardar los comestibles congelados en el congelador.

¿Venden comestibles?

¿Qué piensas del precio de los comestibles?

cuisine

I love Mexican food.

The food's good in this restaurant.

la cocina

Me gusta mucho la cocina mexicana.

Se come bien en este restaurante./ La cocina es muy buena en este restaurante.

foot *n*

[human]

[animal, furniture]

foot of the page

el pie

la pata

la parte inferior/el pie de la página

for *prep*

destined for

He has just left for Spain.

This bus is for Toluca.

Is this book for me?

The train for Barcelona has gone.

Acaba de salir para España.

Éste es el autobús para/de Toluca.

¿Este libro es para mí?

El tren con destino Barcelona ya ha salido.

purpose

What is that machine for?

It's for washing the clothes.

a cure for AIDS

What will you have for dessert?

for sale

for rent

for example

to go for a walk

¿Para que sirve esa máquina?

Sirve para lavar la ropa.

una cura contra el SIDA

¿Qué vas a tomar de postre?

se vende

se renta/se alquila

por ejemplo

darse un paseo

motive

for this reason

the reason for her arrival

He shouted for joy.

for fear of

for fear that

famous for

She went to the market for fruit.

por esta razón

el motivo de su llegada

Gritó de alegría.

por miedo de *[+ infinitive]*

por miedo de que *[+ subjunctive]*

célebre/famoso(a) por

Fue al mercado por fruta.

in exchange for

in exchange for sth

I want to exchange this one for that one.

I'll give you 100 dollars for the picture.

What is the Spanish for "salt"?

to thank for

We thanked him for his help.

a cambio de algo

Quiero cambiar éste por aquél.

Le daré cien dólares por el cuadro.

¿Cómo se dice "salt" en castellano?

dar las gracias por

Les dimos las gracias por su ayuda.

on behalf of

He did it for you.

Lo hizo por ti.

foreign

For God and country

Por Dios y la Patria

for distance covered
He walked for miles and miles [E].

Caminó/Anduvo kilómetros y kilómetros [Sp].

considering
She is very tall for her age.

Es muy alta para su edad.

respect for
They have no respect for their teachers.

No tienen ningún respeto para con sus profesores.

time
It's time for dinner.
I have no time to go to the movies.
forever
forever and ever
I've been living here for six months [and still am].
I lived in Madrid for a year [but no longer do].
He had been living there for six months when he became ill.
I am going to Puerto Rico for a month.
She has reserved a room for two weeks.
They will be in Peru for most of the summer.
I waited for hours.

Es la hora de cenar
No tengo tiempo para ir al cine.
para siempre/por siempre
para siempre jamás
Hace seis meses que vivo aquí./ Vivo aquí desde hace seis meses.
Viví en Madrid durante un año.

Vivía allí desde hacía seis meses cuando se enfermó.
Voy a Puerto Rico para un mes.
Ha reservado una habitación para quince días.
Estarán en el Perú durante gran parte del verano.
Esperé horas y horas.

verb + for
to ask for
to hope for
to look for
to pay for
to pray for
to send for
to send for a doctor
to thank for
to wait for

[Note: "for" is often not translated]
pedir
esperar
buscar
pagar
rogar/orar por
enviar a buscar/mandar a buscar
llamar a un médico
agradecer
esperar

foreign *adj*
foreign
foreign trade
foreign affairs
foreign currency

extranjero(a)
el comercio exterior
los asuntos exteriores
las divisas

forget *v*
to forget
He forgot to buy the paper.
I've forgotten the color.
[to leave behind]
I forgot my umbrella in the café.
And don't you forget it!

olvidar/olvidarse de
Se olvidó de comprar el diario.
He olvidado el color.
dejar
Dejé (olvidado) mi paraguas en el café.
¡Que no se te olvide!

form *n & v*
form *[shape, style, method]*
[vague outline]

la forma
una figura

[document]	un formulario/una hoja
to fill out a form	llenar una hoja
[manner]	la manera
in this form	de esta manera
to form	formar

formal adj

formal dress	el traje formal [LA]
	el traje de etiqueta [men]
	el traje de noche [women]
They were all in formal [evening] dress.	Todos estaban/iban vestidos de etiqueta.
to dress formally	vestirse de etiqueta
[person's manner]	ceremonioso(a)/estirado(a)/formalista
Don't be so formal!	¡No te andes con tantos cumplidos!/ ¡No seas tan formalista!
She spoke to me in a formal manner.	Me habló de una manera ceremoniosa.
a formal visit	una visita oficial/de cumplido
a formal invitation	una invitación formal

Ø **formal** has a number of meanings including "reliable," e.g., **Es un hombre muy formal**. "He's a very reliable man."

former adj

[past, previous]	ex-/antiguo(a) [Note: precedes noun]
the former president	el ex-presidente/el antiguo presidente
the former capital of Spain	la antigua capital de España

former pron

[opposite of "the latter"]	aquél/aquélla
	el primero/la primera
Of the two hotels I prefer the former.	De los dos hoteles prefiero aquél.

fortune n

[fate, luck]	la fortuna/la suerte
[wealth]	una fortuna/un caudal
to cost a fortune	costar un dineral

frame n & v

[framework]	una estructura/un esqueleto
[of eyeglasses]	la montura/la armadura
[of door, window, picture]	el marco
to frame a picture	poner un marco a/enmarcar un cuadro
to frame sb	incriminar a alguien dolosamente

free adj

free of charge	gratis/gratuito(a)/sin gastos
a free ticket	una entrada gratis
a free copy [of book]	un ejemplar gratuito
I got in free.	Entré sin pagar.
duty free	exento/libre de derechos de aduana
post free	franco de porte
tax free	exento/libre de impuestos
released, loose	suelto(a)
The terrorists are free.	Los terroristas están sueltos.

One of the lions is free. — Uno de los leones está suelto.

commerce — libre/franco(a)
a free port — un puerto franco
free trade — el libre cambio
a free gift — una prima

available — libre
Are you free tonight? — ¿Estás libre esta noche?
Is this table free? — ¿Está libre esta mesa?

independent — libre
the free press — la prensa libre
free speech — la libertad de palabra
free expression — la libertad de expresión
the free world — el mundo libre
free and easy — despreocupado(a)

-free preceded by noun — sin + noun
fat-free foods — alimentos sin grasa
lead-free gasoline — la gasolina sin plomo

other
a free translation — una traducción libre
to have a free hand/rein — tener campo libre/carta blanca

freeze/frozen *v*
It's freezing. — Hiela./Hay helada.
I was frozen to the bone. — Estaba helado(a) hasta los huesos.
frozen foods — los alimentos/comestibles congelados

freezer *n*
a freezer — un fríser [LA]/un congelador
[for ice-cream making] — una heladera

friend *n*
a friend — un amigo/una amiga/un(a) camarada/
    un compañero/una compañera/un(a)
    compinche *[fam]*
a close friend — un amigo íntimo/una amiga íntima
a friend of mine — un amigo mío/una amiga mía
He's no friend of mine. — No es de mis amigos.
my boyfriend — mi novio
my girlfriend — mi novia

from *prep*
a place
from the city — de la ciudad
from the school — del colegio
from the stores — de los almacenes
from the provinces — de las provincias
Where are you from? *[place of origin/birth, etc.]* — ¿De dónde eres?
Where have you come from? *[i.e., arrived from]* — ¿De dónde vienes?

with geographic names
from Buenos Aires — de Buenos Aires
from Colombia — de Colombia

from Peru	del Perú
from Mexico City	de la Ciudad de México/de México Distrito Federal

with transport

The train from Santiago has just arrived.	El tren procedente de Santiago acaba de llegar.

to take sth from somewhere

to take sth from the drawer	sacar algo del cajón
Go and get water from the well.	Ve a buscar agua al pozo.

time

from three o'clock to six	De las tres a las seis/desde las tres hasta las seis
from nine o'clock on	a partir de las nueve
from Monday/starting Monday	a partir del lunes
five years from now	dentro de cinco años
from start to finish	desde el principio hasta el final
from then on	desde entonces
from now on	desde ahora en adelante

position

from above	desde arriba/encima
from afar	desde lejos
from below	desde abajo

on behalf of

	de parte de
Say hello to your father from me.	Salúdale a tu papá de mi parte.
He spoke to them on my behalf.	Les habló de parte mía.

other expressions

from bad to worse	de mal en peor
to know good from bad	saber distinguir entre el bien y el mal/saber el bien del mal/saber lo bueno de lo malo
from my point of view	desde mi punto de vista

verb + from

They took my father's watch.	Le quitaron el reloj a mi padre.
I'm going to borrow a ladder from my cousin.	Voy a pedir prestado una escalera a mi primo.
He bought the camera from his neighbor.	Compró la máquina a su vecino.
She stole it from me.	Me lo robó.

front *prep, adv, adj & n*

preposition

in front of	delante (de)
It was in front of us.	Estaba delante de nosotros.

adverb

in front	(por) delante
The mayor was walking in front.	El alcalde iba por delante.
in front [in a vehicle]	delante/en la parte delantera

adjective

	delantero(a)/de delante
the car in front	el coche de delante
[forward part]	delantero(a)
the front seat	el asiento delantero

fruit

[first]
I want to sit in the front row.
The photo was on the front
  page of the paper.

primero(a)
Quiero sentarme en (la) primera fila.
La foto estaba en (la) primera
  plana del diario.

noun
[of vehicle]
[of shirt, dress, etc.]
[business, organization]
His company is just a front.
the front [military]
the popular front [political]

la parte delantera
la pechera
una tapadera
Su empresa no es más que una tapadera.
el frente
el frente popular

Ø **la frente** means "forehead".

fruit n & adj
[botanical]
[for eating]
I like fruit.
I'll have fruit for dessert.
a piece of fruit
a fruit tree
fruit salad
a fruit dish

el fruto
la fruta
Me gusta la fruta.
Voy a tomar fruta de postre.
alguna fruta/una porción de fruta
un árbol frutal
una macedonia de fruta
un frutero

full adj
filled
The glasses were full.

lleno(a)
Los vasos estaban llenos.

no more room
[in bus, theater, restaurant]
We are full.

completo(a)/lleno(a)
Completo./Estamos completos./No
  caben más.

full to overflowing
full house [theater]
"House full"

lleno(a) hasta el tope
el lleno
"No hay localidades"

from eating
I'm full.

No puedo más.

other expressions
full speed
full employment
in full color
full moon
full board
full-length
full-length [of film]
full-scale

a toda velocidad
el pleno empleo
a todo color
la luna llena
la pensión completa
de cuerpo entero
de largo metraje
de tamaño natural

fun n/**funny** adj
[strange, odd]
[amusing]
The play was very funny.
to have fun
They had a lot of fun.
to make fun of sb

curioso(a)/raro(a)
cómico(a)/divertido(a)/gracioso(a)
La comedia fue muy cómica.
divertirse/pasarlo bien
Se divirtieron./Lo pasaron bien.
burlarse de alguien

fur n
fur   el pelo/el pelaje
[of dead animal]   la piel
a fur coat   un abrigo de pieles

furniture n
[in general]   los muebles/el mobiliario
He sells furniture.   Vende muebles.
a piece of furniture   un mueble

future adj
[next]   futuro(a)/venidero(a)
the future champion   el futuro campeón
the future tense   el (tiempo) futuro

future n
the future   el porvenir/el futuro
He has a promising future in   Tiene un porvenir prometedor en la
   the company.   compañía.
in the future   en el futuro/en lo futuro/en lo sucesivo
in the near future   en un futuro próximo/en fecha próxima

fuzzy adj
[of hair]   rizado/crespo
[blurry]   borroso

G

gain *n*
[profit, earning] un logro/una ganancia/un beneficio
[increase] un aumento

gain *v*
[to earn, win] ganar
to gain an objective lograr/conseguir un objetivo

game *n*
in general el juego
the Olympic Games los Juegos Olímpicos (los JJ.OO.)

board & card games una partida
a game of cards una partida de cartas/naipes
a game of chess una partida de ajedrez

ball games un partido
a game of soccer/tennis/ice un partido de fútbol/tenis/hockey
  hockey sobre hielo
game, set and match juego, set y partido

garage *n*
a garage un garaje/un garage *[spelling often
  found in Latin America]*

garbage *n*
household garbage la(s) basura(s)/los desperdicios
[industrial waste] los residuos/los vertidos
[litter, trash] la basura
Don't litter! ¡No tiren/dejen papeles!
a garbage can un cubo de (la) basura
They collect the garbage on Recogen la basura los viernes.
  Thursdays.

gas *n*
a vapor el gas
a gas stove la cocina de gas

gasoline la gasolina/la bencina
  [Chi]/la nafta [Arg & Uru]
to fill up with gas echar gasolina (al coche)
regular/super/unleaded gas la gasolina normal/súper/sin plomo
  *[Note: In Venezuela la nafta means
  "super."]*

gentle *adj*
[of character] amable/benévolo(a)/bondadoso(a)
[mild] suave
a gentle wind un viento suave
a gentle slope una cuesta suave
[soft, sweet] dulce
a gentle voice una voz dulce

84

Ø **gentil** has a number of meanings including "pleasant," "charming," "graceful," and "gentile."

gentleman   n

This gentleman is leaving now.	Este señor se marcha ahora.
Ladies and gentlemen!	¡Señoras y señores!
He's a real gentleman.	Es un cumplido caballero.

Ø **gentilhombre** means "a gentleman at court."

get   v

	[Note: Reflexive verbs often express the idea of "get."]
to get drunk	emborracharse
to get organized	organizarse
to get undressed	desnudarse
to become	[See under **become** for use of **llegar a ser, hacerse, ponerse,** and **volverse.** Alternative forms are often used for "get" in the sense of "become."]
to get excited	emocionarse
to get damaged	dañarse
to get sad	entristecerse
to get wet	mojarse

[See also **angry, big, bored, fat, hungry, interested, old, sick, sleepy, thin, thirsty, tired, used to.**]

to obtain	obtener/conseguir/lograr/procurar/ comprar/sacar
She got her boss's permission.	Obtuvo el permiso de su jefe.
Where did you get your degree?	¿Dónde sacaste el título?
I'll try to get tickets.	Trataré de conseguir localidades.
I got her the raise.	Le procuré el aumento.
We got the books downtown.	Compramos los libros en el centro.
I got a television for my birthday.	Me regalaron un televisor para mi cumpleaños.
to receive	recibir
She gets lots of mail.	Recibe muchas cartas.
You always get good grades.	Siempre sacas buenas notas.
to go, to arrive	
How do I get to the town hall?	¿Cómo puedo llegar al ayuntamiento?
How do you get to San Juan from here?	¿Cómo se llega/se va a San Juan desde aquí?
We can get there by bus.	Podemos ir en autocar.
When will you get here?	¿Cuándo llegarás?
to get sb to come	ir a buscar a/hacer venir a/llamar a
I need to get the doctor.	Hace falta llamar al médico.
Go and get a policeman.	Ve a buscar a un guardia./Haz venir a un guardia./Llama a un guardia.
to go and get sth	ir a buscar
I'll go and get something to drink from the kitchen.	Iré a buscar algo que beber en la cocina.
to grasp (mentally)	comprender/entender
I don't get the joke.	No comprendo/entiendo el chiste.

I've got it!	¡Ya lo comprendo!/¡Ya lo entiendo!
I didn't get her name.	No oí/no llegué a oír su nombre.

to get the chance

She gets to drive the car.	La permiten manejar el coche.
When he's older he'll get to go to the university.	Cuando sea mayor, podrá ir a la universidad.
I got to see the film.	Fui a ver la película./Conseguí ver la película.

to have — tener

Have you got the money?	¿Tienes el dinero?
No, I haven't got it with me.	No, no lo traigo/llevo.

impersonal expressions

It's getting hot/cold.	Empieza a hacer calor/frío.
It's getting dark.	Empieza a hacerse de noche./Se va anocheciendo.
It's getting light.	Empieza a hacerse de día.

to get + adverb

to get about/around	viajar mucho
to get ahead	adelantar
to get along/by	arreglárselas
to get along with sb	llevarse bien con alguien
to get down [lift down]	bajar
to get out [of a place]	salir (de)/bajar (de)/escaparse (de)
to get out [news]	hacerse público
[See also away, back, in, off, on, up]	

to get + past participle — ser + past participle

to get arrested/paid/robbed	ser detenido(a)/pagado(a)/robado(a)
She got fired by the manager.	Fue despedida por el gerente.

gift *n*

[a present]	un regalo/un obsequio
[a talent]	un don/un talento/dotes [fem pl]
I have a gift for languages.	Tengo un don de lenguas.
He has a gift for management.	Tiene talento para la administración.
She has artistic gifts.	Tiene dotes artísticas.

girlfriend *n*

his girlfriend	su novia
[a woman friend]	una amiga

give *v*

to give	dar
[as a present]	regalar
[to donate]	donar
[to pay for]	pagar
to give up [hand over]	ceder
to give up [to stop]	dejar de
to give up smoking	dejar de fumar
to give up [surrender]	rendirse/entregarse
to give up for dead	dar por muerto

glass *n*

[material]	el vidrio/el cristal
It's made of glass.	Es de vidrio/cristal.

glass [window] pane	una luna
glass case	una vitrina
[glassware]	la cristalería/los artículos de vidrio
looking glass [mirror]	un espejo
drinking glass [water, etc.]	un vaso
wine glass	una copa
sherry glass	una copita
beer glass	una caña
eyeglasses	las gafas/los lentes
dark glasses	las gafas negras
sunglasses	las gafas de sol
[binoculars]	los gemelos/los prismáticos

go v

to go (someplace)	ir (a cualquier parte)
Let's go to the beach.	Vamos a la playa.
Let's go!	¡Vámonos!
Go ahead/Go on.	Adelante./Sigue.
It's time to go.	Es la hora de salir.
Things are going well.	Todo marcha bien.
to go abroad	ir al extranjero
to go near to	acercarse a
to go through	pasar por
to go through [endure]	sufrir/experimentar
to go to one's head	subirle a la cabeza
The victory went to his head.	La victoria le subió a la cabeza.
to go under	pasar por debajo de algo
to go under [sink]	hundirse [ship]/ desaparecer por debajo del agua [person]
to go wrong	andar fallando

[see also away, down, in, out, up]

to go + infinitive

They're not going to sell the house.	No van a vender la casa.
I wasn't going to see her.	No iba a visitarla.
Go and see who it is.	Ve/Vaya a ver quién es.
I went out to talk with them.	Salí a hablar con ellos.

goal n

[an aim]	un fin/un objeto/una meta
[ambition]	una ambición
[in sports]	un gol/un tanto
to score a goal	marcar un tanto

good adj

[in general]	bueno(a)
[healthy, wholesome]	sano(a)
Have a good day!	¡Que te vaya bien!
Be good! [well-behaved]	¡Pórtate bien!
a good man/fellow/guy	un buen chico/un buen tío/un buen tipo
a good woman	una buena chica/mujer/persona
to be good at chemistry	ser fuerte en la química
She's good with animals.	Entiende de animales.
He's a good teacher.	Es un buen profesor
She's a good teacher.	Es una buena profesora.
Good Friday	Viernes Santo

good

It's good to be here.	Es agradable estar aquí.
It's good to see you.	Me alegro de verte.
to be good [kind] to sb	ser amable con
It's very good [nice] of you to ...	Eres muy amable de...
to have a good time	divertirse/pasarlo(la) bien
Have a good time!	¡Que lo pases bien!/¡Que te diviertas!
They had a good time.	Lo pasaron bien./Se divirtieron.
good for nothing	inútil
a good deal of	bastante
as good as done	prácticamente terminado

verb + good

to look good [health]	parecer bien
She looks good today. [well-dressed]	Está muy elegante hoy.
to be good-looking	ser guapo(a)/ser de buen parecer
to feel good [health]	sentirse bien
to feel good [emotion]	estar contento(a)/satisfecho(a)
I feel good about my work.	Estoy satisfecho de mi trabajo.
to smell good	oler bien
The meat smells good.	La carne huele bien.
to taste good	ser sabroso(a)

good *n*

good and evil	el bien y el mal
to do good	hacer bien
It's for your own good.	Es por su propio bien.
It'll do you good.	Te sentará bien.
It's no good complaining.	De nada sirve quejarse./No sirve para nada quejarse.
What's the good of it?	¿Para qué sirve?
It's no good worrying about it.	No vale la pena inquietarse por ello.
for good [for ever]	para siempre
goods	los bienes
goods [commerce]	los géneros/los artículos

grade *n*

[in school]	el curso/la clase
to be in sixth grade	estar en el sexto curso
[a score]	una nota
to get bad grades	sacar malas notas
to make the grade	tener éxito/llegar al nivel necesario

Ø **grada** means "step," "stair;" **grado** means "degree" (temperature).

graduate *n & adj*

to be a graduate of the University of Santiago	ser licenciado de la universidad de Santiago
to do graduate studies	hacer estudios graduados

grand *adj*

great, large

the grand hall	grande la gran sala

magnificent

a grand occasion	magnífico(a)/espléndido(a)/grandioso(a) una función magnífica
a grand piano	un piano de cola

grant *n & v*
[scholarship]   una beca
[subsidy]   una subvención
[to concede]   conceder
[to admit]   reconocer
to take sth for granted   dar algo por sentado

gray *adj*
gray — gris
[hair] — cano/canoso
[gloomy] — triste

great *adj*
in general — grande
a great man — un gran hombre
a great novel — una gran novela
> *[Note: **Grande** shortens to **gran** before a noun.]*

They are great paintings. — Son grandes/magníficos cuadros.
to be great friends — ser muy amigos
with great care — con mucho cuidado
with great pleasure — con mucho gusto

excellent — estupendo(a)/maravilloso(a)
a great match — un partido estupendo
a great song — una canción maravillosa
That's great! — ¡Magnífico!/¡Estupendo!/¡Macanudo! [Arg]

gross *adj*
[large, fat] — grueso(a)
[coarse, vulgar] — grosero(a)/ordinario(a)/brusco(a) [Ven]/guarango(a) [Arg, Chi & Uru]/ basto(a) [Sp]
[of error] — craso(a)
[injustice] — flagrante
[commerce] — bruto(a)
gross pay — el salario bruto

ground *n*
[earth, soil] — la tierra/el suelo
[terrain] — el terreno
football ground — un campo de fútbol
on the ground — en/sobre el suelo
the ground floor — la planta baja
[see also **floor**]
[reason] — la causa/el motivo/la razón
grounds [gardens] — los jardines

grow *v intrans*
to grow [people and things] — crecer
My son has grown a lot. — Mi hijo ha crecido mucho.
She's letting her hair grow. — Deja crecerse el pelo.
to grow up — hacerse mayor/hombre/mujer
When they grow up ... — Cuando se hagan mayores...
to grow old — envejecer(se)

of plants — cultivarse

Roses grow well in my garden.	Las rosas se cultivan bien en mi jardín.

to increase aumentar
The population has grown by ten per cent. La población ha aumentado el 10 por ciento.

to grow + adjective: [see get]

grow   *v trans*
to grow plants cultivar
We grow strawberries and raspberries. Cultivamos fresas y frambuesas.

guard   *n & v*
[sentry] un centinela
[escort] una escolta
[soldier] un guardia
the guard [squad] el guardia
to be on guard estar de guardia
a guard dog un perro guardián
to be on one's guard estar en guardia/alerta
off one's guard desprevenido(a)
to guard [place] guardar/proteger
to guard [person] vigilar

guess   *v*
to believe, suppose creer/imaginar/suponer
I guess it's all right. Creo que está bien./Estará bien, supongo.
Has he arrived? – I guess so. ¿Ha llegado? – Creo que sí.
I guess not. Creo que no.

to make a guess adivinar
Guess where she's calling from! ¡A ver si adivinas de dónde llama!
to guess right acertar
You've guessed right. Has acertado.

guest   *n*
the person invited el convidado/la convidada
 el invitado/la invitada
We have guests on Saturday. Tenemos invitados el sábado.
Be my guest. Invito yo.
[at a hotel] el huésped/la huéspeda

guilty   *adj*
[guilty of a wrongdoing] culpable
to have a guilty conscience estar lleno de remordimiento
to feel guilty sentir remordimiento

guy   *n*
[colloquial for a boy or man] un tío/un tipo
a nice guy un buen chico/un buen tío/un buen tipo

H

habit   *n*

a habit
What are his habits?
to be in the habit of doing sth
I usually go to bed late.
to get into the habit
from/out of habit

una costumbre/un hábito
¿Cuáles son sus costumbres?
acostumbrar/soler hacer algo
Acostumbro/Suelo acostarme tarde.
acostumbrarse a
por costumbre

Ø **el hábito** usually means "habit" in the sense of clothing, e.g., "a nun's habit."

hair   *n*

hair *[of the head]*
a single hair
to have brown/blond(e) hair
to have red hair
grey/white hair
My hair was all wet.
He cut his hair.
He had his hair cut.
a haircut
to comb one's hair
to do one's hair
to have one's hair done
a hairstyle
a hairdresser
a hairdresser's
hair *[on chest, arms, etc.]*

el pelo/los cabellos
un pelo
tener el pelo castaño/rubio
ser pelirrojo(a)
las canas
Tenía el pelo todo mojado.
Se cortó el pelo.
Se cortó el pelo./Se hizo cortar el pelo.
un corte de pelo
peinarse
arreglarse el pelo
hacerse arreglar el pelo
un peinado
un peluquero/una peluquera
una peluquería
el vello

half   *adj*

half-
a half-brother/sister
a half-liter of olive oil
a half dozen
a half owner
half ... half ...
half man half beast
half alive
half past two
halfway
halfway measures

medio(a)
un medio hermano/una media hermana
medio litro de aceite de oliva
media docena
un propietario a medias
mitad... mitad...
mitad hombre, mitad animal
medio muerto(a)
las dos y media
a medio camino
medidas parciales

half   *n*

a half
I ate half the orange.
I will pay half (of) the cost.
the first half *[in sport]*

la mitad
Comí la mitad de la naranja.
Pagaré la mitad del coste.
el primer tiempo

hall   *n*

[a passage, a corridor]
[entrance in house]
[a hotel or theater lobby]

un corredor *[LA]*/un pasillo
un hall*[LA]*/un vestíbulo
el hall/el vestíbulo

91

Halt!

[an exhibition or concert hall]　　una sala de exposiciones/conciertos

Halt!　　¡Alto!

hand *n*

a hand	la mano *[Note: feminine]*
the right hand/the left hand	la mano derecha/izquierda
[on a ship]	un tripulante
[worker]	un(a) trabajador(a)/operario(a)
[of clock or watch]	una manecilla
[of writing]	la escritura
to give sb a big hand	darle a alguien una gran ovación/un gran aplauso
on the other hand	por otro lado/por otra parte
She is weak in math; on the other hand she is strong in history.	Es floja en (las) matemáticas; por otro lado es fuerte en (la) historia.
on one hand ... on the other hand	por una parte... por otra parte/por un lado... por otro lado
to be on hand	estar a la mano
one last hand! [cards]	¡la última mano!
not to lift a hand	no mover un dedo
on hands and knees	a gatas/a cuatro patas

Ø **una mano** is used in many Latin American countries to mean "one-way" with regard to traffic.

handle *n*

[of bag, basket, cup]	un asa *[fem]*
[of bicycle]	un puño
[doorknob]	un pomo
[of drawer]	un tirador
to fly off the handle	salirse de sus casillas

handle *v*

to touch　　tocar

Please do not handle the goods.	Por favor no toque/manosee la mercancía.
"Handle with care."	"Manéjese con cuidado."
to handle a boat	dirigir un barco

to take care of, to deal with　　encargarse de/tratar

We'll handle everything.	Nos encargaremos de todo.
I don't know how to handle this problem.	No sé cómo tratar este problema.

to control　　controlar/saber dominar

He cannot handle the students.　　No puede con los estudiantes.

to handle oneself　　comportarse

She handled herself well in that situation.　　Se comportó bien en esa situación.

handlebar *n*

[of bicycle]　　un manillar

handsome *adj*

[of appearance]	guapo(a)/hermoso(a)/apuesto(a)/elegante
[considerable]	considerable/bueno(a)
a handsome amount	una cantidad considerable
a handsome salary	un sueldo muy bueno

handwriting   n
[one's own]   la letra
[writing done by hand]   la escritura
handwritten   escrito(a) a mano

hang   v
[to kill by hanging from the neck]   ahorcar
to hang wallpaper   pegar/poner papel pintado
[to decorate, to hang pictures]   adornar con cuadros
to hang one's head   bajar la cabeza
to be hanging [pending]   estar pendiente
to leave a question hanging   dejar pendiente una cuestión
to hang around   vagar
to hang on   mantenerse firme/resistir/
                                             aguantar

hangover   n
a hangover   un(a) crudo(a) [Mex]/una jaqueca
                                             [Arg & Uru]/un guayabo [Col &
                                             Ecu]/un chucháqui [Col & Ecu]/
                                             un ratón [Ven]/una resaca [Sp]

hang-up   n/hang up   v
to have a hang-up   tener un complejo/una obsesión
to hang up [the phone]   colgar

happen   v
to happen, occur   acontecer/ocurrir/pasar/suceder
What happened?   ¿Qué pasó/sucedió?
That always happens.   Eso siempre ocurre/sucede.
These things happen.   Son cosas que pasan.

to a person
What happened to you?   ¿Qué te pasó?
What happened to [became of]   ¿Que habrá sido de ella?
  her?

by chance   por casualidad
                                           si acaso [+ subjunctive]
If you happen to see her ...   Si la ves por casualidad...
                                           Si acaso la veas...

Ø **suceder** only means "to succeed" in the sense of "to succeed to a title."

happy   adj
[fortunate]   (ser) feliz/dichoso(a)/afortunado(a)
[contented]   (estar) contento(a)/satisfecho(a)
[cheerful]   (estar) alegre
[appropriate]   (ser) feliz/oportuno(a)

hard   adj
[of a substance]   duro(a)
[of a person]   severo(a)/inflexible
[of a situation]   difícil
to have a hard time doing sth   costarle a uno hacer algo/encontrar
                                             difícil hacer algo
He gave us a hard time.   Nos hizo todo muy difícil.

hard *adv*

to work hard	trabajar mucho
to study hard	estudiar mucho/empollar *[fam]*
to try hard to do sth	intentar hacer algo
to try one's hardest to do sth	esforzarse para/por/en hacer algo
	hacer todo lo posible para hacer algo

hardly *adv*

[barely]	apenas
I hardly heard him.	Apenas lo oí.
hardly anyone	casi nadie
hardly anything	casi nada
hardly ever	casi nunca

hardness *n*

[difficulty]	la dificultad
[of winter]	el rigor
[of heart]	la insensibilidad

have *v*

to possess — tener

I have three children.	Tengo tres hijos.
Have you got any money?	¿Tienes dinero? *[Note: There is no equivalent in Spanish of "got".]*
He's got a house by the beach.	Tiene una casa cerca de la playa.

auxiliary verb — haber

I have seen your brother.	He visto a tu hermano.
Have you been to Mexico?	¿Has estado en México?

to have sth done — hacer hacer algo/mandar hacer algo

I have had a tooth out.	Me han sacado una muela.
He should have his watch repaired.	Debería mandar reparar su reloj.
We'll have it done tomorrow.	Mandaremos hacerlo mañana.
He had us read it.	Nos hizo leerlo.

have to *v*

to have to (do sth) — tener que/deber/hay que/hace falta

in the present

I have to leave immediately.	Tengo que/Debo/marcharme al instante/ en seguida.

in the past (habitually)

When we lived in Lima I had to work on Sundays.	Cuando vivíamos en Lima tenía que trabajar los domingos.
She had to visit her aunt every day.	Debía visitar a su tía cada día.

in the past (a specific occasion)

I had to tell you the truth.	Tuve que decirte la verdad.
They had to pay the fine.	Debieron pagar la multa.

in the future

You will have to sell the car.	Tendrás que vender el coche.
I will have to help them.	Deberé ayudarlos.

with a negative

You don't have to come with us.	No es necesario acompañarnos./No tienes que acompañarnos. *[Note: **No debes acompañarnos** would mean "You must not come with us."]*

to have to do with	tener que ver con

hazard n
[danger] — el peligro
[risk] — el riesgo
a health hazard — un peligro/un riesgo para la salud
It's hazardous for your health. — Es peligroso para la salud.

he pron
he — él
He's on vacation at present. — Actualmente está de vacaciones.
He and his wife have gone to Brazil. — Él y su esposa han ido al Brasil.
[Note: *Él, like all the other subject pronouns, is usually omitted; it is used for emphasis and clarification.*]

Ø **él** meaning "he" has an accent to distinguish it from **el** meaning "the;" it can also mean "him" following a preposition, e.g., "It's for him" is translated by **Es para él.**

healthy adj
[of a person] — sano(a)/en buena salud
They are healthy. — Gozan de buena salud.
[of things] — sano(a)
healthy food — el alimento sano

Ø "sane" is translated by **cuerdo(a)**.

hear v
to hear — oír
to hear from sb — tener noticias de/recibir cartas de alguien
I haven't heard from her. — No he tenido sus noticias.
to hear of sb/sth — oír hablar de alguien/algo
I've never heard of her. — Nunca he oído hablar de ella.
to hear that — oír decir que
We heard you had gone away. — Oímos decir que te habías marchado.
I heard he was sick. — Supe/Me enteré que estaba enfermo.
I heard you coming in. — Te oí entrar.
I can hear them. — Los oigo.

heat n & v
heat — el calor
I don't like the heat. — No me gusta el calor.

heating — la calefacción
to turn the (central) heating on/off. — encender/apagar la calefacción central

in cooking
on low heat — a fuego lento
to heat (up) the soup — calentar la sopa

heavy adj
weight — pesado(a)
This case is heavy. — Esta maleta está pesada.
How heavy is he? — ¿Cuánto pesa?

other
The traffic was very heavy. — Había mucho tráfico./El tráfico estaba muy denso.
a heavy schedule — un programa cargado

heel

He's a heavy drinker.	Bebe mucho.
It's a heavy rain.	Está lloviendo fuerte.

heel n
[of foot]	un talón
[of shoe]	un tacón
[a person – slang]	un canalla/un sinvergüenza

hello excl
[in greeting]	¡Hola!/¡Hola, buenos días!
[on the telephone]	¡Bueno! [Mex]/¡Haló! [Ven, Per, Ecu, Bol]/ ¡Holá! [Arg & Uru]¡Diga!/¡Dígame! [Sp]

help v
to help/assist	ayudar
Can I help you? [in shop]	¿En que puedo servirle?

Ø **asistir** means "to attend," "to be present at."

help n
I am grateful for your help.	Te agradezco tu ayuda.
Help!	¡Socorro!

helpful adj
[of a person]	atento(a)/servicial/amable
He's a very helpful waiter.	Es un camarero muy atento.
The doctors were very helpful.	Los médicos eran muy amables.
[of a thing]	útil/provechoso(a)
This book will be most helpful.	Este libro será muy útil.
It would be very helpful to us if you could do it.	Nos serviría mucho si pudieras hacerlo.

her adj
[singular: masc & fem]	su
[plural: masc & fem]	sus
her husband and son	su esposo y su hijo [Note: adjective re-
peated.]	
She lost her books and jewelry.	Perdió su ropa y sus joyas.

Ø As **su** can also mean "his," "its," "your," and "their," you can add **de ella** after the noun if the meaning is not entirely clear, e.g., **su casa de ella** "her house."

her pron
[direct object]	la
[indirect object] to her	le
[disjunctive]	ella/sí
Can you see her?	¿La ves?
Did you give her the money?	¿Le diste el dinero?
Yes, I gave it to her.	Sí, se lo di. [Note: When **le** is followed by **lo, la, los,** or **las** it changes to **se**.]
I lent it to her.	Sí, se lo presté a ella. [Note: As **se** has so many possible meanings you can add **a ella** after the verb to stress that here it means "to her."]
He sat behind her.	Estaba sentado detrás de ella.
She looked around her.	Miró alrededor de sí. [Note: **Sí** is used instead of **ella** as it refers to the same person as the subject of the verb.]

She took the money with her. | Llevó el dinero consigo. *[Note the special form of* **sí** *used after* **con**.*]*

here *adv*

here | aquí/acá
Come here! | ¡Ven aquí!
Here is/are ... | Aquí está/están...
| He aquí...
Here are your documents. | He aquí tus papeles.
Where's the money? – Here it is. | ¿Dónde está el dinero? – Aquí lo tienes.
Is the boss here today? – No, he isn't here. | ¿Está el jefe hoy? – No, no está. *[Note: no Spanish equivalent of "here" used in this sense.]*

around here | por aquí
in here | aquí dentro
near here | aquí cerca
right here | aquí mismo

hers *pron*

[singular] | el suyo/la suya
[plural] | los suyos/las suyas
We all had our passports but Carmen had lost hers. | Todos teníamos nuestros pasaportes pero Carmen había perdido el suyo.
Is this ring yours? – No, it's hers. | ¿Es tuya esta sortija? – No, es suya. *[Note: definite article omitted after the verb* **ser***]*

Ø As **suyo/a/os/as** could also mean "his," "yours," or "theirs," you can replace them with **de ella** if there is any chance of confusion, e.g., "It's hers". **Es de ella.**

herself *[see self]*

high *adj*

[general] | alto(a)
The tower is very high. | La torre es muy alta.
How high is this building? | ¿Qué altura tiene este edificio?/ ¿Cuánto mide este edificio de alto?

It's 10 meters high. | Tiene diez metros de alto/altura.
a high price | un precio elevado
He has a high fever. | Tiene una fiebre fuerte.
a high-rise *[building]* | un rascacielos
high and dry | sin recursos
high and low | de arriba abajo/por todas partes
high and mighty | arrogante
higher education | los estudios universitarios/la enseñanza superior

hill *n*

a hill | un cerro *[LA]*/una colina *[Sp]*
You can see the top of the hill from my room. | Se puede ver la cumbre/la cima del cerro desde mi cuarto.

a hillside, a slope | una cuesta
There are olive trees on the hills. | Hay olivos en las cuestas.
He went up the hill in search of the children. | Subió la cuesta en busca de los niños.
downhill/uphill | cuesta abajo/cuesta arriba

They ran downhill to see me.	Corrieron cuesta abajo a verme.

him *pron*
[direct object]

lo/le *[Note: Lo is far more common than le in Latin America; le is frequently used in Spain.]*

[indirect object] to him
[disjunctive]
Do you know him?
Did you lend him the car?
I read it to him.

le
él/sí
¿Lo/le conoces?
¿Le prestaste el coche?
Se lo leí. *[Note: When le is followed by lo, la, los, or las it changes to se.]*
Se lo leí a él. *[Note: As se has so many possible meanings you can add a él after the verb to stress that here it means "to him."]*

Do you remember him?
He looked around him.

¿Te acuerdas de él?
Miró alrededor de sí. *[Note: Sí is used instead of él as it refers to the same person as the subject of the verb.]*

He took the money with him.

Llevó el dinero consigo. *[Note the special form of sí used after con.]*

himself *[see self]*

his *adj*
[singular: masc & fem]
[plural: masc & fem]
his wife and daughter

su
sus
su esposa y su hija *[Note: adjective repeated.]*

He sold his house and car.

Vendió su casa y su coche.

Ø As **su** can also mean "her," "its," "your," and "their," you can add **de él** after the noun if the meaning is not entirely clear, e.g., **su casa de él** "his house."

his *pron*
[singular]
[plural]
I've got my keys but my husband has lost his.
Is this newspaper yours? – No, it's his.

el suyo/la suya
los suyos/las suyas
Tengo mis llaves pero mi esposo ha perdido las suyas.
¿Es tuyo este diario? – No, es suyo. *[Note: definite article omitted after the verb ser]*

Ø As **suyo/a/os/as** could also mean "hers," "yours," or "theirs," you can replace them with **de él** if there is any chance of confusion, e.g., "It's his." **Es de él.**

hit *v*
[strike]
to hit [targets]
to hit it off with sb

golpear/pegar
alcanzar/acertar/hacer blanco en/dar en
congeniar con/hacer buenas migas con alguien

to hit the ceiling
to hit the hay
to hit the jackpot
to hit the nail on the head
to hit the road

enojarse/perder los estribos
irse a la cama
sacar el premio gordo
acertar
ponerse en camino/largarse

holiday n

a day's holiday	un día libre/un día de descanso
a public holiday	un día feriado [LA]/un día de fiesta/un día festivo
a religious holiday	una fiesta
the Christmas holidays	las Navidades/las Pascuas
the Easter holidays	la Pascua/las Pascuas

home adv

at home	en casa
I was at home last night.	Estaba en casa anoche.
Is your brother at home?	¿Está tu hermano?
Yes, he is.	Sí, está. [Note: The verb **estar** alone is sufficient in such situations.]
home [involving movement]	a casa
Go home at once!	¡Vete a casa en seguida!
I go home at seven o'clock.	Voy/Vuelvo a casa a las siete.
He got home at midnight.	Llegó a casa a medianoche.
She left home in May.	Salió de casa en mayo.

home n

[the building]	la casa
She has a home in Acapulco.	Tiene una casa en Acapulco.
Make yourself at home.	Estás en tu casa.
[the sentiment, the concept]	el hogar
home, sweet home	hogar, dulce hogar
[place of residence]	el domicilio
His home is in Buenos Aires.	Vive en/Es de Buenos Aires.
my home town	mi ciudad natal
the homeland	la patria
a homemaker	un ama de casa [Note: **Un** is used although the noun is feminine, because it begins with a stressed **a**.]
to be homeless	estar sin casa ni hogar
homework	los deberes

hope v

to hope	esperar
I hope to come tomorrow.	Espero venir mañana.
I hope you can come.	Espero que puedas venir. [Note: use of subjunctive.]

Ø **esperar** can also mean "to wait for" or "to expect."

hot adj

[weather, body heat]	el calor [noun]
It was very hot.	Hacía mucho calor.
I'm hot.	Tengo calor.
[things]	caliente
The soup is too hot.	La sopa está demasiado caliente.
There is no hot water.	No hay agua caliente.
a hot day	un día caluroso/de calor
Your head is hot.	Tienes la cabeza caliente.
[of spicy food]	picante
The sauce is very hot.	La salsa es muy picante.
hot line	una línea directa

house

house n

a house	una casa
[commercial]	una casa/una firma
a detached house	una casa independiente/un chalet
housewares	los artículos de uso doméstico/los utensilios domésticos
housework	los quehaceres domésticos
full house [theater]	el lleno
"house full"	"no hay localidades"

house v

to house [a person]	alojar/hospedar
to house [public]	proveer viviendas para

housing n

[act]	el alojamiento/la provisión de viviendas
[houses, apartments]	las casas/las viviendas
the housing shortage	la crisis de la vivienda
They need housing.	Necesitan alojamiento.
student housing	una residencia estudiantil
low-income housing	viviendas a un precio bajo

how adv

How are you?	¿Cómo estás?/¿Cómo está usted?/ ¿Cómo están ustedes?
How's it going?	¿Qué tal?/¿Cómo te va?/¿Cómo le va? /¿Cómo te anda?/¿Cómo le anda?
How do you say "help" in Spanish?	¿Cómo se dice "help" en castellano?
How do you spell it?	¿Cómo se lo escribe?

an exclamation

How beautiful they are!	¡Qué hermosos(as) son!
How terrific!	¡Qué estupendo!

a question: how + adjective

How big is the house?	¿Cómo es de grande la casa?
How big is it?	¿De qué tamaño es?
How far is it to Cancún?	¿Cuánto hay de aquí a Cancún?
How fast was the car going?	¿A qué velocidad iba el coche?
How heavy is the crate?	¿Cuánto pesa el cajón?
How high is the church?	¿Cuánto mide de alto la iglesia?
How long is the corridor?	¿Cómo es de largo el pasillo?
How long is the movie?	¿Cuánto dura la película?
How long is it since you were in Chile?	¿Cuánto tiempo hace desde que estabas en Chile?
How long did they live in Mexico City?	¿Cuánto tiempo vivieron en la Ciudad de México?
How long have you lived here?	¿Desde cuándo vives aquí?/¿Cuánto tiempo hace que vives aquí?
How long did he take to do it?	¿Cuánto tiempo tardó en hacerlo?
How much is it?	¿Cuánto es?/¿Cuánto cuesta?
How much is it worth?	¿Cuánto vale?
How much are the tickets?	¿Cuánto son/cuestan/valen las localidades?
How much does the baby weigh?	¿Cuánto pesa el niño?
How much sugar did you buy?	¿Cuánto azúcar compraste?
How much flour did you buy?	¿Cuánta harina compraste?
How many bulls do they have?	¿Cuántos toros tienen?

How many cows do they have?	¿Cuántas vacas tienen?
How often did you visit her?	¿Cuántas veces la visitaste?
How often do the buses leave for León?	¿Con qué frecuencia salen los autobuses para León?
How old are you?	¿Cuántos años tienes/tiene usted?
How tall is she?	¿Cuánto mide?
How well do you know him?	¿Lo conoces bien?
How wide is the river?	¿Cuánto tiene de ancho el río?

however   *adv*

However you do it, it's all the same to me.	De cualquier modo/manera que lo hagas, me es igual.
However intelligent you are, you will find it difficult.	Por inteligente que seas, lo encontrarás difícil.
However much he tries, he never succeeds.	Por mucho que se esfuerce, nunca tiene éxito.

however   *conj*

[nevertheless]

I can't come today; however I will see you on Friday.	no obstante/sin embargo No puedo venir hoy; sin embargo te veré el viernes.

hug   *n & v*

to hug sb/to give sb a hug	abrazar a/dar un abrazo a alguien
I gave her a big hug.	Le di un fuerte abrazo.
We hugged each other.	Nos abrazamos.

Ø **abrazo** is often used to sign off personal, informal letters, e.g., **un abrazo cordial de...** and at the end of a phone conversation.

humor   *n*/**humorous**   *adj*

humor	el humor
to have a sense of humor	tener un sentido del humor
She has no sense of humor.	No tiene sentido del humor.
humorous *[amusing of person, book, remark, etc.]*	divertido(a)/gracioso(a)/ chistoso(a)
He's a very humorous person.	Es una persona muy divertida.
a humorous poet	un poeta cómico

Ø **humor** also means "mood" or "temperament," e.g., **de buen/mal humor** meaning "in a good/bad mood."

hundred   *n & adj*

a hundred	ciento
a hundred dollars	cien dólares *[Note: Ciento shortensto cien before a noun.]*
I have two hundred dollars and three hundred pesetas.	Tengo doscientos dólares y trescientas pesetas. *[Note: The hundreds agree with the noun they modify.]*
hundreds of people	centenares de personas

hunger   *n*/**hungry**   *adj*

hunger	el hambre *[fem]*
to be very hungry	tener mucha hambre
to get hungry	empezar a tener hambre

hurry *v*
to hurry

apurarse *[LA]*/darse prisa *[Sp]*/
  apresurarse

Hurry up!
to be in a hurry

¡Apúrate!/¡Date prisa!
tener prisa/estar de prisa

hurt *v*
[to cause bodily injury]
to hurt oneself/to get hurt
I hurt my leg.

hacer daño a/hacer mal a/lastimar
hacerse daño/lastimarse
Me lastimé la pierna./Me hice daño
  a la pierna.

My shoes hurt.
[to cause physical pain]
My head hurts.
Does it hurt?
My feet hurt.
Where does it hurt (you)?
[to wound]
[to hurt sb's feelings]
[to hurt sb mentally]

Mis zapatos me hacen daño.
doler
Me duele la cabeza.
¿Te duele?
Me duelen los pies.
¿Dónde te duele?
herir
ofenderle a alguien
doler/herir
causar pena a alguien

Your news hurt her deeply.

Tus noticias le causaron mucha pena.

husband *n*

el esposo/el marido
[Note: **Marido** *is more common in*
  Spain than in Latin America.]

I

I *pron*

I don't want to go to the
 theater; my brother does.
Who is it? – It's me/It is I.
My husband smokes. I don't.

yo   *[Note: Like all the subject pronouns*
 ***yo** is normally only used with a verb for*
 emphasis or in case of confusion.]
Yo no quiero ir al teatro; mi
 hermano sí que quiere ir.
¿Quién es? – Soy yo.
Mi esposo fuma. Yo no.

ice   *n & v*
ice
ice cream
ice-cream parlor
ice cube
iced *[of cake]*
[of drink]
ice hockey
ice skating
icing *[on cake]*
icing sugar
to ice
to ice up
to ice *[drinks]*
to break the ice
to tread on thin ice

el hielo
un helado
una heladería
un cubito de hielo
escarchado(a)
con hielo/enfriado(a)
el hockey sobre hielo
el patinaje sobre hielo
la alcorza/la escarcha/la garapiña
el azúcar de alcorza
helar
helarse
enfriar/echar cubitos de hielo a
romper el hielo
pisar un terreno peligroso

ID   *n*
identification card

Your ID, please.
*[see also **identity**]*

un documento/una tarjeta de identidad/una
 cédula *[Col, Ven & Arg]*/una cartilla *[Mex]*/
 un carnet de identidad *[Sp]*
Sus papeles/documentos, por favor.

idea   *n*
[belief]
[plan]
That's the idea!
not to have the foggiest/slightest
 idea
What's the big idea?

la idea
un plan/un proyecto
¡Eso es!/¡Exacto!
no tener la menor idea

¿A qué viene eso?

identity   *n*
identity
mistaken identity
*[see also **ID**]*

la identidad
la identificación errónea

if   *conj*
If he comes, I will tell him.
I will do it if I can.
He only drinks water if he's thirsty.
If she has done it, she will tell us.

si
Si viene, se lo diré.
Lo haré si puedo.
Sólo bebe agua si tiene sed.
Si lo ha hecho, nos lo dirá.

103

ignore

If I arrived early, I would [i.e., used to] see him.	Si llegaba temprano, lo veía.

[The above are all examples of open conditions, where the action may or may not take place.]

If he came, I would tell him.	Si viniera, se lo diría.
I would do it if I could.	Lo haría si pudiera.
He would only drink water if he were thirsty.	Sólo bebería agua si tuviera sed.
If she had done it, she would tell us.	Si lo hubiera hecho, nos lo diría.
If she had done it, she would have told us.	Si lo hubiera hecho, nos lo habría dicho.
If I arrived early, I would see him.	Si llegara temprano, lo vería.
If only Marta were here.	Ojalá estuviera Marta.

[The above are examples of unfulfilled conditions where the action is unlikely or even impossible. In all these cases si is followed by the imperfect subjunctive.]

ignore *v*

to ignore	no hacer caso de/hacer caso omiso de/desconocer
She ignored my advice.	No hizo caso de mi consejo.
Your brother ignored me.	Tu hermano hizo caso omiso de mí./ Tu hermano me desconoció.
Ignore him!	¡No le hagas caso!

to fail to take into account	no tener/tomar en cuenta
They ignored the fact that we had changed our plans.	No tuvieron en cuenta que habíamos cambiado de proyecto.

to omit, to leave out	pasar por alto
He ignored the details.	Pasó por alto los detalles.

Ø **ignorar** normally means "not to know" or "to be ignorant of," although it will be heard in Latin America meaning "to ignore."

ill *[see sick]*

ill at ease *adj*

ill at ease	molesto(a)/intranquilo(a)
She felt ill at ease in the woods.	Se sintió intranquila en el bosque.

impress *v*

to impress	imprimir
to impress [on sb's mind]	grabar/convencer de
I tried to impress on her the importance of coming on time.	Traté de convencerle de la importancia de llegar a la hora.
I'm not easily impressed.	No me dejo impresionar fácilmente.
He impressed us favorably.	Nos hizo una buena impresión.
How did the product impress you?	¿Qué impresión te produjo el producto?

improve *v*

to improve sth	mejorar/perfeccionar
They want to improve their working conditions.	Quieren mejorar sus condiciones de trabajo.
She needs to improve her Spanish.	Necesita perfeccionar sus conocimientos del castellano.

to undergo improvement	mejorar(se)/perfeccionarse
The economy has improved.	La economía se ha mejorado.

My health is improving.	Mi salud se mejora.
Your Spanish has improved.	Has hecho progresos en el castellano.

in *prep*

in most senses en
in Mexico/in New York/in May — en México/en Nueva York/en mayo

time within dentro de
I'll do it in two hours. — Lo haré dentro de dos horas.
Come back in 20 minutes. — Vuelve dentro de veinte minutos.

in time
in time — a tiempo

time of day
in the morning/in the afternoon — por la mañana/por la tarde
in the evening/in the night — por la tarde/por la noche
eight o'clock in the morning — las ocho de la mañana
five o'clock in the afternoon — las cinco de la tarde
seven o'clock in the evening — las siete de la tarde
in the daytime — de día/durante el día

weather
in the rain — bajo la lluvia
in the sun — bajo el sol
30 degrees in the shade — treinta grados a la sombra
in this weather — con el tiempo que hace
in this heat — con este calor

after a superlative
the biggest country in the world. — el país más grande del mundo
the best team in the league — el mejor equipo de la liga

manner
in this way — de esta manera/de este modo
in writing — por escrito
in ink/in pencil — escrito con tinta/lápiz
painted in white — pintado(a) de blanco
to be in mourning — estar de luto
in alphabetical order — por orden alfabético
covered in — cubierto de
in fashion — de moda
in uniform — de uniforme
dressed in — vestido de

place
in the distance — a lo lejos
in prison — en la cárcel
in bed — en la cama
to arrive in — llegar a
to come/get/go in — entrar en

ratio
one in ten — uno sobre diez

inclined *adj*
to be inclined to [tendency] — inclinarse/tener tendencia a
She's inclined to lie. — Tiene tendencia a mentir.
to be inclined to [choice] — estar dispuesto(a) de
I'm inclined to believe you. — Estoy dispuesto(a) de creerte.

include *v*

to include — incluir
The price includes tax. — El precio incluye impuestos.
The bill includes service. — La cuenta incluye el servicio.
[with a letter] — adjuntar/enviar adjunto

included
[with a letter] — adjunto
service included — servicio incluido/comprendido

including — incluso/inclusive/con inclusión de
Including this one I have six. — Con la inclusión de éste tengo seis.
We're all going, including my grandfather. — Vamos todos, incluso mi abuelo.
[Note: **Incluso** can often be translated by "even."]

income *n*

annual income — los ingresos anuales
gross income — la renta bruta
net income — la renta neta
national income — la renta nacional
income tax — el impuesto sobre la renta
He can't live on his income. — No puede vivir con lo que gana.
to live beyond one's income — gastar más de lo que se gana

inconvenient *adj*

[not convenient] — incómodo(a)/poco práctico(a)
It will be a very inconvenient journey for my boss. — Será un viaje muy incómodo para mi jefe.
[time] — malo(a)/inoportuno(a)
It was an inconvenient time for the meeting. — Fue una hora inoportuna para la reunión.
If it's not inconvenient for you ... — Si no te molesta...

infant *n*

[a baby] — una criatura [Note: used for male or female]
[a small child] — un niño/una niña
[a new-born] — un recién nacido/una recién nacida
infant mortality rate — la mortalidad infantil

Ø **infante** and **infanta** are respectively "prince" (son of a king) and "princess" (daughter of a king or wife of an infante).

informal *adj*

informal dress — el traje de calle
[person's manner] — sencillo(a)/desenvuelto(a)/afable/poco ceremonioso(a)
an informal meeting — una reunión no oficial
She spoke to me informally. — Me habló en tono de confianza.
an informal visit — una visita de confianza
an informal dinner/party — una cena/reunión entre amigos

Ø **informal** usually means "unreliable," "untrustworthy," "bad mannered." It is rarely used of things.

information *n*

information — la información/los informes/los datos
a piece of information — una información/un dato/una noticia

[news]	las noticias
classified information	la información secreta
to ask for information	pedir informes
information office	el centro de informaciones
information desk	las informaciones
information technology	la informática

injure *v*

to injure oneself	hacerse daño/lastimarse
I injured my arm.	Me lastimé el brazo./Me hice daño al brazo.
to be injured	estar lesionado
Ten people were injured when the bomb went off.	Diez personas quedaron lesionadas cuando estalló la bomba.
They took the injured to hospital.	Llevaron a los heridos al hospital.
[see also **hurt**]	

injury *n*

| an injury | una herida/una lesión |
| the injured party | la persona ofendida/perjudicada |

Ø **una injuria** means "an insult," "an offence;" **injuriar** means "to insult."

in-laws [see **law**]

inside *adv*

to wait inside	esperar dentro
Shall we go inside?	¿Vamos adentro?/¿Entramos?
Come inside.	Pasa, por favor.
Look inside.	Mira hacia dentro.
It's very warm inside.	Hace mucho calor por dentro.

inside *prep*

inside	en/dentro de
They're inside the house.	Están dentro de la casa.
Put it inside the box.	Ponlo en la caja.

insist *v*

to insist on sth	insistir en algo
to insist on doing sth	insistir en hacer algo
to insist that	insistir en que [+ subjunctive]
I insist that you pay me now.	Insisto en que me pagues ahora.

instead *adv*

| I bought a car instead. | En cambio/En lugar de eso compré un coche. |
| Her brother went instead. | Su hermano fue en su lugar. |

instead of *prep*

instead of	en lugar de/en vez de
I ordered fish instead of meat.	Pedí pescado en lugar de carne.
They went to Peru instead of Mexico.	Fueron al Perú en vez de México.

insurance *n*

fire insurance	el seguro contra/de incendios
fully comprehensive insurance	el seguro a/contra todo riesgo
life insurance	el seguro de vida/sobre la vida

insure

third party insurance	el seguro contra terceros/contra tercera persona
insurance agent	un agente de seguros
insurance company	una compañía de seguros
insurance coverage	los riesgos cubiertos
insurance policy	una póliza de seguros
insurance premium	una prima de seguros

insure *v*
to insure sth against	asegurar algo contra

intend *v*
to intend to	tener la intención de/pensar
I intend to do it tomorrow.	Pienso hacerlo mañana.
She intends to go alone.	Tiene la intención de ir sola.

Ø **intentar** means "to try," e.g., **Intentó hacerlo.** "He tried to do it."

interest *v*
to interest	interesar
to be/get interested in	interesarse en/por
He's not interested in baseball.	No le interesa el béisbol./No se interesa en el béisbol.
to be interested in *[financially]*	estar interesado(a) en

intermission *n*
[interruption]	una intermisión/una interrupción
[in movies]	el descanso
[in theater]	el descanso/el entreacto

intoxicated *adj*
[drunk]	borracho(a)/ebrio(a) *[more formal, legal term]*

Ø **intoxicado(a)** usually has the sense of "poisoned."

introduce *v*
to introduce sb to sb	presentar alguien a alguien
May I introduce my wife?	Permíteme presentarte a mi esposa./ Te presento a mi esposa.
He introduced me to his sister.	Me presentó a su hermana.
Let me introduce myself.	Me presento.
I'd like to introduce Alfonso.	Quisiera presentarte a Alfonso./Te presento a Alfonso.
to introduce a new fashion/ product	introducir una moda nueva/un producto nuevo
[to insert]	introducir
She introduced the key into the lock.	Introdujo la llave en la cerradura.

involve *v*
to concern	concernir/atañer
This problem involves you too.	Este problema te atañe a ti también.
those involved	los interesados
to imply	suponer
This job involves living abroad.	Este trabajo supone que tengo que vivir al extranjero.

to require
Your plan will involve a lot
of money.

requerir/exigir
Tu proyecto requerirá mucho dinero.

to implicate
He was involved in the murder.

implicar/meter/involucrar
Estaba implicado/metido/involucrado
en el homicidio.

to get involved in
They got involved in the
argument.
Don't get involved in that!
[to have an affair with sb]
He got involved with an actress.

meterse en/enredarse en/embrollarse en
Se metieron en la disputa.

¡No te metas en eso!
tener un lío con alguien
Tuvo un lío con una actriz.

involved *adj*
[complex]
This is very involved.

complicado(a)
Esto es muy complicado.

issue *n*
a question, a topic
It's a political issue.

una cuestión/un asunto/un problema
Es una cuestión política.

a copy of a publication
in this issue of the magazine

un número
en este número de la revista

shares, stamps, notes
an issue of shares

una emisión
una emisión de acciones

it *pron*
[subject]

él *[masculine]*
ella *[feminine]*
ello *[neuter]*
*[Note: Even more than the other subject
pronouns, él, ella, and ello meaning "it"
are usually omitted.]*

Where's the money? – It's on
the table.
Have you seen my scarf? – Yes,
it's in the car.
I didn't like it. *[the whole
business]*
It was all over and done with.

¿Dónde está el dinero? – Está en la
mesa.
¿Has visto mi bufanda? – Sí, está
en el coche.
Ello no me gustó.

Ello se acabó. *[Note: Ello does not
refer to a specific object but to an idea,
concept, the whole business, etc.]*

[direct object]

lo *[masculine & neuter]*
la *[feminine]*

My passport? I've lost it.
Your jacket? I haven't seen it.

¿Mi pasaporte? Lo he perdido.
¿Tu chaqueta? No la he visto.

[indirect object]
Give it a kick!

le
¡Dale una patada!

[disjunctive]

él/sí *[masculine]*
ella/sí *[feminine]*
ello/sí *[neuter]*

He'll see to it.

Se ocupará de ello.

its *adj*

[singular: masc & fem]	su
[plural: masc & fem]	sus
its main street	su calle mayor
its rivers and mountains	sus ríos y sus montañas [Note: adjective repeated]

it's (it is)   [see it]

itself   *pron*

	él mismo/ella misma/ello mismo
	sí/sí mismo(a)
in itself/per se	de por sí/en sí

J

jacket *n*
a jacket
[a sport coat]
[of woman's suit]
[of pajamas]
a sheepskin jacket

un saco *[LA]*/una chaqueta/una americana
una americana de sport
una chaqueta
una chaqueta
una chamarra

jam *n*
[food]
a traffic jam
[a blockage]
[fig.]
to be in a jam
to get into/out of a jam

la mermelada
un embotellamiento
un atasco
un apuro/un lío
estar en un apuro
meterse en/salir de un apuro

jam *v*
to jam sth into

meter algo a la fuerza en

jeans *n*
jeans

el bluyín *[LA]*/los tejanos/
   los pantalones vaqueros *[Sp]*

jerk *n*
[sudden movement]
[sudden pull]
[a shove]
[a fool]

una sacudida
un tirón
un empujón
un idiota

job *n*
a job
to look for a job
to lose one's job
to be laid off [from a job]
to do a good job
to be out of a job
a full-time job

a part-time job

un trabajo/un empleo/un puesto
buscar trabajo/un empleo
perder su trabajo
ser despedido(a)
hacer un buen trabajo/hacer algo bien
estar sin trabajo/estar desocupado(a)
un trabajo de jornada completa/de
   plena dedicación
un trabajo a media jornada/de
   dedicación parcial

join *v*
[two things together]
[a club or society]
[a political party]
[the armed forces]
[to meet someone]
I'll join you at six.
They joined him at the café.
Would you like to join us?
May I join you?
Join the club!

unir/juntar/poner juntos
ingresar en/hacerse socio de
afiliarse a/hacerse miembro de
alistarse en
reunirse con/unirse a/juntarse con
Me reuniré contigo a las seis.
Se reunieron con él en el café.
¿Te gustaría acompañarnos?
¿Se permite?
¡No faltaba más!

journey   n
a journey
Ø **una jornada** means "a working day."

un viaje

juice   n
[in general]
[fruit juice]
[gas]
[electricity]

el jugo
el jugo [LA]/el zumo [Sp]
la gasolina
la corriente

junior   adj & n
[in age]
[in terms of service on staff]
[of a championship]
the junior soccer championship
a junior

menor/más joven
más nuevo(a)
juvenil
el campeonato juvenil de fútbol
un(a) menor/un(a) joven

at the university
the junior year
a junior
He's a junior.
Ø Spanish has no real equivalent for a "junior" at high school.

el tercer año
un/una estudiante de tercer año
Es estudiante del tercer año.

junk   n
[cheap goods]
That car is junk.
The film was a load of junk.
You're talking a lot of junk.
a junk market
a junkshop

las baratijas
Ese coche es una porquería.
La película era una porquería.
No dices más que tonterías.
un rastro
un baratillo

just   adv
It's just what I wanted.
It's just the same.
She's just leaving.
I was just leaving.
It's just here.
The library is just past the
  museum.
just a little (bit)
just a few
I'm just as capable as you.
He plays the piano just as
  well as his brother.
She just missed the train.
They arrived just in time.
Just a moment!
They were here just now.
just around the corner
just because
Why don't you do it? – Just because.

Es exactamente lo que quería.
Es exactamente igual.
Sale ahora mismo.
Estaba a punto de salir.
Está aquí mismo.
La biblioteca está un poco más allá
  del museo.
un poquito
unos pocos/unas pocas
Soy tan capaz como tú.
Toca el piano tan bien como su
  hermano.
Acaba de perder el tren.
Llegaron justamente con tiempo.
¡Un momentito!
Estaban aquí hace un momento.
a la vuelta de la esquina
porque sí
¿Por qué no lo haces? – Porque no.

to have just
I have just seen her.
He had just left the office
  when I telephoned.

acabar de [+ infinitive]
Acabo de verla.
Acababa de salir de la oficina
  cuando telefoneé.[Note: **acabar de** is only
  used in two tenses, the present and the
  imperfect, and translates "have just" and
  "had just" respectively.]

112

K

keep *v intrans*

to keep quiet	callarse
Keep quiet!	¡Cállate!
Keep straight ahead for the hotel.	Sigue todo derecho para el hotel.
Keep to the left/right.	Sigue por la izquierda/derecha.
Keep out!	¡Prohibida la entrada!
Keep off the grass!	¡No pisar la hierba! *[Note: Public signs often use the infinitive form instead of the imperative.]*

to keep at it	perseverar
to keep fit	mantenerse en forma
to keep in mind	tener en cuenta/tener presente

to keep (on) doing sth — seguir haciendo algo
She kept on talking. — Siguió hablando.
Keep on looking for it! — ¡Sigue buscándolo!

to last — conservarse/durar
These apples won't keep. — Estas manzanas no se conservarán frescas.
Buy some fruit that will keep. — Compra fruta que durará.

keep *v trans*

to keep a promise/one's word	cumplir una promesa/lo prometido
to keep an appointment	acudir a una cita
to keep company with	tener relaciones con
to keep house	llevar la casa
to keep one's chin up	no desanimarse
to keep order	mantener/imponer orden
to keep the ball rolling	mantener el interés/animar la conversación
to keep sb waiting	hacer esperar a alguien/hacer que alguien espere *[Note: use of subjunctive]*

She kept me waiting an hour. — Me hizo esperar una hora./Hizo que esperara yo una hora.

to keep sb informed/posted about sth — tener a alguien al corriente de algo
Keep me informed! — ¡Tenme/Téngame al corriente!
I don't know where she keeps her jewels. — No sé dónde guarda sus joyas.

[to keep domestic animals] — tener
They keep a dog and two cats. — Tienen un perro y dos gatos.
[to rear animals] — criar
He keeps sheep and cows. — Cría ovejas y vacas.

to save — tener guardado(a)/reservar
He was keeping the book for me. — Tenía guardado el libro para mí.
Keep me a seat! — ¡Resérvame un asiento!

to retain
Keep the change! — ¡Quédese con la vuelta!

to keep sth hot/cold — tener algo caliente/frío
I've kept the soup hot. — He tenido caliente la sopa.
You must keep this juice cold. — Debes tener frío este jugo.

113

to keep (sb) warm
You must keep (yourself) warm.

abrigar(se)/mantener(se) el calor
Debes mantener el calor del cuerpo.
/Debes abrigarte.

This blanket will keep you
warm.

Esta cobija te mantendrá el calor.
/te abrigará.

kid *n*
a kid *[child]*

un(a) chaval(a) *[LA & Sp]*/un(a)
chamaco(a) *[Mex]*/un(a) pibe *[Arg & Uru]*/
un(a) patojo(a) *[Gua]*/un(a) guambito(a)
[Col]/un(a) nene(a) *[Arg, Uru, Sp]*

kill *v*
to kill
He killed his wife.
He killed himself.
The President has been killed.

matar
Mató a su esposa.
Se mató.
Le han matado al Presidente./Se
mató al Presidente.

to kill time

pasar el rato

kind *adj*
to be kind
You're very kind./That's very
kind of you.
to be kind to
He's very kind to me.
to be kind to animals
Please be so kind as to ...
Would you be so kind as to ...?

ser amable/bondadoso(a)
Eres/Es usted muy amable.

ser amable con
Es muy amable conmigo.
tratar bien a los animales
Ten/Tenga la bondad de...
¿Me haces/hace el favor de... ?

kind *n*
a kind
What kind of car do you have?
He's interested in animals of
that kind.
I'm not that kind of person.
He's the sort of person who
would not do that.
I like films of all kinds.

una clase/una especie/un género/un tipo
¿Qué clase/tipo de coche tienes?
Le interesan los animales de esa
especie/ese género.
No soy de esa clase de personas.
Es de los que no podrían hacer eso.

Me gustan películas de toda clase./
Me gusta toda clase de películas.

all kinds of people
She's a kind of detective.
It's kind of awkward.

toda clase de gente
Es algo así como una detective.
Es algo difícil.

kiss *n & v*
a kiss
to kiss sb/give sb a kiss
to kiss sb goodbye
They kissed.

un beso
besar/dar un beso a alguien
dar un beso de despedida a alguien
Se besaron./Se dieron un beso.

knock *n & v*
to knock
to knock at the door
There's a knock at the door.
Did you hear a knock?

golpear
llamar a la puerta
Llaman/Se llama a la puerta.
¿Oíste una llamada (a la puerta)?

know *v*

to be acquainted with
Do you know my boss?
I know him by name/sight.
I've known your parents for
  twenty years.

She knows Spain very well.
I don't know Gabriel García
  Márquez's novels.

to get to know (people/places)
We got to know them last
  summer.

to recognize
I knew them at once.

to know facts
Do you know how much it costs?
He doesn't know the price.
Do they know German?
Who knows?
How should I know?
to know sth by heart
If only I had known ...!

to let know
I'll let you know.
Why didn't you let me know?

to get to know sth
How did you get to know that?

to know how to
Does he know how to swim?
She doesn't know how to play
  the piano.
I don't know how to repair it.

to know about/to understand
He knows all about cars.

to know one's business/job

not to know/be unaware of
I didn't know about their
  problems.

conocer
¿Conoces a mi jefe?
Lo conozco de nombre/vista.
Conzco a tus padres desde hace
  veinte años./Hace veinte años que
  conozco a tus padres.
Conoce bien España.
No conozco las novelas de Gabriel
  García Márquez.

(llegar) a conocer
Los conocimos/Llegamos a conocerlos
  el verano pasado.

reconocer
Los reconocí en seguida.

saber
¿Sabes cuánto cuesta?
No sabe el precio.
¿Saben alemán?
¿Quién sabe?
¿Qué sé yo?
saber algo de memoria
¡De haberlo sabido antes...!

avisar
Te avisaré.
¿Por qué no me avisaste?

enterarse de algo
¿Cómo te enteraste de eso?

saber
¿Sabe nadar?
No sabe tocar el piano.

No sé cómo repararlo.

entender de
Entiende mucho de coches.

conocer/saber su oficio

ignorar/no saber
Ignoraba sus problemas.

115

L

label *n*
[on goods, clothes, bottles]   una etiqueta/un rótulo

Ø **etiqueta** also means "etiquette," "formality."

lady *n*
a lady   una señora
a lady [distinguished, old]   una dama
the ladies' restroom   las señoras
Ladies and gentlemen!   ¡Señoras y señores!
The First Lady   La primera dama
Our Lady   Nuestra Señora

land *n*
[in general]   la tierra
[nation]   un país
[region]   una región/una tierra
[soil]   la tierra/el suelo
[property]   tierras/una estancia [LA]/una
                                              hacienda [LA]/una finca

[countryside, agricultural]   el campo
[piece/tract of land]   un terreno
native land   la patria

land *v*
[of aircraft]   aterrizar
to land a job   conseguir un trabajo

lane *n*
[in the country]   un camino/una vereda
[in town]   un callejón/una callejuela
[traffic]   un carril/una vía/una banda/una senda
the left-hand lane   el carril de la izquierda
[in track and field, swimming]   una calle/una banda
[in bowling]   una pista

language *n*
[of country or region]   la lengua/el idioma
the Spanish language   la lengua castellana/el idioma
                                              castellano/el español

modern languages   las lenguas modernas/los idiomas modernos
to be good at languages   ser fuerte en los idiomas

[faculty of speech]   el lenguaje
bad language   el lenguaje indecente/las palabrotas
scientific/technical language   el lenguaje científico/técnico

large *adj*
large   grande
a large house   una casa grande
a large family   una familia grande/numerosa

116

a large quantity	una gran cantidad
a large sum of money	una gran cantidad de dinero
[see also **big**]	

Ø **largo** means "long."

last   adj
final · último(a) [Note: precedes the noun]

in the last days of the war	en los últimos días de la guerra
It was Galdós' last novel.	Fue la última novela de Galdós.
It will take place on the last Sunday of the month.	Tendrá lugar el último domingo del mes.
the last three numbers	las tres últimas cifras [Note the word order.]
the last straw	la última gota/el final/el colmo [Sp]

most recent · pasado(a)

last Saturday	el sábado pasado
last month	el mes pasado
last year	el año pasado
last week	la semana pasada
last night	anoche/ayer en la noche
the night before last	anteanoche
Did you like her last film?	¿Te gustó su película más reciente?

late   adj & adv
to arrive/be late

[person]	llegar tarde
She is always late.	Siempre llega tarde.
I'm sorry I'm late.	Siento llegar tarde.
[of transportation]	llegar con retraso
The train arrived ten minutes late.	El tren llegó con diez minutos de retraso.
His plane will be half an hour late.	Su avión llegará con media hora de retraso.

It's late. · Es tarde.

It was getting late.	Se estaba haciendo tarde.
to work late at the office	trabajar en la oficina después de la hora acostumbrada/hasta una hora tardía
late at night/in the night	ya muy entrada la noche
late into the night	hasta muy entrada la noche
late in the afternoon	a última hora de la tarde
in the late eighties	en los últimos años ochenta

to be late (in) doing something · tardar en hacer algo

I was late (in) getting up.	Tardé en levantarme.

miscellaneous

to be in one's late thirties	acercarse a los cuarenta
See you later!	¡Hasta pronto!/¡Hasta más tarde!
at the latest	a lo más tarde/a más tardar
the latest fashion	la última moda/la moda más reciente
my late husband/wife	mi esposo difunto/mi esposa difunta

latter   pron

[as opposed to former]	éste/ésta/éstos/éstas
Of the two dishes, I prefer the latter.	De los dos platos, prefiero éste.

law n

the law(s) *[of a country]*	la ley/las leyes
[subject for study, body of law]	el derecho/la jurisprudencia

civil/commercial/constitutional/
  criminal/international law
	el derecho/civil/mercantil/político
	  penal/internacional

martial law	la ley marcial/el gobierno militar
by law	según la ley
court of law	un tribunal (de justicia)
to study law	estudiar derecho
law school	una escuela/facultad de derecho
to practice law	ejercer de abogado
the law of gravity	la ley de la gravedad
in-law	político(a)
brother-in-law	el cuñado/el hermano político
sister-in-law	la cuñada/la hermana política
father-in-law	el suegro/el padre político
mother-in-law	la suegra/la madre política

lawyer n

[an attorney]	un(a) abogado(a)
[out-of-court legal adviser]	un(a) licenciado(a) *[Mex]*
[notary]	un(a) notario(a)

lazy adj

lazy	flojo(a) *[LA]*/perezoso(a)

least adj, adv & n

adverb

	menos
the least important matter	el asunto menos importante

the least expensive shirts in
  the store
	las camisas menos costosas de la
	  tienda *[Note: de after a superlative]*

These are the least expensive.	Éstos/Éstas son los/las menos costosos(as).
This is the least interesting.	Éste/Ésta es el/la menos interesante.
He's the one who works least.	Es él que trabaja menos.
She did it least efficiently.	Fue ella quien lo hizo menos eficientemente.

adjective

	menos/menor/(más) mínimo(a)
He has the least money.	Es el que tiene menos dinero.

I have the least chance of
  going to Colombia.
	Tengo la menor oportunidad de ir a
	  Colombia.

noun

	lo menos
The least you can do is ...	Lo menos que puedes hacer es...
to say the least	para no decir más
not in the least!	¡en absoluto!/¡de ninguna manera!

least (at) adv

at least	a lo menos/al menos/por lo menos
He's at least fifty.	Tiene por lo menos cincuenta años.
At least it's not raining.	Por lo menos no llueve.
At least, that's what I think.	De todos modos, eso es lo que pienso yo.

leave v

to go away

	irse/marcharse
They left yesterday.	Se fueron/marcharon ayer.

to leave a place
We left Madrid this morning.

salir de
Salimos de Madrid esta mañana.

to take one's leave
I must leave you now.

despedirse de
Tengo que despedirme de ustedes ahora.

to leave sb or sth somewhere
They left me at the airport.
I left your money on the table.

dejar
Me dejaron en el aeropuerto.
Dejé su dinero en la mesa.

to leave for good
My friend has left his wife.

abandonar
Mi amigo ha abandonado a su esposa.

to leave unintentionally
I left my umbrella in the
 train.
I've left my books behind.
They left their friends behind.

dejar (olvidado)/olvidar/dejar atrás
Dejé (olvidado) mi paraguas en el
 tren.
He olvidado mis libros.
Dejaron atrás a sus compañeros.

to leave + adjective
She left the door open.
Leave me alone!

dejar
Dejó abierta la puerta.
¡Déjame en paz!

to bequeath
His father left him 50,000
 dollars.

dejar/legar
Su padre le legó cincuenta mil
 dólares.

lecture   n
[in general]
[university lecture]
to go to a lecture
to go to lectures on ...
a lecture hall

una conferencia
una clase
asistir a una conferencia
seguir un curso sobre/de...
una sala de conferencias/un aula [fem]

Ø **lectura** means "reading."

left   adj, adv & n
opposite of right
your left arm
the left(-hand) drawer
on the left
to the left
to keep to the left
the left-hand side
left turn
left-handed
to be on the left [politics]
left-winger

izquierdo(a)
tu brazo izquierdo
el cajón de la izquierda
a la izquierda
a la izquierda
circular por la izquierda
la izquierda
una vuelta a la izquierda
zurdo(a)
ser de izquierdas
un(a) izquierdista

remaining
to be left
Is there any money left?
We have enough money left.
I'm sorry, there's no rice
 left.

quedar
¿Queda dinero?
Nos queda bastante dinero.
Lo siento, no queda arroz.

to be left over [to spare]
Is there any fruit left over?
There was a lot of food left.
I have no time left.
leftovers

sobrar
¿Sobra fruta?
Sobraba mucha comida.
No me sobra tiempo.
las sobras/los restos

lend *v*
to lend sth to sb   prestar algo a alguien
Will you lend me the car?   ¿Quieres prestarme el coche?
to lend a hand   echar una mano

less *adj, adv & n*
in comparisons   menos... que
I have less money than you.   Tengo menos dinero que tú.
He is less intelligent than   Es menos inteligente que su
   his sister.   hermana.
It cost less than 10 dollars.   Costó menos de diez dólares. *[Note:*
     use of **de** *when a number follows.]*

the less ... the less   mientras/cuanto menos... menos
The less you work, the less   Mientras menos trabajas, menos
   you earn.   ganas.

less and less   cada vez menos
I am less and less interested   Me interesan cada vez menos los
   in business.   negocios.

let *v*
to allow   dejar/permitir
Let me help you!   ¡Déjame ayudarte!/¡Permíteme ayudarte!
He didn't let me go to the game.   No me permitió ir al partido.
Let us in!   ¡Déjanos pasar!
Let them come in!   ¡Déjalos pasar!/¡Que pasen!

in suggestions   ¡Vamos!
Let's go!   ¡Vamos!/¡Vámonos!
Let's go to the beach!   ¡Vamos a la playa!
Let's see!   ¡Vamos a ver!/¡A ver!
Let's play tennis!   ¡Vamos a jugar al tenis!

to let go [set free]   soltar
They are letting the prisoners go.   Sueltan a los prisioneros.

to let go of   soltar
He let go of the rope.   Soltó la cuerda.

to let sb down   fallar/desilusionar/defraudar a alguien
The train let me down.   El tren me falló/defraudó.
Her brother let us down.   Su hermano nos falló/defraudó.

other
Let's face it!   ¡Seamos realistas!

let alone *adv*
let alone   mucho menos
He can't go for a week, let   No puede ir por una semana, y mucho
   alone a month.   menos un mes.

letter *n*
[correspondence]   la carta
[of alphabet]   la letra

library *n*
a library   una biblioteca

Ø **una librería** means "bookstore."

license n

[general]
una licencia/un permiso/una autorización

driver's license
un brevete [Per]/un carnet [Chi & Sp]/una libreta [Arg & Uru]/una licencia [Mex]/un carnet de conducir [Sp]/un título [Ven]

license plate [of car]
una placa (de matrícula)

license number
la matrícula/el número de matrícula

light adj & adv

not heavy
liviano(a) [LA]/ligero(a)

lightweight clothes
ropa liviana/ligera

a light wind
un viento suave

to be a light sleeper
tener un sueño ligero

to travel light
viajar con poco equipaje

not dark
claro(a)

a light room
una habitación clara

light blue
azul claro/azul celeste

a light complexion
una tez blanca

to grow light
amanecer/hacerse de día

[illuminated/well lit]
bañado(a) de luz/con mucha luz

light n

in general
la luz

daylight
la luz del día

sunlight
la luz del sol

lighting
la iluminación

[lamp]
una luz/una lámpara

to turn on the light
encender la luz

to turn off the light
apagar la luz

floodlight
un foco

street light
un farol

traffic lights
los semáforos

the red/green light
la luz roja/verde

headlight [car]
un faro/una linterna [Col]

rear light [car]
un piloto/una calavera [Mex]/un cocuyo [Ven]

lighthouse
un faro

flame
el fuego/la lumbre

Do you have a light? [for a cigarette, etc.]
¿Tienes fuego?

pilot light [in an oven]
un mechero/un encendedor

light v

to set light to
pegar fuego a/encender

to light a fire/the gas/a match
encender un fuego/el gas/una cerilla

to light a room
iluminar una habitación

like v

to find pleasurable
gustar(le) a uno/agradar(le) a uno [Mex]

I like fruit.
Me gusta la fruta.

He likes potato chips.
Le gustan las papas fritas.

121

We like swimming.	Nos gusta nadar.
Do you like it/them?	¿Te gusta?/¿Te gustan?

acquaintances

Do you like Mr. Ramírez?	gustar(le) a uno
	¿Te gusta el señor Ramírez?/¿Le tienes simpatía al señor Ramírez?/¿Te es simpático el señor Ramírez?

close friends, relations

Do you like your cousins?	querer/gustar(le) a uno
She likes my brother.	¿Quieres a tus primos?
	Le gusta mi hermano.

to want

Would you like an ice-cream?	querer/gustar(le) a uno
I'd like some strawberries.	¿Quieres un helado?/¿Te gustaría un helado?
They would like to stay.	Quisiera unas fresas.
	Les gustaría quedarse.

likely *adj*

likely	probable
It's quite likely.	Es muy probable.

likewise *adv*

likewise	igualmente

line *n*

[in general]	una línea
a dotted line	una línea de puntos
a straight line	una línea recta
to draw a line	dibujar/trazar una línea
a line of poetry	un verso
lines [of a play]	el papel
a line of traffic	una cola de coches
to stand/wait in line	hacer cola
to line up	alinearse/ponerse en fila

liquor *n*

[alcoholic]	el licor/las bebidas alcohólicas
hard liquor	el licor espiritoso

Ø **licor** is also used to mean "a cordial."

listen *v*

to listen to	escuchar a [people]
	escuchar [Note: no preposition when used with objects]
He never listens to his boss.	Nunca escucha a su jefe.
I want to listen to the music.	Quiero escuchar la música.

litter [see *garbage*]

little *adj, adv & n*
small

It's a small house.	chico(a) [LA]/pequeño(a)
	Es una casa chica.

not much

He eats very little.	poco
She has little patience.	Come muy poco.
	Tiene poca paciencia.

a small amount/quantity

	un poco (de)

I have a little bread.	Tengo un poco de pan.
Would you like a little wine?	¿Te gustaría un poco de vino?
– Yes, just a little.	– Sí, sólo un poco/un poquito.
a little bit (of)	un poquito (de)
little by little	poco a poco

live v

to live	vivir
They live in this appartment.	Viven en este apartamento.
to live a happy life	llevar/tener una vida feliz
to live well	darse buena vida/vivir en el lujo
as long as I live	mientras viva
Long live the president!	¡Viva el presidente!

living n

to make a living	ganarse la vida
to work for a living	ganarse la vida trabajando
What do you do for a living?	¿Cómo te ganas la vida?/A qué te dedicas?
the cost of living	el coste de vida

loan n

a loan [between people]	un préstamo
a loan [commercial]	un empréstito
on loan	prestado(a)
[see also **borrow** and **lend**]	

lobby n [see **hall**]

locate v

to locate	encontrar
to locate a place on the map	encontrar un sitio en el mapa
Where is it located?	¿Dónde se encuentra?/¿Dónde está?

location n

[a site]	una localización/un solar
a location for the factory	un solar para la fábrica
It's in a good location.	Está bien situado(a).
to be on location [filming]	estar rodando

lock n & v

to lock	cerrar con llave
The doors are locked.	Las puertas están cerradas con llave.
to lock sb or sth in	encerrar a alguien/encerrar algo
I'll lock my money in the drawer.	Voy a encerrar mi dinero en el cajón.
to lock up [in prison]	encarcelar
a lock	una chapa [LA]/una cerradura

lonely adj

[general]	solitario(a)/solo(a)
to feel lonely	sentirse solo(a)
It's a lonely life.	Es una vida solitaria.
[place]	aislado(a)/remoto(a)
We live in a lonely place.	Vivimos en un sitio aislado.

long adj

long	largo(a)

long

a long journey	un viaje largo
a long story	una historia larga
She has long hair.	Tiene el pelo largo.

long *adv*
[for a long time]

I've been waiting a long time.	Hace mucho tiempo que estoy esperando.
I won't be long. *[returning]*	Vuelvo pronto.
I won't be long. *[finishing]*	Termino pronto.
a long time ago	hace mucho tiempo
He cannot wait any longer.	No puede esperar más (tiempo).
I'll wait a little longer.	Esperaré un poco más (tiempo).
How much longer must I wait?	¿Hasta cuándo tengo que esperar?

how long ... ?

mucho tiempo

¿desde hace cuánto tiempo... ?/¿cuánto
   tiempo hace que... ?

How long has he lived in San Juan?	¿Desde hace cuánto tiempo vive en San Juan?/¿Cuánto tiempo hace que vive en San Juan?
How long did he live in San Juan?	¿Durante cuánto tiempo vivió en San Juan?

as long as

As long as you work here, you will do what the boss says.	Mientras trabajes aquí harás lo que diga el jefe.
Stay as long as you like.	Quédate hasta cuando quieras.
[provided that]	con tal que *[+ subjunctive]*
You can go to the dance as long as you are back by midnight.	Puedes ir al baile con tal que vuelvas antes de medianoche.

long *v*

to long for sth	anhelar algo
I'm longing for her return.	Anhelo su regreso.
to long to do sth	anhelar hacer algo
She's longing to see you again.	Anhela verte otra vez.

look *v*
to seem

That book looks interesting.	Ese libro parece interesante.
You look ill.	Pareces enfermo(a).

to look like

She looks like her aunt.	Se parece a su tía.

parecer

parecerse a

to look at

mirar a *[people]*
mirar *[Note: no preposition when used
   with objects]*

Look at Maria!	¡Mira a María!
I was looking at the photos.	Miraba las fotos.
He was looking out of the window.	Miraba por la ventana.

to look after sb

He looks after his parents.	Cuida de sus padres.

cuidar de alguien

to look up

I looked up that word in the dictionary.	Busqué esa palabra en el diccionario.

consultar/buscar

to look up to

They look up to their teacher.	Respetan a su profesor(a).

respetar/admirar

to look forward to *[see forward]*

124

lost adj
to get lost
They got lost in the woods.
I think they're lost.
the lost and found department

perderse/extraviarse
Se perdieron en el bosque.
Creo que se han perdido.
la oficina de objetos perdidos

lot adv
[a great deal]
She smokes a lot.
I liked the hotel a lot.

mucho
Ella fuma mucho.
Me gustó/agradó mucho el hotel.

lot(s) n
[much; many]
They have a lot/lots of money.
I have a lot/lots of relations
  in Cuba.

mucho/mucha/muchos/muchas
Tienen mucho dinero.
Tengo muchos parientes en Cuba.

loud adj
loud
a loud voice
a loud noise
He spoke in a loud voice.
The music is very loud.
[noisy]
a loud district
loudspeaker

alto(a)/fuerte/ruidoso(a)
una voz fuerte
un ruido fuerte
Habló en voz alta.
La música está muy alta.
ruidoso(a)
un barrio ruidoso
un altoparlante/un altavoz/una magnavoz

love v & n
to love sb
He loves his children.
to fall in love with sb
She fell in love with him.
to be in love in with sb
I'm not in love with her.
to make love (to sb)
to love sth
I love Mexican food.
I love Chinese food.

querer a alguien
Quiere a sus niños.
enamorarse de alguien
Se enamoró de él.
estar enamorado(a) de alguien
No estoy enamorado de ella.
hacer el amor (a alguien)
adorar algo/encantarle a uno algo
Adoro la comida mexicana.
Me encanta la comida china.

lovely adj
of appearance

How lovely she is!
It's a lovely beach.

lindo(a) [LA]/bonito(a)/hermoso(a)/
  precioso(a)
¡Qué linda es!
Es una linda playa.

of personal qualities
His father is a lovely person.

encantador(a)
Su padre es una persona encantadora.

pleasant
It was a lovely trip.
to have a lovely time
We had a lovely time in Spain.

agradable
Fue un viaje agradable.
pasarlo muy bien/divertirse
Lo pasamos muy bien en España.

lover n
a lover
to be lovers
[an enthusiast]

un/una amante
ser amantes
un(a) aficionado(a)

lucky

a lover of soccer

She's a music lover.
She's a great lover of the guitar.

un(a) aficionado(a) al fútbol/un(a)
  hincha del fútbol
Es aficionada a la música.
Tiene mucha afición a la guitarra.

lucky   *adj*
lucky
He's a very lucky person.
to be lucky
You were very lucky.
She was lucky enough to get
  tickets.
How lucky!
a lucky charm
It's not my lucky day.

afortunado(a)
Es una persona afortunada.
tener suerte
Tuviste mucha suerte.
Tuvo la suerte de conseguir
  entradas.
¡Qué suerte!
un amuleto que trae suerte
Hoy no traigo buena estrella.

luggage   *n*
luggage
hand luggage
excess luggage
a piece of luggage
luggage check-in
luggage locker

el equipaje/las maletas
los bultos de mano/el equipaje de mano
el exceso de equipaje
una maleta
la consigna
la consigna automática

luxury   *adj & n*
luxury
a luxury apartment/hotel
to live in luxury
I can't afford luxuries.

el lujo
un apartamento/hotel de lujo
vivir en (el) lujo
No tengo con que comprar artículos
  de lujo.

Ø **la lujuria** means "lust."

M

mad *adj*

angry

She'll be mad if you arrive late.

to be mad at sb

to get mad at sb

furioso(a)

Estará furiosa si llegas tarde.

estar furioso(a) con alguien

enojarse/enfadarse/ponerse enojado(a)/
ponerse enfadado(a) con alguien

crazy

His father is mad.

Are you mad?

[idea, plan]

[hurriedly]

to go mad

a mad dog

loco(a)

Su padre es loco. *[Note: **Ser** is used to
refer to a permanent state of insanity.]*

¿Estás loco(a)? *[Note: **Estar** is used where
permanent insanity is not referred to.]*

insensato(a)

precipitadamente

volverse loco(a)

un perro rabioso

enthusiastic

to be mad about

I'm mad about her.

He's mad about music.

andar/estar loco(a) por

Ando loco por ella.

Está loco por la música.

mail *n*

[in general]

[letters]

airmail

by airmail

el correo/la correspondencia *[Arg]*

las cartas/la correspondencia

el correo aéreo

por avión/por correo aéreo

mail *v*

[to send through the mail]

[to put in mail box]

echar/mandar por correo

echar/depositar al buzón

main *adj*

main course

main office

main street

el plato principal

la oficina central

la calle mayor

major *n*

academic studies

What is your major?

to change one's major

la especialidad

¿Cuál es tu especialidad?

cambiarse de especialidad

person studying

He is a chemistry major.

Se especializa en la química.

military rank

a major

un comandante

major *v*

to major in *[a subject at a
university]*

She majored in Spanish.

especializarse en

Se especializó en español.

127

make   n
a make [brand]   una marca

make   v
[general]   hacer
to make a journey/a noise   hacer un viaje/un ruido
[manufacture]   fabricar
They make cars here.   Fabrican coches aquí.
"Made in Venezuela"   "Fabricado en Venezuela"
to make a mistake   equivocarse/cometer una falta
to make money   ganar dinero
to make an appointment with   citarse con/darse una cita con
to make friends with   trabar amistad con/hacerse amigo de
to make up one's mind   decidirse
to make a meal   preparar una comida
to make fun of sb   burlarse de alguien
to make good grades   sacar buenas notas
to make a living   ganarse la vida

to make sb do sth   hacer/obligar a alguien
to make sb leave   obligar a alguien a salir
She made him cry.   Le hizo llorar.
I made him apologize to the   Le hice disculparse con el cliente.
  customer.

to cause/provoke   causar
to make trouble   causar problemas

to cause to be
to make sb ill/sad   poner a alguien enfermo(a)/triste
Don't make me laugh!   ¡No me hagas reír!
to make sb hungry/thirsty   darle hambre/sed a alguien

to make out
I can't make that out.   No lo entiendo./No me lo explico.
Can you make out his writing?   ¿Puedes descifrar su letra?

to make up
[with cosmetics]   maquillarse/pintarse
[after a quarrel]   hacer las paces
to make up for lost time   recuperar el tiempo perdido
to make up a story   inventar un cuento
You're making it up!   ¡Puro cuento!

to make up for   compensar

make-believe   n
make-believe   la fantasía/la invención

male   n
[animal, plant]   un macho
[person]   un varón
[adj: male sex]   masculino

manage   v
to run [a business]   administrar/dirigir/llevar
He manages three businesses.   Dirige tres empresas.
My daughter manages a hotel in   Mi hija lleva un hotel en Cancún.
  Cancún.

128

to manage one's own affairs — llevar sus negocios

to succeed (in getting) — conseguir
He managed to get a good job. — Consiguió un buen trabajo.

to succeed in doing sth — conseguir/lograr hacer algo
They managed to find the museum. — Consiguieron/lograron encontrar el museo.
Did you manage to see the doctor? — ¿Conseguiste ver al médico?

to handle a tricky situation — arreglarse
How did you manage at the meeting? — ¿Cómo te arreglaste en la reunión?
I managed very well. — Me arreglé muy bien.

to manage people — manejar/manejarse con
She manages her employees very well. — Maneja muy bien a sus empleados./Se maneja muy bien con sus empleados.
They can't manage the children. — No pueden con los niños.

manager *n*
[of a company] — el director/la directora
el/la gerente
el encargado/la encargada
[owner, boss of small business] — el dueño/la dueña
[of estate] — el administrador/la administradora
sales manager — el gerente de ventas
[of sports team] — el/la entrenador(a)

Ø **el mánager** is also used to refer to a "manager" in the sport and entertainment fields.

mane *n*
[of a horse] — una crin
[of a lion] — una melena

man-made *adj*
[lake] — artificial
[fabric, etc.] — sintético(a)

manners *n*
bad manners — la mala educación
good manners — la educación
He has good manners. — Tiene educación.
You have no manners. — No tienes educación.
It's bad manners to interrupt. — Es de mala educación interrumpir.

manufacture *v*
[in general] — fabricar
[for clothes] — confeccionar
[for food] — elaborar

many *adj & pron*
There are many people in the square. — Hay mucha gente en la plaza.
I have many friends in Spain. — Tengo muchos amigos en España.
Many houses have air conditioning. — Muchas casas tienen aire acondicionado.
Many of them/us/you — Muchos de ellos/nosotros/ustedes
Muchas de ellas/nosotras/ustedes

129

| many times | muchas veces |

as many as
She has as many friends as you.
I have as many as you.

tantos(as) como
Tiene tantos amigos como tú.
Tengo tantos como tú.

map   *n*
[general]
a map of the world
[of town/streets/transport system]
a map of the subway

un mapa [Note: masculine]
un mapamundi
un plano
un plano del Metro

march   *n*
[military]
[walk]
[demonstration]
[of time]

una marcha
una caminata
una manifestación
una marcha/un paso

march   *v*
to march in and out
to march past

entrar y salir enojado
desfilar

mark   *n*
[stain]
[imprint]
[from a blow]
[education]
On your marks!
to make one's mark

una mancha
una huella
una señal
una nota/una calificación
¡Preparados!
distinguirse

market   *n*
[general]
an open-air market
[stock market]
a supermarket
a hypermarket
[small grocery store]
the corner market
to be on the market

el mercado
un mercado al aire libre
la bolsa
un supermercado
un hipermercado
una tienda de ultramarinos
la tienda de la esquina
estar a la venta

marry   *v*
to marry/get married
Peter is marrying Teresa today.
We are getting married on Saturday.
They got married in Las Vegas.

casarse con
Pedro se casa con Teresa hoy.
Nos casamos el sábado.
Se casaron en Las Vegas.

**to conduct the marriage
  ceremony**
The priest married them.
The bishop will marry my sister.

casar a

El cura los casó.
El obispo casará a mi hermana.

to be married
I am not married.
They've been married for fifty years.

estar casado(a)(os)(as)
No estoy casado(a).
Hace cincuenta años que están
  casados.

master's   *[see degree]*

match n
[game]   un partido/un encuentro
[for striking]   un fósforo/un cerillo [Mex]/una cerilla [Sp]
a box of matches   una caja de fósforos
[marriage]   un partido
to be a good match   ser un buen partido

match v
to equal   igualar/corresponder a
Her words don't match her   Sus palabras no corresponden a sus
   actions.   acciones.

of clothes/colors   hacer juego con/ser a tono
His tie matches his shirt.   Su corbata hace juego con su camisa.
These colors do not match.   Estos colores no son a tono/no hacen juego.

material n & adj
[information, ideas]   el material
[cloth]   el tejido/la tela
[substance]   la materia
raw materials   las materias primas
writing materials   los efectos de escritorio
[important]   material

matter n & v
[substance]   la materia
[subject, affair]   el asunto/la cuestión
as a matter of fact ...   en realidad.../el caso es que...
What's the matter?   ¿Qué hay?/¿Qué pasa?
What's the matter with you?   ¿Qué te pasa?/¿Qué tienes?/¿Te pasa algo?
Nothing's the matter.   No pasa nada.
It doesn't matter.   No importa./Da igual.
It's a matter of opinion.   Es cuestión de opinión.
It's a matter of time.   Es cuestión/cosa de tiempo.
It's a serious matter.   Es cosa seria.
no matter how   como sea
No matter where I go ...   Dondequiera que vaya...

matter-of-fact adj
matter-of-fact   práctico(a)/realista

mature adj
[person, fruit]   maduro(a)
a mature person   una persona madura/de edad madura
[commerce, finance]   vencido(a)

may v
permission   poder/permitir a alguien
May I ... ?   ¿Me permite(s)... ?
You may go in now.   Puedes entrar/pasar ahora.
May I come in?   ¿Me permite(s) pasar?/¿Se puede pasar?

possibility   es posible que/puede ser que
I may be able to help you.   Es posible que pueda ayudarte.
                                             [Note: subjunctive]
She may have said so.   Es posible que lo haya dicho.
                                             [Note: subjunctive]/Puede haberlo dicho.

me   *pron*

[direct object]	me
[indirect object] to me	me
[disjunctive, object of preposition]	mí
He saw me in the street.	Me vio en la calle.
She gave the money to me.	Me dio el dinero.
Give it to me!	¡Dámelo!
Don't give them to me!	¡No me los des!
These are for me.	Éstos son para mí.
He came with me.	Vino conmigo.

mean   *adj*

petty
	mezquino(a)
It's very mean of you.	Es muy mezquino de tu parte.

bad/unkind
a mean trick	malo(a)/antipático(a)
	una mala jugada
Her boss was a very mean guy.	Su jefe era un tío muy malo.

with temperature
	medio(a)
the mean temperature	la temperatura media

mean   *v*

to signify
	querer decir/significar
What does this mean in English?	¿Qué quiere decir esto en inglés?
These instructions don't mean anything.	Estas instrucciones no significan nada.

to intend
They mean well.	Tienen buenas intenciones.
Do you mean it?	¿Lo dices en serio?
I didn't mean to do it.	Lo hice sin querer.
Does she mean to be difficult?	¿Quiere ser difícil?

means   *n*

[manner]	el medio/la manera
[resources]	los medios
economic means	los recursos económicos
a person of means	una persona acaudalada
By all means!	¡Naturalmente!

medicine   *n*

field of study
	la medicina

medication
	el medicamento/la medicina
You must take this medicine twice a day.	Debes tomarte esta medicina dos veces al día.

meet   *v*

to get to know
	conocer
I met them in Acapulco.	Los conocí en Acapulco.
We met at the university.	Nos conocimos en la universidad.
I'm very pleased to meet you.	Tengo mucho gusto en conocerte/lo/la.
Juan, meet Lola.	Juan, quiero presentarte a Lola.
Pleased to meet you!	¡Mucho gusto!/Encantado(a)/ Encantado(a) de conocerte/lo/la.

by arrangement
	reunirse (con)/ir a recibir/esperar/venir a buscar/entrevistarse con

Let's meet later.	Vamos a reunirnos más tarde.
We can meet them at the café.	Podemos reunirnos con ellos en el café.
I'm meeting my wife at the airport.	Voy a recibir a mi esposa en el aeropuerto.
They're meeting me at the museum.	Vienen a buscarme en el museo.
I'll meet you at the theater.	Te espero en el teatro.
The President is meeting them at four o'clock.	El Presidente se entrevista con ellos a las cuatro.

accidentally
I met my cousin in the street.

encontrar/encontrarse con
Encontré a mi primo en la calle./Me encontré con mi primo en la calle.

We met in the market.

Nos encontramos en el mercado.

meeting n
a group of people
a mass meeting
to hold a meeting

una reunión/una sesión
una reunión/un mitin popular
celebrar una reunión/sesión

individuals
[accidental]
[arranged]

un encuentro
una cita

mellow adj
[voice]
[person]

suave
sereno(a)

memorize v
to memorize

aprender de memoria

memory n
the mental faculty
I have a good memory.
He has a bad memory for names.

la memoria
Tengo buena memoria.
No recuerda bien los nombres.

something remembered
We have happy memories of Mexico.

Tenemos felices recuerdos de México.

menu n
the menu
[fixed price]
today's menu
tourist menu
What's on the menu?

la lista de platos/la carta
el menú/el cubierto [Mex]
el menú del día
el menú turístico
¿Qué hay de comer?

middle n
in the middle of
in the middle of the field
in the middle of the night
in the middle of summer
in the middle of June
in the middle of Bogotá
the middle class
the Middle Ages

en medio de
en medio del campo
en medio de la noche
en pleno verano
a mediados de junio
en el centro de Bogotá
la clase media
la Edad Media

to be busy doing sth

estar + gerund

133

They were in the middle of lunch when I arrived.	Estaban comiendo cuando llegué.

might *v*

It might be true.	Podría ser verdad.
It might be that he'll come tomorrow.	Podría ser que viniera mañana. *[Note: subjunctive]*
She said she might be able to help you.	Dijo que pudiera ayudarte. *[Note: subjunctive]*
She might have said so.	Podría haberlo dicho.

mind *n*

mind	la mente
What's on your mind?	¿Qué es lo que te preocupa?
to be out of one's mind	estar fuera de juicio
to change one's mind	cambiar de opinión
It crossed my mind that ...	Se me ocurrió...que
to go out of one's mind	volverse loco
to make up one's mind to	decidirse a
Have you made up your mind?	¿Te has decidido?

mind *v*

Do you mind if I open the window?	¿Te molesta si abro la ventana?
Where do you want to go? – I don't mind.	¿Adónde quieres ir? – Me es igual./ No me importa.
I don't mind waiting.	No tengo inconveniente en esperar.
Would you mind ... ?	¿Serías tan amable de... ?

mine *pron*
[possessive]

	el mío/los míos
	la mía/las mías
His house is bigger than mine.	Su casa es más grande que la mía.
These books are mine.	Estos libros son míos. *[Note: The definite article is omitted after the verb **ser**.]*
Is this your glass? – No, mine is in the kitchen.	¿Es tuyo este vaso? – No, el mío está en la cocina.
a friend of mine	un amigo mío/una amiga mía

minister *n*

[religious title]	el pastor
[political]	el ministro

miserable *adj*

[sad]	triste
[unfortunate]	desdichado(a)/desgraciado(a)
[wretched]	miserable
a miserable room	una habitación miserable

miss *v*
to fail to catch

	perder
They missed the bus.	Perdieron el autobús.

to be absent

	faltar a
They missed the meeting.	Faltaron a la reunión./No asistieron a la reunión.

She missed her appointment.	Faltó a su cita./No asistió a su cita.
to miss the boat	perder el tren
to be missing	faltar
Two people are missing.	Faltan dos personas.
[absent]	ausente
There are three students missing.	Tres estudiantes están ausentes.
[lost]	perdido(a)
Four tourists are missing in the desert.	Cuatro turistas están perdidos en el desierto.
to feel the absence of	echar de menos
We miss her.	La echamos de menos.
I missed you this morning.	Noté tu ausencia esta mañana.

mistake n

a mistake	una equivocación/un error/una falta
a spelling mistake	una falta de ortografía
There must be some mistake.	Ha de haber algún error.
to make a mistake	equivocarse/cometer un error/pelarse [Ven]

mistake v

to mistake sb for sb else	tomar a alguien por/confundir a alguien con/equivocar a alguien con
I mistook her for her sister.	La tomé por su hermana.

mix v

to mix a drink	preparar una bebida
a mixed salad	una ensalada mixta
to mix [socially]	llevarse bien con la gente
He doesn't mix well.	No se lleva bien con la gente.
to mix up	mezclar/confundir
He gets the two brothers mixed up.	Confunde a los dos hermanos.
I mix up ser and estar.	Confundo ser con estar.
to be mixed up	estar totalmente confuso(a)
to be mixed up in sth	estar metido en algo
to get mixed up in sth	meterse en algo

mixed adj

mixed	variado(a)
[with feelings]	contradictorio(a)

model n

a model	un modelo
[of plane, ship, etc.]	en miniatura
[exemplary]	un ejemplar
a model home	una casa piloto

money n

[in general]	el dinero/la plata [in many parts of LA]
paper money	el papel moneda
ready money	el dinero contante
money payment	un pago en metálico
to make money	ganar dinero

Ø **la moneda** means "currency," "coinage", and "coin:" note **la moneda suelta** meaning "small change."

135

monitor *n & v*

a monitor *[TV, computer]*	un monitor
[student]	un estudiante responsable
[to listen to]	escuchar
[to follow]	seguir de cerca

mood *n*

to be in a good/bad mood	estar de buen/mal humor
to be in the mood to do sth	tener ganas de hacer algo
I'm not in the mood to do it.	No tengo ganas de hacerlo.

more *adj, adv & pron*

in comparisons

más... que
más... del que/de la que/de los que
  /de las que/de lo que

He has more money than you.	Tiene más dinero que tú.
They drink more wine than beer.	Beben más vino que cerveza.
She is more intelligent than her brother.	Es más inteligente que su hermano.
I have more money than she thinks.	Tengo más dinero del que piensa.
They visited more factories than they expected.	Visitaron más fábricas de las que esperaban.
He is more intelligent than you think.	Es más inteligente de lo que piensas.

[Note how the forms del que/de la que/de los que/de las que are used when the comparison is made between a noun and a following clause; de lo que is used when the comparison is between two clauses.]

before a number

más de

I have more than 50 dollars.	Tengo más de cincuenta dólares.
More than 100,000 people went to the game.	Más de cien mil personas asistieron al partido.
more than half	más de la mitad

additional

más

four more	cuatro más
Would you like some more wine?	¿Quieres más vino?
a few more days	algunos días más
I have one more thing to do.	Tengo una cosa más que hacer.
once more	una vez más

remaining

Is there any more coffee?	¿Queda café?
There are more potatoes left.	Quedan papas.

in negative sentences

I have no more money.	No tengo más dinero.
She doesn't go to the beach any more.	Ya no va a la playa.
There are no more than five left.	No quedan más de cinco.

more and more

cada vez más

He became more and more excited.	Se puso cada vez más emocionado.

the more ... the more ...

cuanto más... (tanto) más

The more you study the more you learn.	Cuanto más estudias (tanto) más aprendes.
the more the merrier	cuantos más mejor

morning n

the morning	la mañana
[before dawn]	la madrugada
in the morning	por la mañana
in the morning [with time by the clock]	de la mañana
at eight o'clock in the morning	a las ocho de la mañana
early in the morning	muy de mañana
very early in the morning	muy de madrugada
this morning	esta mañana
tomorrow morning	mañana por la mañana
yesterday morning	ayer por la mañana
I spent every morning in the library.	Pasaba todas las mañanas en la biblioteca.
I spent the whole morning at the office.	Pasé toda la mañana en la oficina.
Good morning!	¡Buenos días! [Note: plural]

Ø **mañana** also means "tomorrow."

most adj, adv & n
with a noun

[with a singular noun]	más
My brother has the most money.	Mi hermano tiene más dinero.
[with a plural noun]	los más/las más/la mayor parte de/ la mayoría de
Most students will be there.	La mayoría de los estudiantes estarán allí.

with an adjective

	más
It's the most enjoyable film I have seen.	Es la película más divertida que he visto.
It's the tallest building in the world.	Es el edificio más alto del mundo. [Note: **de** is used to mean "in" after a superlative.]
[meaning "very"]	muy
The film was most enjoyable.	La película fue muy divertida.

with a verb or adverb

His sister spent the most.	Es su hermana que ha gastado más.

most (of) n

[with a singular noun]	la mayor parte (de)
most of the time	la mayor parte del tiempo
He paid for most of the wine.	Pagó la mayor parte del vino.
at the very most	como máximo
[with a plural noun]	la mayoría de
Most of these teachers are from Mexico.	La mayoría de estos profesores son de México.

mostly adv
for the most part

They are mostly Peruvians.	en su mayor parte/en su mayoría En su mayoría son peruanos.

mainly

	casi siempre/la mayoría de las veces generalmente/en general/por lo general
We mostly go to the movies.	Generalmente vamos al cine.
He mostly drinks coffee.	Casi siempre bebe café.

mother *n & v*
a mother | una madre/una mamá *[Note: In Mexico the word **madre** is very often used in an insulting fashion; it is therefore better to use **mamá** to refer to one's mother.]*

mother country | la madre patria
to mother | mimar

mother tongue | la lengua materna

mountain *n*
a mountain | una montaña/un monte
The Appalachians | Los Montes Apalaches
a chain/range of mountains | una sierra/una cordillera
Let's go to the mountains. | Vamos a la sierra.
I spent my vacation in the mountains. | Pasé las vacaciones en la sierra.

mouth *n*
a mouth | una boca
[of a river] | una desembocadura
by word of mouth | de palabra
to keep one's mouth shut | no decir esta boca es mía/tener la boca cerrada

to mouth *[to articulate]* | articular

move *v trans*
physical
I couldn't move the piano. | mover
No pude mover el piano.

emotional
to move to tears | hacer llorar a alguien
The music moved me to tears. | La música me hizo llorar.

move *v intrans*
to move | moverse
Don't move! | ¡No te muevas!/¡No se mueva!/¡No se muevan!

to move house | mudarse de casa
They moved last week. | Se mudaron de casa la semana pasada.
She's moved to San Diego. | Se ha trasladado a San Diego.
to move in | instalarse en una casa
When did you move in? | ¿Cuándo se instalaron ustedes?

movie *n*
a movie | una película
a movie theater | un cine
to go to the movies | ir al cine
a movie star | un astro de cine *[man]*/una estrella de cine *[woman]*

much *adj, adv & pron*
He doesn't sleep much. | No duerme mucho.
I don't drink much coffee. | No tomo mucho café.
There isn't much to do here. | Aquí no hay mucho que hacer.
How much do you need? | ¿Cuánto necesitas?

in comparisons
as much as
I didn't eat as much as you.
as much ... as
They don't buy as much fruit
  as they used to.

so much
He drank so much coffee that
  he couldn't sleep.
There is so much to do.

too much
[adj]
They eat too much rice.
[adv & pro]
You smoke too much!
She has too much to do.

musical adj
a musical instrument
She is very musical.
I come from a musical family.
a musical [show]

must v
obligation
I must speak to him at once.
You must not go alone.

probability
They must be very rich.
You must have been mistaken.

my adj
[masc & fem]
my son/family
my parents/sisters

myself [see self]

tanto como
No comí tanto como tú.
tanto(a)... como
No compran tanta fruta como antes.

tanto(a)
Bebió tanto café que no pudo
  dormir.
Hay tanto que hacer.

demasiado(a)
Comen demasiado arroz.
demasiado
¡Fumas demasiado!
Tiene demasiado que hacer.

un instrumento músico
Tiene mucho talento para la música.
Soy de familia de músicos.
una comedia musical

deber/tener que
Debo/Tengo que hablarle en seguida.
No debes ir solo(a).

deber de
Deben de ser muy ricos.
Debías de haberte equivocado.

mi/mis
mi hijo/familia
mis padres/hermanas

N

nail *n & v*

[finger, toe] una uña
[animal's claw] una garra
[metal] un clavo
to be as hard as nails ser muy resistente/tener el corazón de piedra

to bite one's nails comerse las uñas
to hit the nail on the head dar en el clavo/acertar
to nail clavar
to nail together fijar con clavos

name *n*

[general] el nombre
first name el nombre de pila
family name/surname el apellido
maiden name el apellido de soltera
married name el apellido de casada
nickname el apodo
pet name el nombre cariñoso
by name de nombre
I know her by name. La conozco de nombre.
a man named Morales un hombre de nombre/llamado Morales
What's your name? ¿Cómo te llamas?/¿Cómo se llama usted?
My name is ... Me llamo...
name [of book] el título

narrow *adj*
narrow angosto(a) [LA]/estrecho(a)

native *adj*
native country el país natal/la patria
native language la lengua materna/nativa
native born de nacimiento
She's a native born Venezuelan. Es venezolana de nacimiento.

native *n*
She is a native of Lima. Es natural de Lima./Nació en Lima./ Es limeña.
I'm a native of Panama. Soy natural de Panamá.
He speaks Spanish like a native. Habla español como si fuera su primera lengua.
the natives (of a country) los indígenas/los aborígenes

near *adj & prep*
of places
I live near the park. cerca de
  Vivo cerca del parque.
near here aquí cerca

of time
near the end of the month hacia fines del mes
in the near future en fecha próxima

140

other
a near relative — un pariente cercano

nearby adv
They live nearby. — Viven cerca/aquí cerca.

nearly [see *almost*]

neat adj
[room, garden, etc.] — bien cuidado(a)/arreglado(a)
[personal appearance] — pulcro(a)/esmerado(a)
neat handwriting — la escritura/letra clara

necessary adj
it's necessary — es necesario/preciso/hace falta
It's necessary to have a passport. — Es necesario tener un pasaporte./ Hace falta tener un pasaporte.
It's necessary for you to come alone. — Es necesario que vengas solo(a).
[Note: use of subjunctive]
It wasn't necessary for him to do it. — No era necesario que lo hiciera.
They will do everything necessary. — Harán todo lo necesario.

need v
to need sth — necesitar
We need money. — Necesitamos dinero.

to demand, to require — requerir/exigir
This needs care. — Esto requiere/exige cuidado.

to need to do sth — haber de/necesitar
Do we need to be there? — ¿Hemos de asistir?/¿Necesitamos asistir?
The car needs repairing. — Hay que reparar el coche.

neighborhood n
[district] — el barrio
[area] — la vecindad
a neighborhood movie theater — un cine del barrio

neither (one) adj & pron
Neither of them has any money. — Ninguno de ellos tiene dinero.
Which of the shirts do you prefer? – Neither. — ¿Cuál de las camisas prefieres? – Ni la una ni la otra.

neither ... nor conj
neither ... nor — ni... ni
I neither drink nor smoke. — Ni bebo ni fumo.
She had neither the time nor the opportunity. — No tenía ni el tiempo ni la oportunidad.
Neither my brother nor my sister lives here. — Ni mi hermano ni mi hermana vive aquí.
You don't play tennis? – Neither do I./Me neither. — ¿No juegas al tenis? – Ni yo tampoco.

nerve n
[anatomical] — un nervio
It gets on my nerves. — Me pone los nervios en punta.
They get on my nerves. — Me fastidian terriblemente.

141

nervous

What nerve!
[courage]

¡Qué desvergüenza!
el valor

nervous adj
apprehensive
to get nervous
Don't be nervous!
It makes me nervous.

miedoso(a)/nervioso(a)
ponerse nervioso(a)/sentir miedo
¡No sientas/tengas miedo!
Me da miedo.

medical
a nervous breakdown

nervioso(a)
una depresión nerviosa

by nature

tímido(a)

never adv
never
He never eats meat.

nunca/jamás
Nunca come carne./No come nunca
   carne. [Note: If **nunca** or **jamás** follow the
   verb, **no** precedes it.]

never mind
Never mind!

¡No te molestes, olvídalo!/¡No importa,
   déjalo!

nevertheless adv
[however]

no obstante/sin embargo

new adj
brand-new
I have bought a new car.

nuevo(a)
He comprado un coche nuevo.
   [Note: here **nuevo** follows the noun.]

newly acquired
What color is your new car?

nuevo(a)
¿De qué color es tu nuevo coche?
   [Note: here **nuevo** precedes the noun.]

other expressions
What's new?
There's nothing new.
It's as good as new.

¿Qué hay de nuevo?
No hay nada nuevo.
Está como nuevo.

news n
the news
a piece of news
What news?
a news bulletin [radio]
a newscast [TV]
a newscaster
a newspaper [general]
a newspaper [daily]

las noticias
una noticia
¿Qué hay de nuevo?
un noticiario
un telediario/un noticiero
un(a) locutor(a) de telediario
un periódico
un diario

next adj
of future time
next week/month/year

next Thursday
the next ten days
next time

próximo(a)/que viene/que entra
la semana próxima/el mes próximo/el
   año próximo
la semana/el mes/el año que viene
el jueves que viene/el jueves que entra.
los diez días que vienen
la próxima vez

142

of past time
the next day
On the next day they got up
  early.

of place
He lives next door.
You must get off at the next stop.

of order
He caught the next train.
Look at the next page.

next *adv*
[then, after that]
Next he heard a shot.
What did you do next?
Give it to him when you next
  see him.
When I saw her next ...

next *prep*
next to
She lives next to the café.
He's sitting next to his brother.
next to nothing
We got it for next to nothing.

nice *adj*
[likeable]
She is very nice.
[kind]
They are such nice people.
[attractive of people]
She looks very nice.
[attractive of things]

The house is very nice.
[of food]
The meals were very nice.

night *n*
the night
tonight
last night
the night before last
tomorrow night
in the night
at eleven o'clock at night
It's night.
at night
to work nights
to spend the night
to have a bad night
the night before
good night
to be a night owl

siguiente
el día siguiente
Al día siguiente se levantaron
  temprano.

próximo(a)/vecino(a)/de al lado
Vive en la casa vecina/de al lado.
Debes bajar en la próxima parada.

próximo(a)
Tomó el próximo tren.
Mira la página siguiente.

luego/después/la próxima vez
Luego oyó un tiro.
¿Qué hiciste después?
Dáselo la próxima vez que lo
  veas.
Cuando volví a verla...

junto a/al lado de
Vive al lado del café.
Está sentado junto a su hermano.
casi nada
Lo adquirimos por casi nada.

simpático(a)
Es muy simpática.
amable
Son personas tan amables.
guapo(a)
Es muy linda/guapa.
agradable/bonito(a)/chulo(a)
  [Mex]/regio *[LA]*/sabroso *[Ven]*
La casa es muy agradable/bonita.
rico(a)
Las comidas fueron muy ricas.

la noche
esta noche
anoche/ayer en la noche
anteanoche
mañana por la noche
por la noche/durante la noche
a las once de la noche
Es de noche.
de noche
trabajar de noche
pasar la noche
dormir mal/pasar una noche mala
la víspera
buenas noches
trasnochar

no *adj*
[not any]
No honest man would do that.

He has no money.

There are no tickets left.

There's no problem.
[for emphasis]
We have no money at all.
He made no reply.
in public notices
no entry
no parking/smoking

ninguno(a)/ningunos(as)
Ningún hombre honrado haría
 eso. [Note: **Ninguno** shortens to **ningún**
 when it precedes a noun.]
No tiene ningún dinero. [Note: **No**
 precedes the verb when **ninguno(a)**
 comes after.]
No tiene dinero.
No quedan localidades. [Note: The
 ninguno forms are frequently not used.]
No hay problema.
alguno(a)/algunos(as)
No tenemos dinero alguno.
No hizo respuesta alguna.
prohibido(a)
prohibida la entrada
prohibido aparcar/fumar

nobody (no one) *pron*
nobody
Nobody will help me.
There was nobody in.

nadie
Nadie quiere ayudarme.
No estaba nadie. [Note: **No** precedes
 the verb when **nadie** comes after.]

none *pron*
[not any, not one]
Have you any bread? – There is
 none left.
Where are the grapes? – There
 are none left.
None of my friends is going to
 the party.
None of the tourists came.
none of them
none of us
none of you

ninguno(a)
¿Hay pan? – No queda ninguno.

¿Dónde están las uvas? – No queda
 ninguna.
Ninguno de mis amigos va a la
 fiesta.
No vino ninguno de los turistas.
ninguno(a) de ellos/ellas
ninguno(a) de nosotros/nosotras
ninguno(a) de ustedes

nose *n*
[of person]
[of animal]
to have a good nose for

una nariz
un hocico
tener buen olfato para

note *n*
[annotation]
to take notes
[musical note/footnote]
[letter]
a banknote
a hundred peso note

un apunte/una nota
sacar/tomar apuntes
una nota
una nota/una carta
un billete
un billete de cien pesos

note *v*
[to notice]
[to note down]

notar/observar/advertir
apuntar/anotar

nothing   *pron*

[not anything]	nada
I said nothing.	No dije nada.
Nothing interested me.	Nada me interesó./No me interesó nada. *[Note: **No** precedes the verb when **nada** comes after.]*
I have nothing to do.	No tengo nada que hacer.
nothing else	nada más
nothing much	poca cosa
nothing to write home about	nada extraordinario/nada del otro mundo

notice   *n*

[a sign]	un letrero
[a poster]	un cartel
[in a newspaper]	un anuncio
[information/warning]	un aviso
"Notice to the public"	Aviso al público
until further notice	hasta nuevo aviso
to give notice *[to quit work]*	dimitir
to give notice *[to employee]*	despedir a alguien
to dismiss sb without notice	despedir a alguien sin aviso
to give notice *[to a tenant]*	dar aviso a alguien
She gave him notice to leave.	Le dio el aviso de que se marchara.
at short notice	a corto plazo
without previous notice	sin previo aviso
a week's notice	una semana de anticipación
to take notice of someone	hacer caso a alguien
Don't take any notice of him!	¡No le hagas caso!
to take notice of something	prestar atención a/hacer caso de algo
They took no notice of the paintings.	No prestaron atención a/no hicieron caso de los cuadros.

Ø **noticia** means "an item of news;" **las noticias** means "the news."

notice   *v*

[to see/realize]	darse cuenta de
I noticed that it was raining.	Me di cuenta de que llovía.
[to take note of]	fijarse en/reparar en/notar/observar
Did you notice his shoes?	¿Te fijaste en sus zapatos?
I didn't notice the color.	No reparé en el color.
Notice how it moves.	Observa cómo se mueve.
[to see sb/sth]	ver
She noticed you in the street.	Te vio en la calle.

now   *adv*
as expression of time

now	ahora/ya
What are you doing now?	¿Qué haces ahora?
She's a university student now.	Ya es universitaria.
right now	ahora mismo/ahorita *[LA]*
Do it right now!	¡Hazlo ahora mismo!
at present	actualmente/en este momento
He'll be in the office now.	En este momento estará en la oficina.
now and then/again	de vez en cuando
up to now	hasta ahora
I'm off now.	Ya me voy.

now

They're coming now.	Ya vienen.

without any sense of time
Now!	¡A ver!
Now then!	¡Vamos a ver!

now *conj*
Now that you've arrived ...	Ahora que has llegado...

nowadays *adv*
nowadays	hoy día/hoy en día/actualmente

nowhere *adv*
[no place]
Where are you going? – Nowhere.	¿Adónde vas?— A ninguna parte.
They went nowhere.	No fueron a ninguna parte.
Nowhere in Spain will you see such a thing.	En ninguna parte de España verás tal cosa.
She's nowhere to be seen.	No se la encuentra por ningún lado.

nuisance *n*
of a situation or happening
	una molestia/un fastidio/una incomodidad/una lata/una pesadez
What a nuisance!	¡Qué lata!/¡Qué fastidio!/¡Qué pesadez!/¡Qué macana! *[Arg]*
It's a nuisance having to get up early.	Es una molestia tener que levantarme temprano.

of a person
What a nuisance you are!	¡Qué pesado(a) eres!
to make a nuisance of oneself	dar la lata

number *n*
in mathematics
	un número
whole number	un número entero
even/odd number	un número par/impar
cardinal/ordinal number	un número cardinal/ordinal

digit, figure
	una cifra/un número
Arabic/Roman numbers	cifras arábigas/romanas
It consists of ten numbers.	Consiste en diez cifras.

for house, telephone
	un número
They live in number eight.	Viven en el número ocho.
What's your phone number?	¿Cuál es tu número de teléfono?

an amount or quantity
	algunos(as)/varios(as)/un número de
a number of people	algunas/varias personas
a large number of people	buen número de personas

nuts *n*
[botanical]
	frutos secos
Brazil nut	una nuez de Brasil
chestnut	una castaña
hazelnut	una avellana
peanut	un cacahuate *[Mex]*/un maní *[other LA countries]*/un cacahuete *[Sp]*
walnut	una nuez/una nuez de Castilla *[Mex]* *[Note: In Mexico* **nuez** *refers to "pecan nuts."]*

You're nuts.	Estás chalado(a)/chiflado(a). [fam.]
to be nuts about sb/sth	estar chalado(a)/chiflado(a) por alguien/algo
He's nuts about Teresa.	Está chalado/chiflado por Teresa.
She's nuts about music.	Está chalada/chiflada por la música.

O

object *n*
a thing
a round/square object

aim

My object is to win.

grammar
a direct/indirect object

object *v*
to object
The students objected.
I object!
to object to sth
We objected to their decision.

obvious *adj*
obvious
It's obvious.
It's all very obvious.

obviously *adv*
obviously
He obviously can't do it.

occasion *n*
time
It was the last occasion I saw them.
On that occasion I was late.
on occasion

function
It will be a very important
  occasion.

suitable occasion/opportunity
Wait for the right occasion!

occasionally *adv*
occasionally

odd *adj*
strange
How odd!
He's an odd person.
That's a very odd way to do it.

of numbers
an odd number

un objeto/una cosa/un artículo
un objeto redondo/cuadrado

un objeto/un objetivo/un próposito/un
  intento
Mi próposito es ganar.

un complemento
un complemento directo/indirecto

hacer objeciones/oponerse/protestar
Los estudiantes hicieron objeciones.
¡Yo protesto!
oponerse a/protestar contra
Nos opusimos a su decisión./
  Protestamos contra su decisión.

evidente/claro(a)
Es evidente.
Todo cae de su peso.

claro/evidentemente
Claro está que no sabe hacerlo.

la ocasión/la vez
Fue la última vez que los vi.
Esa vez/En aquella ocasión llegué tarde.
de vez en cuando

un acontecimiento/una función
Será un acontecimiento muy
  importante.

una ocasión/una oportunidad
¡Espera el momento propicio!

de vez en cuando/a veces

curioso(a)/extraño(a)/raro(a)
¡Qué raro!
Es una persona rara/extraña.
Es una manera muy rara de
  hacerlo.

impar
un número impar

other

I write the odd article.	Escribo algún que otro artículo.
These are odd gloves.	Éstos son guantes desparejados.
at odd moments	a ratos perdidos
odd jobs	pequeños arreglos/reparaciones
to do odd jobs around the house	hacer pequeños arreglos en toda la casa
odd jobs [casual work]	trabajitos

odds n

The odds are against it.	Es muy poco probable.
The odds are against/with you.	Tienes pocas/muchas probabilidades.

of prep

[in most senses]	de
a friend of mine	un amigo mío/una amiga mía
all of us	todos nosotros/todas nosotras
all of them	todos ellos/todas ellas
Some of us went to the movies.	Algunos fuimos al cine.
It's ten of six.	Son las seis menos diez.
a love of music	un amor a la música
a smell of garlic	un olor a ajo
a taste of honey	un sabor a miel
to smell of [see smell]	
to taste of [see taste]	
to think of [see think]	
It's very kind of you.	Eres muy amable./Es muy amable de tu parte.
of course	por supuesto/naturalmente
of no avail	inútil
It's of no avail.	Es inútil.

off adj & adv

power [lights, etc.]

	apagado(a)
The lights were off.	Las luces estaban apagadas.
to turn off	apagar
Turn the gas off before you leave.	Apaga el gas antes de salir.

to be off

I'm off now.	Ya me voy.
We must be off.	Debemos marcharnos.
They're off to Brasil tomorrow.	Salen para el Brasil mañana.
Be off!	¡Fuera de aquí!
Off we go!	¡Vamos!

not to be present

to be off	estar ausente/no estar (en la oficina, etc.)
a day off	un día de descanso
to take a day off	tomarse un día de descanso

reduction, removal

twenty per cent off	un descuento del veinte por ciento
with my shoes off	sin zapatos
with her hat off	sin sombrero

to be cancelled

The match is off. [cancelled]	El partido está cancelado.
The match is off. [postponed]	El partido está aplazado.

off   *prep*

to fall off	caerse de
He fell off the roof.	Se cayó del tejado.
It fell off the desk.	Se cayó del pupitre.
She took it off the table.	Lo tomó de la mesa.
to get off *[vehicles]*	bajar (de)
They got off the train.	Bajaron del tren.
We got off at the main square.	Bajamos en la plaza mayor.
to jump off	saltar de
The cat jumped off the wall.	El gato saltó del muro.
Keep off the grass!	¡Prohibido pisar la hierba!
off the cuff	improvisado(a)
off the record	en confianza/entre nosotros(as)
off season	fuera de temporada
off color	de mal gusto
[see also **take off***]*	

offense   *n*

to give offense	ofender
to take offense at	ofenderse por/resentirse de
[insult]	una ofensa
[crime]	un delito/un crimen
to commit an offense	cometer un delito

Ø **crimen** is a major felony, not a misdemeanor.

offer   *v*

to offer sth to sb	ofrecer algo a alguien
to offer to do sth	ofrecerse a hacer algo

office   *n*

[place of work]	una oficina
[private office]	un escritorio *[Arg & Uru]*/un despacho *[Sp]*
main office	la central
office worker	un/una oficinista
box/ticket office	la taquilla
information office	el centro de informaciones
post office	correos/la casa de correos/la oficina de correos/la central de correos *[Arg]*
tourist office	la oficina de turismo
an office block	un bloque de oficinas
[public office]	un cargo público
to hold office	ocupar un cargo

Ø **el oficio** means "office" in the sense of "trade" or "occupation."

official   *adj*

official	oficial

official   *n*

an official	un oficial/un funcionario

officially   *adv*

officially	oficialmente/de modo autorizado

often   *adv*

often	a menudo/frecuentemente/muchas veces

I often go to the beach.	Voy a menudo a la playa.
very often	muy a menudo/muchísimas veces
how often?	¿cuántas veces?
How often did you visit her?	¿Cuántas veces la visitaste?

oil n
[in general]	el aceite
[geological]	el petróleo
crude oil	el petróleo bruto
vegetable oil	el aceite vegetal
oil painting	un cuadro al óleo
to check the oil [in a car]	revisar el nivel de aceite

okay (O.K.) adj & excl
exclamation
	¡Está bien!/¡Bueno!/¡Vale!
O.K. I'm ready.	¡Bueno! Estoy listo(a).
Shall we go? – Yes, O.K.	¿Vamos? – Sí, vale.

as agreement
	de acuerdo
Is it O.K. with you?	¿Estás de acuerdo?
Is it O.K. with you if I go?	¿Te importa/molesta que vaya?
It's O.K. with me.	Estoy de acuerdo.

not bad
What do you think of the hotel? – It's O.K.	¿Qué te parece el hotel? – No está mal.

in response to an apology
	no hay de qué
I'm very sorry to have troubled you. – It's O.K.	Siento mucho haberte molestado. – No hay de qué.

physical condition
Are you O.K.?	¿Estás bien?
I feel O.K. now.	Me siento bien ahora.

old adj
age [people]
	viejo(a)/anciano(a)
an old man	un viejo/un anciano
an old woman	una vieja/una anciana
old John	el viejo Juan
older/oldest	más viejo(a)/mayor
his older/oldest daughter	su hija mayor
to get/grow old	envejecerse
How old are you?	¿Cuántos años tienes?
I'm 15 years old.	Tengo quince años.
He's older than his wife.	Tiene más años que su esposa.
He's two years older than I.	Tiene dos años más que yo.
to get older [children]	hacerse mayor

age [things]
	viejo(a)
an old house	una casa vieja
old clothes	ropa vieja/usada

old-established
	viejo(a)/antiguo(a)
an old friend of mine	un(a) viejo(a) amigo(a) mío(a)

former
	antiguo(a)
an old student	un antiguo estudiante
my old school	mi antiguo colegio
in the old days	antaño/en el pasado

151

old-fashioned   anticuado(a)/pasado(a) de moda
That skirt is old-fashioned.   Esta falda está pasada de moda.

Ø **anticuado(a)** is close to obsolete.

omelet   *n*
an omelet   una torta de huevos *[Mex]*/una tortilla *[Sp]*

Ø In Mexico and many other parts of Latin America **una tortilla** is a corn pancake.

on   *prep*
place   en/sobre/encima de
on the table   en/sobre la mesa
[on top of]   encima de
The box is on (top of) the cupboard.   La caja está encima del armario.
on the ceiling   sobre el techo
on the wall   en la pared
hanging on the wall   colgado(a) de la pared
[with sense of "in"]   en
on the street/square   en la calle/plaza
on the bus/plane/train   en el autobús/avión/tren
on the other side of the street   al otro lado de la calle
on the left/right   a la izquierda/derecha

means of transport
to get on   subir a
They got on the bus.   Subieron al autobús.
on horseback   a caballo
on foot   a pie

time
on time   a tiempo/a la hora
on Monday   el lunes *[Note: no preposition]*
I'm going to Lima on Monday.   Voy a Lima el lunes.
on Sundays   los domingos *[Note: no preposition]*
On Sundays they go to the beach.   Los domingos van a la playa.
on the next day   al día siguiente

concerning
on *[about/on the subject of]*   sobre/acerca de
a book on the history of Peru   un libro sobre la historia del Perú
What did he say on the subject   ¿Qué dijo acerca del accidente?
  of the accident?

with gerund
On seeing her, he crossed the   Al verla cruzó la calle. *[Note: The
  street.   infinitive is used in Spanish.]*

other
on the telephone   al teléfono
on sale   de/en venta
on business   de negocios
on vacation   de vacaciones
on the house   la casa invita
on the level   sincero(a)/en serio

verb + on
to be on *[apparatus, TV, radio]*   estar conectado(a)/puesto(a)/enchufado(a)
to be on *[light]*   estar encendido(a)
to be on *[at the movies]*   poner
"Casablanca" is on at the movies.   Ponen "Casablanca" en el cine.

to be on [at the theater]	representar
What's on at the theater?	¿Qué representan en el teatro?
to be on [a show]	estrenarse
The show is now on in New York.	Se ha estrenado el espectáculo en Nueva York.
to be on a diet	seguir un régimen
to be on duty	estar de servicio
to go on [continue]	seguir adelante
Go on as far as the park.	Sigue hasta el parque.
She went on reading.	Siguió leyendo.
to put on [clothes]	ponerse
to try on [clothes]	probarse
to spend money on	gastar dinero en
to spend time on	dedicar tiempo a
to switch/turn on [electrical apparatus, TV, radio, etc.]	encender/conectar/poner
to switch/turn on the engine	arrancar el motor
to switch/turn on the light	encender la luz
to live on	vivir con/de
I live on 500 dollars a month.	Vivo con quinientos dólares al mes.
They live on fruit.	Viven de fruta.
to congratulate sb on sth	dar la enhorabuena/felicitar a alguien por algo
to depend on	depender de

once   adv

once [on one occasion]	una vez
once or twice	algunas veces
once again	una vez más/otra vez
once a week	una vez por semana
at once	en seguida
at once [at the same time]	de una vez
They all spoke at once.	Todos hablaron de una vez.
all at once	de repente
He got up and left all at once.	De repente se levantó y se marchó.
once [formerly]	antes/antiguamente/en otro tiempo
The farm was prosperous once.	Antes la estancia era próspera.
Once upon a time there was...	Érase un vez.../Hubo una vez...
once in a blue moon	casi nunca/muy de tarde en tarde
once-over	un vistazo/una ojeada
He gave the hotel a once-over.	Dio/Echó un vistazo al hotel.

one   pron

One must insist.	Se debe insistir.
One never knows.	Nunca se sabe. [Note: **Nunca** precedes the pronoun.]
These cakes/oranges are good. – Do you want one?	Estos pastelitos/Estas naranjas son ricos(as). – ¿Quieres uno/una?
One of them will come.	Uno(a) de ellos(as) vendrá.
any one of us	cualquiera de nosotros(as)
Have you found the one you need?	¿Has encontrado el/la que necesitas?

[See also **the one, that one, this one, which one.**]

one another   [see **each other**]

153

one-way *adj*
a one-way ticket
[of direction]
This street is one-way.

un boleto de ida
de dirección única/de sentido único
Esta calle es de dirección única.

only *adj & pron*
only
his only son
They are the only two books I
  have left.
the only one(s)
I was not the only one to hear it.

único/solo
su hijo único
Son los dos únicos libros que me
  quedan. *[Note word order.]*
el único/la única/los únicos/las únicas
No fui el único/la única en oírlo.

only *adv*
only
Only my father can do it.
She only said that you would
  help me.
I only asked him for money.
They only have 500 pesos.

You only have to ask.
not only ... but also
Not only Juan but his wife.
If only he were here.

sólo/solamente/no... más que
Sólo mi padre sabe hacerlo.
Dijo solamente que me ayudarías.

No hice más que pedirle dinero.
Tienen solamente quinientos pesos./No
  tienen más de quinientos pesos. *[Note: use
  of **de** when a number follows]*
No hay sino preguntar.
no sólo... sino también *[Note: use of **sino**]*
No sólo Juan sino también su esposa.
Ojalá estuviera aquí. *[Note: imperfect
  subjunctive is used after **ojalá**.]*

opening *n*
[a job]
"Openings"
"Opening for a carpenter"

una vacante
"Se ofrece trabajo"
"Búscase un carpintero"

operation *n*
[medical, military]
to carry out an operation on sb (for)
to have an operation (for)

una operación
operar a alguien (de)
ser operado(a) de/sufrir una operación (de)

opinion *n*
opinion
in my opinion
What's your opinion of ... ?
to change one's opinion

la opinión/el parecer
en mi opinión/a mi parecer/a mi ver
¿Qué piensas de... ?
cambiar de opinión

opportunity *n*
opportunity
to have the opportunity to do sth
to take the opportunity to do sth
equal opportunities

la oportunidad/la ocasión
tener la oportunidad de hacer algo
aprovechar la ocasión para hacer algo
la igualdad de oportunidades

opposite *adj & n*
[adjective]
He lives in the house opposite.
The museum is on the opposite
  bank of the river.
the opposite page

opuesto(a)/de enfrente
Vive en la casa de enfrente.
El museo está en la ribera
  opuesta del río.
la página opuesta/de enfrente

in the opposite direction
[noun]
She always says the opposite.

en sentido contrario/opuesto
lo contrario
Siempre dice lo contrario.

opposite *adv & prep*
I sat down opposite the boss.
They were sitting opposite the
  entrance.
We were sitting opposite each
  other.
My office is opposite the town
  hall.

Me senté enfrente del jefe.
Estaban sentados(as) enfrente de
  la entrada.
Estábamos sentados(as) uno(a)
  enfrente del otro/de la otra.
Mi oficina está enfrente del
  ayuntamiento.

or *conj*
or
What do you want, fruit or cheese?
seven or eight

He didn't eat or drink.

o/u
¿Qué quieres, fruta o queso?
siete u ocho *[Note: **u** is used before a
  word starting with "o" or "ho".]*
No comió ni bebió. *[Note: **ni** is used after a
  negative.]*

*[See also **either** and **neither**.]*

order *n*
in succession
in alphabetical/chronological/
  numerical order

un orden
por orden alfabético/cronológico/
  numérico

peace
law and order

el orden público

command
on the orders of
to obey orders

una orden *[Note: feminine in this sense]*
por orden de
cumplir las órdenes *[Note: accent
  in the plural]*

to be under the orders of

estar bajo el mando de

business/commercial
an order
to give/place an order
made to order

un pedido/un encargo
pedir algo/hacer un pedido de algo
hecho(a) por encargo especial/
  hecho(a) a la orden

to the order of
banker's order

a la orden de
una orden bancaria

to be out of order
The elevators are out of order.

no funcionar
Los ascensores no funcionan.

in order to
You will have to save a lot of
  money in order to buy a house
  in this neighborhood.

para *[+ infinitive]*
Tendrás que ahorrar mucho dinero
  para comprar una casa en este
  barrio.

in order that/so that
I loaned him a thousand
  dollars in order for him/so
  that he could buy a computer.

para que *[+ subjunctive]*
Le presté mil dólares para que
  pudiera comprar una
  computadora.

order *v*
to order sb to do sth

mandar/ordenar a alguien hacer algo

155

I ordered them to go home.
[to request]
She ordered a mixed salad.

Les mandé volver a casa.
pedir
Pidió una ensalada mixta.

other   *adj & pron*
other

otro(a)/otros(as)
demás

He sold the other car.
We prefer the other house.
I've read all the other books.

Vendió el otro coche.
Preferimos la otra casa.
He leído todos los otros libros/
    todos los demás libros.

She washed my other shirts.

Me lavó las otras camisas/las
    demás camisas.

I don't like this carpet. I want the
    other one.
The others will be here soon.

No me gusta esta alfombra. Quiero
    la otra.
Los otros/Los demás estarán aquí
    pronto.

one after the other
Some are hungry, others are
    thirsty.
Some man or other gave it to me.

uno tras otro
Unos tienen hambre, otros tienen
    sed.
Algún hombre me lo dio.

otherwise   *conj*
[in other respects]
Otherwise the hotel was very good.
[if not]
We must leave now, otherwise
    we'll miss the plane.

por otra parte/por lo demás
Por lo demás el hotel era muy bueno.
si no
Tenemos que salir ahora, si no
    perderemos el avión.

ought   *v*
ought to
You ought to go to see her.

We ought to have bought it.

deber
Deberías ir a verla. *[Note:conditional]*
Debieras ir a verla. *[Note: imperfect
    subjunctive as an alternative to the
    conditional]*
Deberíamos haberlo comprado./
    Habríamos debido comprarlo. *[Note:
    alternative forms]*

*[see also **should**]*

our   *adj*
our
our money/our house
our friends

nuestro(a)/nuestros(as)
nuestro dinero/nuestra casa
nuestros amigos/nuestras amigas

ours   *pron*
[possessive]

el nuestro   la nuestra
los nuestros   las nuestras

Your garden is prettier than
    ours.
Those cases are ours.

Tu jardín es más linda que la
    nuestra.
Esas maletas son nuestras.
    *[Note: The definite article is omitted after
    the verb **ser**.]*

a friend of ours
some friends of ours

un amigo nuestro/una amiga nuestra
unos amigos nuestros/unas amigas
    nuestras

ourselves [see **self**]

out   adv

to be out	estar fuera/no estar/haber salido
They're out.	Están fuera/No están/Han salido.
to come/go out	salir

out of   prep

out of	fuera de
to be out of danger	estar fuera de peligro
to get out of bus/car/train	bajar del autobús/del coche/del tren
to go out of the house	salir de la casa
to go out of the door	salir por la puerta
She ran out of the room.	Salió corriendo de la habitación.
to jump out of the window	saltar por la ventana
to look out of the window	mirar por la ventana/asomarse a la ventana
to take sth out of a drawer	sacar algo de un cajón
He took the money out of his pocket.	Sacó el dinero de su bolsillo.
to be out of work	estar sin trabajo/estar parado(a)
seven out of ten	siete sobre diez
out of print	agotado(a)
out of the blue	inesperadamente/sin saber cómo

outdoor(s)   adj & adv

outdoors	al aire libre/fuera de casa
to eat outdoors	comer al aire libre
an outdoor concert/restaurant	un concierto/restaurante al aire libre
Go and play outdoors!	¡Ve/¡Vayan a jugar fuera!

outside

	prep
outside (of)	fuera de/al exterior de
outside the store	fuera de la tienda
He's outside the door.	Está a la puerta.

outside

	adv
outside	fuera
to be outside	estar fuera/estar en la calle
to go outside	salir fuera/salir a la calle

over   adv

[above]	encima/por encima
Does this go over or under?	¿Éste pasa por encima o por debajo?
[finished]	terminado/acabado
Is the game over?	¿Está terminado el partido?
As soon as the film is over ...	En cuanto termine la película...
The storm is over.	Ya pasó la tormenta.
It's all over (and done with)!	¡Ya se acabó!
She's over here/there.	Está acá/allá.
all over (the place)	por todas partes
to invite sb over	invitar a alguien a casa
Come over tonight.	Pasa a casa esta noche.
I ache all over.	Me duele todo el cuerpo/en todas partes.
to do sth over again	volver a hacer algo
Write it over again!	¡Vuelve a escribirlo!

157

over *prep*
place

over	encima de/por encima de
It's over your head.	Está por encima de tu cabeza.
He jumped/looked over the wall.	Saltó/Miró por encima de la tapia.
They live over the shop.	Viven por encima de la tienda.
[in contact with]	sobre
There was a sign over the door.	Había un letrero sobre la puerta.
[other]	
to cross over	atravesar/cruzar
I crossed over the street.	Atravesé/Crucé la calle.
to fall (trip) over sth	tropezar con algo
to fall over a cliff	caer por un precipicio
to fly over	sobrevolar
They will fly over the Andes.	Sobrevolarán los Andes.
all over Europe	por toda Europa
all over the world	en todo el mundo/en el mundo entero
over the counter	de venta libre/sin receta

number

past/over	más de
My mother is past eighty.	Mi madre tiene más de ochenta años.
the numbers over ten	los números superiores a diez

time

over the last few weeks	durante las últimas semanas
over the weekend	durante el fin de semana

overlook *v*

[of building]	dar a/tener vista a
The library overlooks the river.	La biblioteca da al río.
[to forget]	olvidar
I overlooked your keys.	Olvidé tus llaves.

own *adj & pron*
one's own

	propio(a)
I have my own house.	Tengo mi propia casa.
The money is all his own.	El dinero es el suyo propio.
This is all my own.	Esto es todo lo mío.

on one's own

	solo(a)
Are you on your own?	¿Estás solo(a)?
I live on my own.	Vivo solo(a).
Do it on your own!	¡Hazlo solo(a)!

own *v*
in general

	poseer/tener
He owns ten cars.	Posee/Tiene diez coches.
Do you own a computer?	¿Tienes computadora/ordenador [Sp]?
Who owns this dog?	¿A quién pertenece este perro?

real estate, company

	ser dueño de
He owns a large farm.	Es dueño de una estancia grande.
Who owns this publishing company?	¿Quién es dueño de esta casa editorial?

owner *n*

owner	el dueño/la dueña
	el propietario/la propietaria
His wife is the owner of the hotel.	Su esposa es propietaria del hotel.
Is the owner around?	¿Está el dueño/propietario?

P

pad *n & v*
[of paper]   un taco/un bloc
[of brake]   una zapata
to pad   acolchar

pain *n*
physical pain   el dolor/el sufrimiento
to be in pain   tener dolor/estar con dolor
to be out of pain   haber dejado de sufrir/no sufrir más
I have a pain in my arm.   Me duele el brazo.

mental pain   la pena/el dolor
It caused her great pain.   Le causó mucha pena.

nuisance
He's a pain in the neck.   Es un pesado.
It's a pain.   Es una lata.

other
to take pains to do sth   hacer grandes esfuerzos/darse
                                        mucho trabajo para hacer algo

[see also **ache**]

painful *adj*
[physically]   doloroso(a)/dolorido(a)
a painful blow/illness   un golpe doloroso
a painful illness   una enfermedad dolorosa
[difficult]   difícil/penoso(a)
a painful decision   una decisión difícil
It was very painful for me.   Me causó mucha pena.
[duty]   desagradable/nada grato(a)
It is my painful duty to tell   Tengo el deber desagradable de
  you that ...   decirte que...

pair *n*
a pair of gloves/shoes/stockings   un par de guantes/zapatos/medias
a pair of pants   un pantalón/unos pantalones
a pair of scissors   unas tijeras
[two people, a couple]   una pareja
What a strange pair!   ¡Qué pareja tan extraña!

pancake *n*
pancake   un panqueque [LA]/una torta/una
                                        hojuela
corn/maize pancake [in Mexico]   un taco/una tortilla/una enchilada

pants *n*
pants   el pantalón/los pantalones

paper *n*
[material, general]   el papel
It's made of paper.   Es de papel.

parents

a piece of paper	un papel/una hoja de papel
writing paper	el papel de escribir
waste paper	papeles usados
[document]	un papel/un documento
identity papers	los papeles/la documentación
exercise paper [school/college]	un ejercicio/un ensayo
examination paper	un examen/una prueba
to give a paper [academic]	leer una comunicación
written paper	un artículo
newspaper	un diario/un periódico

parents n

my parents	mis padres/mis papás [LA]
parent company	la casa central

Ø **los parientes** means "relatives" or "relations."

park v trans

to park	aparcar/estacionar(se)/parquear [LA]/atracar [Arg & Uru]/cuadrar [Per] el coche
I parked the car on the street.	Aparqué/Estacioné el coche en la calle.
Where did you park?	¿Dónde aparcaste/te estacionaste?
You can't park here.	No se puede aparcar/estacionar aquí.

parking adj & n

parking	el aparcamiento/estacionamiento
No parking!	¡Prohibido estacionarse/aparcar!
parking lot	un aparcamiento/un estacionamiento/ una playa de estacionamiento [LA]
parking meter	un parquímetro/un parcómetro/un contador de aparcamiento
parking place	un sitio para aparcar
to look for a parking place	buscar dónde aparcar
I couldn't find anywhere to park.	No encontré dónde aparcar.
parking ticket [fine]	una multa por estar mal aparcado

part n

[general]	una parte
the best/worst/funniest part is ...	lo mejor/lo peor/lo más gracioso es...
the greater part	la mayor parte
[role in theater, etc.]	un papel
to play a part	hacer/interpretar un papel
in these parts	por aquí
Are you from these parts?	¿Eres de aquí?
to take part in	tomar parte en/participar en/intervenir en
to be part of	formar parte de
spare parts [for car, etc.]	las piezas de recambio/repuesto

part v

[to separate]	separarse
They parted last year.	Se separaron el año pasado.
[to say good bye]	despedirse
They parted at the airport.	Se despidieron en el aeropuerto.

Ø **partir**, as well as meaning "to leave," means "to part" in the sense of "to split or break apart."

partner n
[in marriage]

el esposo/la esposa
el/la cónyuge

[companion]
[business]
[in dancing, tennis, etc.]
silent partner

un(a) compañero(a)
un(a) socio(a)
una pareja
un socio comanditario

party n & v
a social event
to give/have/throw a party
to party
a pot-luck party

una fiesta/una reunión [formal]
organizar una fiesta
hacer la fiesta
una fiesta donde cada invitado(a)
   contribuye un plato

law
party [to a dispute/agreement]
a third party
an interested party

una parte
una tercera persona
un(a) interesado(a)

group
a party of tourists
We're a party of fifty.

un grupo
un grupo de turistas
Somos un grupo de cincuenta.

politics
a political party
Democratic/Republican Party
to be a member of the party
to join the party

un partido
un partido político
el Partido Demócrata/Republicano
ser miembro del partido
hacerse miembro del partido

pass v
[general]
Pass me the sugar, please.
to pass an exam

pasar
Pásame el azúcar por favor.
aprobar en/ser aprobado(a) en un
   examen [Note: not **pasar**]

[to move past]
They are passing the White
  House.
He passed her on the street.
We passed each other on the way.
[to overtake]
We passed the truck at 100
  miles an hour.

pasar/pasar por delante de
Pasan por delante de la Casa
  Blanca.
Se cruzó con ella en la calle.
Nos cruzamos en el camino.
pasar/adelantar a
Adelantamos al camión a cien
  millas (a ciento sesenta kilómetros)
  por hora.

No passing!
[to spend time]
I spent two weeks in Quito.

¡Prohibido adelantar!
pasar
Pasé quince días/dos semanas en Quito.

patron n
[customer]
[supporter of a cause/business]
[of the arts]
patron saint

un cliente/un parroquiano
un patrocinador
un mecenas
un santo patrón/una santa patrona

Ø **un patrón/una patrona** also means "boss".

pay n
[general]

la paga/la remuneración/la retribución

161

pay

[salary of professional person]	el sueldo
[wages of working person]	el salario/el sueldo
equal pay	la igualdad de retribución
pay rise	un aumento de sueldo

pay v
to pay	pagar
I have to pay the rent.	Tengo que pagar el alquiler.
to pay sb	pagar a alguien
You must pay the landlord.	Tienes que pagar al propietario.
to pay for sth	pagar algo [Note: no preposition]
They paid for the tickets.	Pagaron las entradas.
to pay back [money]	devolver
to pay by check	pagar con cheque
to pay by installments	pagar a plazos
to pay in advance	pagar por adelantado
to pay in cash	pagar al contado
to pay attention to	prestar atención a

peaceful adj
[quiet]	tranquilo(a)
[not warlike]	pacífico(a)

peas n
peas	los guisantes/las arvejas [LA]/los chícharos [LA]
green peas	los guisantes
chickpeas	los garbanzos/los chícharos [LA]
split peas	los guisantes secos

people n
general
	la gente
many people	mucha gente
There are many people who want to see that film.	Hay mucha gente que quiere ver esa película.
What will people say?	¿Qué dirá la gente?
There are few people around.	Hay poca gente por aquí.

countable number
	las personas
How many people are coming to the party?	¿Cuántas personas vienen a la fiesta?
There were thousands of people in the square.	Había miles de personas en la plaza.
I know several people who speak Portuguese.	Conozco a varias personas que hablan portugués.

politics
	el pueblo
the people of the United States	el pueblo de los Estados Unidos
government by the people	el gobierno del pueblo

race
	el pueblo/la nación
the Mexican people	el pueblo mexicano/la nación mexicana
the peoples of Europe	las gentes de Europa

inhabitants
	los habitantes
the people of Córdoba	los habitantes de Córdoba
All the people of the village agreed.	Todos los habitantes de la aldea se pusieron de acuerdo.

pepper   n
[the spice/condiment]	la pimienta
black pepper	la pimienta negra
[the vegetable/green pepper]	el pimiento/el chile
red pepper	el pimiento rojo
sweet pepper	el pimiento morrón
red pepper/paprika	el pimentón

performance   n
carrying out of duties
in the performance of my duties	en el ejercicio de mi cargo

                                              el ejercicio

session at the movies
	la sesión
continuous performance	una sesión continua
the late performance	la sesión de la noche
What time is the first performance?	¿A qué hora es la primera sesión?

session at the theater
	la función
the late performance	la función de la noche
first performance	el estreno [Note: **estreno** refers to the first ever performance of a particular play or film at a specific theater, not to the first performance of the day.]

by actor, dancer, singer
	la actuación/el desempeño/la interpretación
Her performance as Carmen was magnificent.	Su interpretación del papel de Carmen fue magnífica.

by musicians
	la ejecución/la interpretación
a good performance of the concerto	una buena interpretación del concierto

in sport
	la actuación
The team gave a poor performance in Guadalajara.	El equipo tuvo una mala actuación en Guadalajara.

of machines
	el comportamiento/el funcionamiento
[of car engine]	el rendimiento
[of car in a race]	la performance

perhaps   adv
[maybe]	quizá(s)/tal vez/puede ser (que)
Perhaps he'll come tomorrow.	Quizás/Tal vez venga mañana.
Perhaps they are away.	Puede ser que estén ausentes.
Perhaps Juan did it.	Quizás lo hizo Juan. [Note: the subjunctive is used when the speaker is expressing a strong sense of doubt.]

person   n
a person	una persona [Note: always feminine]
The mayor is a strange person.	El alcalde es una persona extraña.

pet   n
a pet	un animal (doméstico)/un animalito de compañía/una mascota
a pet dog	un perro de casa
No pets!	¡Animales prohibidos!
teacher's pet	el/la favorito(a) del maestro/de la maestra

163

phone υ

to phone	telefonear/llamar por teléfono/ llamar al teléfono
to phone sb/sth	telefonear a alguien/algo
I phoned you last night.	Te telefoneé/llamé anoche.
I must phone the airport.	Debo telefonear al aeropuerto.

phone call   n

a phone call	un llamado telefónico [LA]/una llamada telefónica [Sp]/un golpe de teléfono [Arg]

photograph   n & υ

a photograph/a photo	una fotografía/una foto
to photograph/take a photograph	fotografiar/sacar una foto

photographer   n

photographer	un(a) fotógrafo(a)

phrase   n

[a saying]	un dicho/una locución/un refrán
[a set phrase]	una frase hecha
[in music]	una frase
[in grammar]	una frase

Ø **frase** can also mean "a sentence."

physical   [see checkup]

physician   n

[medical doctor]	un(a) médico(a)
I'm a physician.	Soy médico(a).

Ø **un físico** is "a physicist."

physics   n

[field of study]	la física [Note: singular]

pick   υ

to choose/select

	escoger/seleccionar
Which car did you choose?	¿Qué coche escogiste?
Who is picking the team?	¿Quién selecciona el equipo?

to gather

	recoger
I'm going to pick some roses.	Voy a recoger unas rosas.
We went to pick some pears.	Fuimos a recoger unas peras.

pick up   υ

to pick up sth from the floor	recoger algo del suelo
[to collect]	recoger
I went to pick up my books at the bookstore.	Fui a recoger mis libros en la librería.
Go and pick up your mother at the station!	¡Ve a buscar a tu madre en la estación!
[to learn]	aprender
She picked up a few words of Arabic.	Aprendió unas palabras de árabe.

[to acquire]   adquirir/comprar
We picked it up cheap.   Lo adquirimos/compramos por muy
    poco dinero.

[to arrest]   detener
He was picked up at the frontier.   Fue detenido en la frontera.

picture   n
[a painting]   un cuadro/una pintura
[a drawing]   un dibujo
[a portrait]   un retrato
[a book/magazine illustration]   una ilustración
[a film]   una película
[a photograph]   una fotografía/una foto
to take pictures   sacar fotos
[on TV]   la imagen

piece   n
[general]   un pedazo/un trozo
a piece of bread   un pedazo/trozo de pan
a piece of cake   una porción de tarta
a piece of chocolate   una porción de chocolate
a piece of paper   una hoja de papel
a piece of advice   un consejo
a piece of furniture   un mueble
a piece of information   una información
a piece of land [for building on]   un terreno/un solar
a piece of news   una noticia
[an extract from a book, etc.]   un trozo
a piece of luck   un poco de suerte
a piece of music   una pieza de música
a chess piece   una pieza de ajedrez
a piece of fabric/material   una pieza de tejido
a piece of crockery   una pieza
[a piece for the theater]   una pieza

pill   n
a pill   una píldora/una pastilla

Ø **un pillo** means "a rogue;" **una pila** means "a battery."

pitch   n
[music]   el tono
[degree]   un grado/un nivel
[slope]   una pendiente
[throw]   un lanzamiento

Ø **un pendiente** means "an earring."

pitch   v
[to throw]   tirar/arrojar
[to set]   fijar
to pitch a tent   armar una tienda

place   n
general   un lugar/un sitio
This is a very peaceful place.   Éste es un lugar muy tranquilo.
It was a good place to camp.   Fue un buen sitio para acampar.

plain

English	Spanish
Any place will do.	Cualquier sitio será conveniente.
I don't see it any place.	No lo/la veo en ninguna parte.
specific place	un sitio/un local
This is the place for the new factory.	Éste es el local/sitio para la nueva fábrica.
place of business	la oficina [office]/el comercio [shop]/la fábrica [factory]
place of residence	el domicilio/la residencia
We went to their place in the country.	Fuimos a su casa en el campo.
in order	
in first/second/third place	en primer/segundo/tercer lugar
everything in its place	todo en su lugar
seat	un asiento/una plaza
The theater has only 200 places.	El teatro tiene sólo doscientos asientos.
There are no places left.	Ya no quedan plazas.
other	
to take place	tener lugar/verificarse
in place of	en lugar de/en vez de

plain *adj*

English	Spanish
clear, obvious	claro/evidente
It was plain that ...	Era evidente que.../Estaba claro que...
of food	sencillo
I like plain cooking.	Me gusta la cocina sencilla.
simple	sencillo/llano/sin adornos
a plain dress	un vestido sencillo

plan *n*

English	Spanish
architectural plan	un plano
He made a plan of the palace.	Trazó un plano del palacio.
schedule	un programa
today's plan	el programa de hoy
economic, political	un plan
to draw up a plan	hacer un plan
a development plan	un plan de desarrollo
personal plan	un proyecto
to make plans	hacer proyectos
I have no plans for the vacation.	No tengo proyectos para las vacaciones.
to change one's plan	cambiar de proyecto

plan *v*

English	Spanish
to make plans	planear/idear
My wife planned the trip.	Mi esposa ideó el viaje.
What have you planned for the weekend?	¿Qué has planeado para el fin de semana?
to intend	tener intención de/pensar
I don't plan to pay for it.	No tengo intención de pagarlo.
How long do you plan to stay?	¿Cuánto tiempo piensas quedarte?

plant n
[botanical]   una planta
[factory]   una fábrica
[equipment, machinery]   el equipo/la maquinaria/la instalación

plate n
[for eating off]   un plato
gold/silver plate   la vajilla de oro/plata

Ø **plato** also means "a dish" on a menu; **la plata** means "silver;" **un platillo** means "a saucer."

play v
games, sports   jugar a
Do you play golf?   ¿Juegas al golf?
We spent the evening playing chess. Pasamos la tarde jugando al ajedrez.
[to play with sb]   jugar con
I played tennis with her.   Jugué con ella al tenis.

musical instruments   tocar a
He plays the guitar very well. Toca muy bien a la guitarra.

a piece of music   tocar
They played my favorite piece. Tocaron mi pieza favorita.

at a theater
What's playing at the theater ¿Qué ponen en el teatro esta
 tonight?   noche?

please adv
The check, please.   La cuenta, por favor.
Please tell him I've arrived. Haga el favor de decirle que he llegado.
Pass the sugar please.   ¿Me hace el favor de pasar el azúcar?

plug n
[electric]   un enchufe/una chavija [Mex]
[bath, wash basin, etc.]   un tapón

plus adv, n & prep
two plus two equals four   dos más dos son cuatro
I've got 30 plus.   Tengo treinta y pico.
He cost me 50 dollars plus. Me costó cincuenta dólares y algo más.
[besides/in addition]   además
Plus, he can't drive.   Además, no sabe manejar/conducir.
[an advantage]   una ventaja
Being able to cook well is a plus. Saber cocinar bien es una ventaja.

P.M.
It will begin at five p.m.   Empezará a las cinco de la tarde.
The train arrived at ten p.m. Llegó el tren a las diez de la noche.
It's four p.m.   Son las cuatro de la tarde.
It's 11.30 p.m.   Son las once y media de la noche.

point n
general   un punto
decimal point/dot   un punto decimal/una coma

167

point

She scored 9.6 points.	Ganó 9,6 (nueve coma seis) puntos. *[Note the Spanish punctuation and means of expression.]*

in sport and games
	un punto
to win on points	ganar por puntos
They won by 50 points to ten.	Ganaron por cincuenta puntos a diez.

sharp end
	una punta
the point of a knife	la punta de un cuchillo
the point of a pen	la puntilla de una pluma
five-point star	una estrella de cinco puntas

purpose
What's the point of asking?	¿De qué sirve preguntar?
There's no point in doing it.	No vale la pena hacerlo.

place and time
point of departure	el punto de partida
point *[of the compass]*	una cuarta
at this/that point in time	en este/aquel momento
to be on the point of doing sth	estar para hacer algo

point of argument/discussion
	un punto
point at issue	el punto en cuestión
point of view	un punto de vista
from my point of view	desde mi punto de vista
to make a point	hacer una observación/establecer un punto
to be beside/off the point	no venir al caso
That's not the point.	Eso no es el caso.

characteristics
He has some good points.	Tiene algunas cualidades buenas.

matter of importance or significance
The important point is ...	Lo importante es...
This is the essential point.	Esto es lo esencial.

point *v*
to point out sth to sb	indicar/señalar algo a alguien
The guide pointed out the ruins to us.	El guía nos indicó las ruinas.
She pointed out my mistakes.	Me señaló mis errores.
I should like to point out that ...	Permíteme observar que...
to point at	señalar con el dedo
He pointed at the sign.	Señaló el letrero con el dedo.
I didn't point at you.	No te señalé con el dedo.
[to point at with a gun]	apuntar
He pointed the rifle at us.	Nos apuntó con el fusil.

poisonous *adj*
[of snakes, insects, etc.]	venenoso(a)
[drugs, fumes, substances, etc.]	tóxico(a)

police *n*
the police force	la policía
police headquarters	la jefatura de policía
police station	la comisaría/la estación de policía *[LA]*
police officer	un(a) policía/un(a) guardia/un(a) agente

168

police record — los antecedentes penales
The police have arrested two men. — La policía ha detenido a dos hombres. [Note: singular verb]

policy n
[political] — la política
economic policy — la política económica
foreign policy — la política exterior
government policy — la política del gobierno
[approach, system] — el sistema
This is our policy. — Esto es nuestro sistema.
insurance policy — una póliza de seguros

politics n
politics — la política [Note: singular]
to talk politics — hablar de política
to go into politics — dedicarse a la política

poor adj
[impoverished] — pobre
a poor man — un pobre
a poor woman — una mujer pobre [Note: **pobre** follows noun]

the poor/poor people — los pobres
[unfortunate] — pobre
Poor man/woman! — ¡Pobre hombre/mujer!
Poor María! — ¡Pobre María! [Note: **pobre** precedes noun]
Poor you/him/her/old thing! — ¡Pobrecito(a)!
Poor Teresa is ill. — La pobre Teresa está enferma. [Note: use of definite article]

[bad] — malo(a)/de baja calidad
I have a poor memory. — Tengo una mala memoria.
to be in poor health — estar mal

positive adj
[opposite of negative] — positivo(a)
a positive result — un resultado positivo
[certain, sure] — seguro(a)
I'm positive about it. — Estoy seguro(a) de ello.

possibility n
possibility — una posibilidad
[outcome] — un resultado posible
to foresee the possibilities — prever los resultados posibles

possible adj
to be possible — ser posible
Is it possible to talk with the manager? — ¿Es posible hablar con el gerente?
Is it possible for your brother to come? — ¿Es posible que venga tu hermano? [Note: subjunctive]
It's not possible for me to do it. — No me es posible hacerlo.
as soon as possible — lo más pronto posible

possibly adv
possibly — posiblemente

169

postpone

I'll do it if I possibly can.
They did all they possibly could.
We'll do all we possibly can.

Lo haré si me es posible.
Hicieron todo lo que pudieron.
Haremos todo lo que podamos.
   [Note: subjunctive]

[perhaps]
Will they win? – Possibly.

quizá(s)/tal vez
¿Ganarán? – Quizás.

postpone *v*
[to put off]
The game has been postponed
   until Sunday.

aplazar
Se ha aplazado el partido hasta
   el domingo.

potato *n*
potato
potato chips

la papa *[LA]*/la patata *[Sp]*
las papas/las patatas fritas/las papas
   colochas *[ES]*/las papalinas *[Gua]*

[French fries]

las papas/patatas francesas

Ø In Latin America **una batata** means "sweet potato." Remember **el papá** means
"Dad" and **El Papa** is "the Pope."

power *n*
general

el poder

ability
Birds have the power of flight.
I have the power to do it.
mental powers

el poder/la facultad
Los pájaros tienen la facultad de volar.
Tengo el poder de hacerlo.
las facultades mentales

physical strength
He doesn't have the power to
   lift it.

la fuerza/la energía/el vigor
No tiene la fuerza para
   levantarlo.

nations
The USA is a world power.

la potencia
Los Estados Unidos son una potencia
   mundial.

the nuclear powers

las potencias nucleares

authority
political power
to be in power

el poder/el poderío
el poder político
estar en el poder

energy
electrical power
power cut/failure
They've cut off the power.
nuclear power
power station
nuclear power station

la fuerza/la energía/el fluido
la fuerza/energía eléctrica
un corte de corriente
Han cortado el fluido.
la energía nuclear
una central eléctrica
una central nuclear

mechanical force

effective power
attractive/motive power
The engine is operating at
   half power.

la potencia/la energía/la fuerza/ el
   rendimiento
la potencia real
la fuerza atractiva/motriz
El motor funciona a medio
   rendimiento.

cars
power brakes
power steering

los frenos asistidos
la dirección asistida

powerful   adj
[people, organizations, etc]	poderoso(a)
a powerful president/government	un presidente/gobierno poderoso
[engines, etc.]	potente

practice   v
to practice a profession	ejercer una profesión
to practice medicine	ejercer de médico/ejercer la medicina/practicar la medicina
to practice a musical instrument	hacer ejercicios en/estudiar un instrumento
to practice a sport	entrenarse en un deporte
to practice a religion	practicar una religión
to be a practicing Christian	ser un cristiano practicante
to practice one's Spanish	practicar el castellano

Ø **practicar** used with the name of a sport usually means "to take part in" or "to play;" **Practico el fútbol.** "I play soccer."

prejudice   n/**prejudiced**   adj
[bias in favor]	la parcialidad
[biased view]	el prejuicio
[bias against]	la mala voluntad/la prevención
racial prejudice	el prejuicio racial
to be prejudiced	tener prejuicios
She's very prejudiced.	Tiene muchos prejuicios.
to be prejudiced against sth	estar predispuesto(a) contra algo
to be prejudiced in favor of sth	estar predispuesto(a) a favor de algo

prescription   n
prescription	una receta

Ø **receta** does not mean "receipt," for which the word is **el recibo.**

presently   adv
[now/at the present moment]	ahora/actualmente
[soon]	dentro de poco

preservative   n
[in food]	un producto de conservación/para la conservación

Ø **un preservativo** means "a condom."

pressure   n & v
[physical, technical, meteorological]	la presión
tire pressure	la presión de los neumáticos
[influence]	la influencia/la persuasión
to be under pressure from sb	ser presionado(a) por alguien
to put pressure on sb to do sth	hacer presión sobre alguien (que haga algo)
to work under pressure	trabajar con urgencia
pressure group	el grupo de presión
[stress]	la tensión nerviosa
blood pressure	la tensión arterial
high/low blood pressure	la tensión alta/baja

pretend   v
to pretend	fingir
to pretend to be ill	fingir estar enfermo(a)

171

pretty

to pretend to be asleep	fingir(se) dormido(a)
to pretend to be a reporter	darse de periodista/decirse periodista/ hacerse el/la periodista
[to claim]	pretender
I do not pretend to know.	No pretendo saber.

Ø **pretender** also means "to claim the throne," or "to have pretensions."

pretty   adj

pretty	lindo(a) [LA]/mono(a) [Sp]/ bonito(a)/guapo(a)/chulo(a) [Mex]

Ø **mono** means "vain" in Venezuela.

prevent   v

to prevent	evitar/prevenir/impedir
to prevent an accident/illness	evitar/prevenir un accidente/una enfermedad
to prevent sb from doing sth	impedir a alguien hacer algo

Ø **prevenir** also means "to warn," "to foresee."

primary   adj

[first]	primario(a)
primary school	la escuela primaria
primary color	el color primario
[fundamental]	principal
the primary reason	la razón principal
of primary importance	sumamente importante

privacy   n

privacy	la soledad/la intimidad
in search of privacy	en busca de soledad
desire for privacy	el deseo de estar a solas
in the privacy of one's home	en la intimidad de su casa
There is no privacy here.	Aquí no se puede estar en privado.
in the strictest privacy	en el mayor secreto

private   adj

not public	privado(a)
private enterprise	la empresa privada
private life	la vida privada
personal	particular/personal
a private arrangement	un acuerdo particular
a private car	un coche particular
Private!	¡Propiedad particular!
private secretary	un(a) secretario(a) particular
my private opinion	mi opinión personal
a private citizen	un(a) particular

Ø **especial** is used to mean "particular," e.g., **una razón especial** "a particular reason."

confidential	secreto(a)/confidencial/privado(a)
a private report	un informe secreto/confidencial
private and confidential	privado y confidencial

in private	
in private	en privado/en secreto
[confidentially]	confidencialmente
The meeting was held in private.	La reunión se celebró a puerta cerrada.

The ceremony will be held in private.	La ceremonia se celebrará en la intimidad.

Ø **privado** in Latin America also means "mad" or "senseless."
Ø **privativo** means "exclusive."

probably *adv*

probably	probablemente
Is she ill? – Probably.	¿Está enferma? – Probablemente.
They've probably forgotten.	A lo mejor lo habrán olvidado.

problem *n*

problem	un problema *[Note: masculine]*
No problem!	¡No hay problema!
the housing problem	el problema de la vivienda
a problem child	un niño difícil

process *n*

[proceeding]	el procedimiento/el proceso
the process of the mind	el proceso de la mente
the manufacturing process	el procedimiento de fabricación
data processing	el proceso de datos
in course of construction	bajo/en construcción
in course of demolition	está siendo derribado(a)
[method]	el procedimiento/el proceso/el método/el sistema
the technical process	el proceso técnico
[law]	el proceso

program *n*

[computer, list of events]	un programa *[Note: masculine]*
[radio/TV show]	una emisión

progress *n*

[general]	el progreso/los progresos
to make progress	hacer progresos
to make slow progress	avanzar despacio
[events]	la marcha/el desarrollo
to be in progress	estar en marcha
The work is in full progress.	El trabajo está en plena marcha.

prohibit *v*

to prohibit	prohibir
to prohibit sb from doing sth	prohibir a alguien hacer algo
It is forbidden to feed the animals.	Se prohíbe dar de comer a los animales.
Smoking prohibited!	¡Prohibido fumar!/¡Se prohíbe fumar!

proper *adj*

right, suitable

at the proper time	en el momento oportuno
proper shoes for the occasion	zapatos apropiados para la ocasión
the proper word	la palabra exacta
in proper condition	en buen estado

seemly

proper behavior	la conducta correcta

173

public

That's not proper.	Eso no está bien.
to do what is proper	hacer lo que se debe
[see also **right**]	

public   adj
[general]	público(a)
public holiday	un día de fiesta/un día festivo/una fiesta legal
public school	un instituto
public spirit	el civismo

Ø **el público** not only means "the public," but also "the audience."

publish   v
to publish	publicar/editar
published by	editado por
My first book has just been published.	Mi primer libro acaba de salir.
When is the magazine published?	¿Cuándo sale la revista?

publisher   n
[company]	una casa editorial
[person]	un editor
newspaper publisher	el propietario de un periódico

purple   adj
purple	púrpura [inv]/purpúreo(a)/morado(a) [Sp]

purpose   n
[intention]	el propósito/la intención/el objeto
My purpose in doing this ...	Mi propósito al hacer esto...
on purpose	a propósito
[sense of purpose]	la resolución

purse   n
a purse	un bolso [LA]/una bolsa [Sp]

put   v
[to place]	poner/colocar/meter
to put away	devolver a su lugar
to put back	devolver a su lugar
to put down (on ground)	poner en tierra/en el suelo
to put in	meter/introducir
to put off [postpone]	aplazar
to put on [clothes]	ponerse
to put on [shoes]	ponerse/calzarse
to put on [light, appliances]	encender/poner
to put on [play]	representar/poner en escena
to put on weight	engordar/echar carnes
to put out [light, fire]	apagar
to put through [phone]	poner con
to put sb up	hospedar/alojar a alguien
Can you put me up for the night?	¿Me puedes dar una habitación para esta noche?
to put up with sb or sth	aguantar
I can't put up with her any more.	No la aguanto más.
I can't put up with (it) any more.	No aguanto más.

Q

qualification n
[of a person]
He doesn't have the
  qualifications for the job.
[paper qualifications]
What are your qualifications?
[for membership]
Do you have the qualifications
  for membership?

la capacidad/la aptitud
No tiene las aptitudes para el
  puesto.
los títulos
¿Qué títulos tienes?
el requisito
¿Tienes los requisitos para ser
  miembro?

qualified adj
Are you qualified for that job?
a qualified engineer
in a qualified sense
to be qualified to vote

¿Tienes los requisitos para ese puesto?
un ingeniero titulado
en un sentido limitado
estar capacitado(a) para votar

qualify v
to qualify [academically]
He qualified as a lawyer.
to qualify for the finals

obtener el título de...
Obtuvo el título de abogado.
satisfacer los requisitos/clasificarse
  para los exámenes finales

quality n & adj
[nature, kind]
of good quality
a quality jacket
[characteristic, e.g. moral]
They have some good qualities.

la calidad
de buena calidad
una chaqueta de calidad
la cualidad
Tienen unas buenas cualidades.

quantity n
quantity

la cantidad

quarter n
[fraction]
a quarter of a kilo of flour
the first quarter of the moon
a quarter [coin]
a quarter of an hour
a quarter after/past four
a quarter of/to four
[division of academic year]
[of town]
the old quarter

un cuarto/una cuarta parte
un cuarto de kilo de harina
el primer cuarto de la luna
una moneda de 25 centavos
un cuarto de hora
las cuatro y cuarto
las cuatro menos cuarto
el trimestre
el barrio
el barrio viejo

question n
to ask sb a question
I asked him many questions.
[matter, subject]
the Cuban question
The question is, ...

hacer una pregunta a alguien
Le hice muchas preguntas.
el asunto/la cuestión/el problema
el problema cubano
El caso es, ...

175

question

It's a question of knowing whom to ask.	Se trata de saber a quién preguntar.
It's not a question of money.	No se trata de dinero/No es cuestión de dinero.
That's not the question.	No se trata de eso.
It's out of the question.	Es imposible.
without question	sin duda/indudablemente

question *v*

to question sb	hacer preguntas a alguien
The police questioned me.	Los guardias me interrogaron.
[to doubt]	cuestionar/dudar de
Do you question his motives?	¿Dudas de sus motivos?

questionable *adj*

questionable	cuestionable/dudoso(a)/discutible
It's questionable whether they are right.	Es dudoso si tengan razón. *[Note: use of subjunctive]*

quick *adj*

[fast]	rápido(a)/veloz/ligero(a)
a quick reflex	un reflejo rápido
be quick!	¡date prisa!
to be quick about sth	hacer algo rápidamente
a quick temper	un genio vivo
[clever]	agudo(a)/ágil/listo(a) *[Note: **Listo** is used with **ser** when it means "clever," and with **estar** when it means "ready."]*
[early]	pronto(a)
a quick reply	una pronta contestación

quickly *adv*

[fast]	de prisa/rápidamente
[soon]	pronto
as quickly as possible	lo más pronto posible

quiet *adj*

[silent]	silencioso(a)/callado(a)
[of a person by nature]	callado(a)/reservado(a)
a quiet place	un lugar tranquilo
to keep quiet	callarse
Be quiet!	¡Cállate!/¡Silencio!

quit *v*
to resign from

I've quit my job.	He abandonado mi puesto./He dimitido.

to stop

Why don't you quit doing that?	¿Por qué no dejas de hacer eso?
Quit saying that!	¡Deja de decir eso/hablar así!
I quit!	¡Me rajo!
¡Quit fooling!	¡Déjate de tonterías!

quite *adv*
completely

	totalmente/completamente

This is completely new.	Esto es completamente nuevo.
We quite understand.	Lo comprendemos perfectamente.
She is quite right.	Está en lo cierto.
Quite so!	¡Así es!/¡Efectivamente!
He's quite a hero.	Es realmente un héroe/todo un héroe.

rather	bastante
He is quite rich.	Es bastante rico.
quite a few	bastantes
There were quite a few books.	Había bastantes libros.
quite a while	un buen rato/bastante tiempo

quiz n

[in school]	una prueba/un examen
a quiz show	un concurso de televisión/un concurso radiofónico
to quiz sb about sth	interrogar a alguien sobre algo
They quizzed him about the theft.	Le interrogaron sobre el robo.

quotation n

[passage or sentence cited]	la cita/la citación
[financial]	la cotización
today's quotation	la cotización del día
[business estimate]	un presupuesto
They gave us a quotation.	Nos dieron un presupuesto.
quotation marks	las comillas
in quotation marks	entre comillas
to open/close quotation marks	abrir/cerrar las comillas

quote v

to cite exactly

	citar
to quote (from) Lorca	citar a Lorca
You can quote me.	Puede Ud. mencionar mi nombre.
Don't quote me!	¡No me menciones!
You must quote the number of the invoice.	Debes expresar el número de la factura.

to name a price

	estimar un precio
They quoted a very high price.	El precio que estimaron fue muy alto.
This is the best price I can quote you.	Éste es mi mejor precio.

financially

The dollar is quoted at X pesos.	La cotización del dólar está a X pesos.
It is not quoted on the stock exchange.	No se cotiza en la Bolsa.
What is today's price?	¿A cuánto está la cotización del día?

R

race *n*
[sporting]   una carrera
horse race   una carrera de caballos
long-distance race   una carrera de fondo
relay race   una carrera de relevos
to run a race   tomar parte en una carrera
human race   la raza humana/el género humano

radio *n*
radio [waves]   la radio
radio [set]   el radio [most of LA]/la radio [Sp]

Ø **el radio** also means "radius" in geometry.

raise *n & v*
to raise one's hands   levantar las manos
to raise the flag   alzar la bandera
to raise prices   aumentar los precios/el sueldo
to raise sb's salary   aumentar el sueldo a alguien
to raise funds   reunir fondos
raise in salary   un aumento de sueldo

rank *n & v*
[line]   una fila
[military position]   una graduación
[status]   la posición/la categoría
ranking   una clasificación
to rank   figurar/estar
to outrank   ser de categoría superior a

rare *adj*
rare   poco frecuente/poco común
a rare visitor   un visitante poco frecuente
This bird is rare in Cuba.   Este pájaro es poco común en Cuba.

Ø **raro** means "odd," "strange."

rate *n*
[price]   un precio/una tasa
[at hotel, etc.]   la tarifa
rate for the job   el sueldo justo
rate of exchange   el cambio/el tipo de cambio
rate of interest   el tipo de interés
postage rate   la tarifa
birth rate   el índice de natalidad
at any rate   de todas formas/de todos modos

rather *adv*
with an adjective   algo/bastante/un poco
I'm rather glad.   Estoy bastante contento(a).
He's rather strange.   Es algo raro.

178

to indicate preference

| I would rather go to Mexico. | Preferiría/Me gustaría más ir a México. |
| She would rather the red ones. | Preferiría los rojos. |

to correct a statement

| These are his books, or rather his fiancée's. | Éstos son sus libros, o mejor dicho los de su novia. |

reach n

to be within reach	estar al alcance de
to be within arm's reach	estar al alcance de la mano
to be out of reach	estar fuera del alcance
within easy reach of the hotel	a corta distancia del hotel
It's within easy reach by car.	Es fácilmente accesible en coche.

reach v

We reached Cancún on Saturday.	Llegamos a Cancún el sábado.
You can reach me by phone.	Puedes telefonearme/llamarme.
Your letter didn't reach me until yesterday.	Tu carta no llegó a mis manos antes de ayer.
to reach one's goal	llegar a la meta/realizar una ambición

reading n

reading	la lectura
I like reading.	Me gusta leer.
I have a lot of reading to do.	Tengo mucho que leer.

ready adj

to be ready	estar listo(a)/preparado(a)
Are you ready?	¿Estás listo(a)?
to get ready to leave	prepararse para salir
to get sth ready	preparar algo

Ø **listo** means "clever" when used with **ser.**

real adj

real	real/verdadero(a)/auténtico(a)
She's a real friend.	Es una verdadera amiga.
the real world	el mundo real
It's the real McCoy.	Es lo auténtico.

Ø **real** also means "royal."

realize v

[to comprehend, learn]	darse cuenta de/hacerse cargo de
I didn't realize he was here.	No me di cuenta de que estaba aquí.
Didn't you realize that?	¿No te diste cuenta de eso?
They realized the danger.	Se dieron cuenta del peligro.
[to convert into money]	realizar
to realize one's assets	realizar sus bienes
to realize an ambition	realizar una ambición
My ambitions were realized.	Mis ambiciones se realizaron/se hicieron realidad.

really adv

really	de verdad/realmente/en realidad
I don't really know.	En realidad no lo sé.
The play was really good.	La comedia fue verdaderamente buena.

179

reason

Really?	¿De veras?/¿De verdad?
Not really?	¿Lo dices en serio?

reason n
[faculty]	la razón
to lose one's reason	perder la razón
[motive]	la razón/el motivo/la causa
the reason for my visit	el motivo de mi visita
for this reason	por esta razón/por esto
the reason why	el por qué/la razón por qué
We have reason to believe that ...	Tenemos motivo para creer que...
It stands to reason.	Es evidente.

receipt n
a receipt	un recibo
on receipt of the goods	al recibo de/al recibir los géneros
I acknowledge receipt of your letter.	Acuso recibo de su carta.
receipts [money received]	los ingresos

Ø **una receta** means "recipe" or "prescription."

receiver n
[addressee of letter, etc.]	un(a) destinatario(a)
radio receiver	un receptor
telephone receiver	el auricular
to pick up/hang up the receiver	descolgar/colgar el auricular

recipe n
[in cooking]	la receta

Ø **receta** also means "prescription."

record n
[music]	un disco
to make a record	grabar un disco
to play a record	tocar un disco
record player	un tocadiscos
[sport]	un récord/una marca
world record	el récord/la marca mundial
to beat the record	batir el récord/superar la marca
a record time	un tiempo récord
an academic/professional record	un expediente académico/ profesional

record v
to record [music, voice]	grabar
to record on tape	grabar en cinta

Ø **recordar** normally means "to remember" or "to remind," but is also found in Latin America with the meaning "to record."

recover v intrans
to recover from an illness	recuperarse/reponerse/restablecerse de una enfermedad
I have completely recovered.	Me he curado del todo.
He is recovering slowly from the operation.	Está reponiéndose poco a poco de la operación.

Shares have recovered.	Las acciones han vuelto a subir.

recover *v trans*

to recover one's health	recobrar la salud/reponerse
to recover consciousness	recobrar el conocimiento/volver en sí
to recover one's appetite/strength	recobrar el apetito/las fuerzas
to recover lost/stolen property	recuperar un objeto perdido/los géneros robados

red *adj*

red	rojo(a)/colorado(a)
red-haired	pelirrojo(a)
redhead	una pelirroja
red wine	el vino tinto

refer *v*

to refer to	referirse a/mencionar/hacer referencia a
What are you referring to?	¿A qué te refieres?
He referred to your absence.	Se refirió a tu ausencia.
I won't refer to it again.	No volveré a mencionarlo.
Refer to page nine.	Véase la página nueve.

regard(s) *n*

[attention, care]	la atención
without regard to	sin hacer caso de/sin considerar
having regard to	en atención a/considerando/ teniendo en cuenta
[esteem]	el respeto/la consideración/la estimación
to have a high regard for sb	respetar mucho a alguien/tener a alguien en gran estima
I have a high regard for them.	Les tengo en gran estima.
to show no regard for others	no tener ninguna consideración con los demás
[greetings]	recuerdos
Please give my regards to your wife.	Recuerdos a tu esposa/Saluda de mi parte a tu esposa.
with regard to/as regards	en cuanto a/por lo que se refiere a/con respecto a

register *v*

[instruments]	marcar/indicar
The thermometer registered 12 degrees.	El termómetro marcó doce grados.
to register for a course/class	matricularse en una asignatura/ una clase
to register at a hotel	firmar el registro en un hotel
to register mail	recomendar *[LA]*/certificar una carta
a registered letter	una carta recomendada *[LA]*/ certificada *[Sp]*
to register luggage	facturar el equipaje
registered trademark	una marca registrada
to register for the draft	ingresar/ingresarse *[Mex]*

Ø **registrar** normally means "to search" in the police sense of searching luggage, premises, etc.

registration   n

registration number [car]	la matrícula
registration [for a course, etc.]	el registro/la inscripción/la matrícula
registration fee	los derechos de matrícula

regular   adj

[habitual, regular, usual]	asiduo(a)/habitual/acostumbrado(a)
the regular customers	los clientes habituales
the regular staff	los empleados permanentes
the regulars [bar/café/club]	los asiduos/las asiduas
regular bus/train service	un servicio regular de autobuses/trenes
regular job	un empleo fijo/seguro/permanente
I arrived at my regular time.	Llegué a mi hora acostumbrada.
This is my regular work.	Éste es mi trabajo acostumbrado.
[normal/ordinary]	normal/corriente
regular gas	la gasolina normal
a regular day	un día corriente
regular size	de tamaño regular/medio

Ø **regular** often means "so-so."

relation/relationship   n

[link, connection]	la relación/la conexión
the relation between the government and the unions	la relación entre el gobierno y los sindicatos
It bears no relation to the facts.	No tiene nada que ver con los hechos.
[relationship between people]	la relación/las relaciones
to have a good relationship with sb	tener buenas relaciones con alguien
to break a relationship with sb	romper con alguien
business/diplomatic/political relations	las relaciones comerciales/ diplomáticas/políticas
to break off/establish relations	romper/establecer relaciones
family relationship	el parentesco
What is his relationship to your family?	¿Qué parentesco hay entre él y tu familia?
[family member: see **relative**]	

relative   n

my relatives	mis parientes
They're relatives of mine.	Son parientes míos.

Ø **parientes** does not mean "parents," which is rendered by **padres.**

relax   v

[to rest]	descansar
I relaxed by swimming every evening.	Descansé nadando todas las tardes.
[to calm down]	calmarse
Relax!	¡Cálmate!/¡No te apures!

rely   v

to rely on	confiar en/contar con/fiarse de
You can't rely on the weather.	No puede fiarse del tiempo.
I am relying on you.	Cuento contigo./Confío en ti.
I am relying on you to do it.	Cuento contigo para hacerlo./ Confío en que lo hagas.

remain v

[to stay]	quedar(se)/permanecer
I remained in bed for a week.	(Me) Quedé en cama una semana.
She remained standing/sitting.	Permaneció de pie/sentada.
[to survive]	quedar
Many people remained in the village.	Quedó mucha gente en la aldea.
[to be left over]	sobrar
Very little bread remained.	Sobró muy poco pan.

remark n & v

[comment]	una observación
to make a remark	hacer una observación
He made some remarks on her behavior.	Hizo unas observaciones sobre su conducta.
She remarked to us that it was cold.	Nos observó que hacía frío.

Ø **remarcar** is an anglicism which is found in Latin America.

remember v

to remember	acordarse de/recordar
Do you remember his name?	¿Te acuerdas de su nombre?
I don't remember the color.	No recuerdo el color.
He remembered to phone his wife.	Se acordó de telefonear a su esposa.
Did you remember to buy the wine?	¿Recordaste comprar el vino?

Ø **acordarse de** and **recordar** are interchangeable for "to remember."

remind v

This reminds me of the summer.	Esto me recuerda el verano.
Your brother reminds me of the president.	Tu hermano me recuerda al presidente.
He reminded us that it was getting dark.	Nos recordó que anochecía.
to remind sb to do sth	recordar a alguien que haga algo
Remind me to go to the bank.	Recuérdame que vaya al banco.
	[Note: subjunctive]
That reminds me ...!	¡Y a propósito...!

Ø **acordarse de** cannot be used in place of **recordar** with the meaning of "to remind."

rent n & v

to rent *[car, house, etc.]*	alquilar/rentar *[LA]*
the rent	el alquiler/la renta *[LA]*
to pay the rent	pagar el alquiler/la renta
House/Appartment to rent	Se alquila casa/apartamento
	Se renta casa/apartamento

Ø **la renta** also means "income" (from property, dividends, etc.) and is not used for "rent" in Spain.

rental n

car rental	el alquiler del coche
[income from rents]	la renta

repair(s) n
repairs [car]
Closed for repairs!
The house is in good repair.

las reparaciones/las composturas [Mex]
¡Cerrado por reformas!
La casa está en buen estado.

report n
[account]
[official]
newspaper report
school report
weather report

un relato/una relación
un informe
un reportaje/una crónica
un boletín
un boletín meteorológico

representative n
[elected]
[salesperson]

un diputado/un representante
un viajante/un representante
  comercial

require v
to demand
The officials require that you
  fill out this form.

exigir
Los oficiales exigen que rellenes
  este formulario. [Note: subjunctive]

to need
I require 100 dollars.

necesitar
Necesito cien dólares.

required adj
[necessary]
the required qualifications
a required course [college/school]
within the required time

necesario(a)
los requisitos necesarios
un curso obligatorio
dentro del plazo prescrito

resign v
to resign [from a job]
to resign oneself to

dimitir
resignarse a

resort n
holiday resort
seaside resort
ski resort
summer resort
winter resort
tourist resort
as a last resort

una estación/un punto de veraneo
una estación balnearia/una playa
una estación de esquiar
una estación veraniega
una estación de invierno
un centro de turismo
en último caso

Ø **un resorte** means "a coiled spring."

resort v
to resort to bribery

recurrir al soborno

rest n & v
the remainder
the rest of the students
Where are the rest?
the rest of the day/time
Tell me the rest!

el resto/lo demás/los demás
los demás estudiantes
¿Dónde están los demás?
el resto del día/tiempo
¡Cuéntame lo demás!

relaxation

el descanso/el reposo

to rest/have a rest   descansar
May he/she rest in peace.   Descanse en paz.

Ø **restar** means "to subtract," "to deduct."

restrooms   *n*
ladies' room   el baño para señoras/damas
men's room   el baño para caballeros
[public]   el baño/los servicios

resumé   *n*
[summary]   un resumen
[news summary]   un resumen de noticias
[CV]   un currículum vitae

resume   *v*
to resume   continuar/comenzar de nuevo

retire   *v*/retirement   *n*
to retire from a job   jubilarse
to retire from the armed forces retirarse
I'm retired.   Soy jubilado(a).
[act of retirement]   la jubilación
[state of retirement]   el retiro
to retire for the night   ir a acostarse

return   *v intrans*
[to come back, go back]   volver/regresar
to return home   volver a casa

return   *v trans*
[to give/send/take back]   devolver
Have you returned the books? ¿Has devuelto los libros?
Return to sender.   Devuélvase al remitente.
[to pay back]   devolver/reembolsar
I returned the money to him. Le reembolsé el dinero.

reverse   *adj, n & v*
[direction]   contrario(a)/opuesto(a)
They went in the reverse   Fueron en sentido contrario.
  direction.
to reverse/drive in reverse dar marcha atrás
to reverse the car   dar marcha atrás al coche
[order]   inverso(a)/invertido(a)
in reverse order   en orden inverso
[opposite]   contrario(a)
It's quite the reverse.   Es todo lo contrario.
to reverse one's decision   revocar su decisión

review   *n & v*
review *[of play, film, show]* una reseña
to review a play/film   reseñar una comedia/una película
review *[journal]*   una revista
[to reconsider]   reconsiderar
They reviewed their policy. Reconsideraron su política.
[to take stock of]   examinar/estudiar

rich

| Let's review the situation. | Estudiemos la situación. |
| to review for an exam | repasar los libros para un examen |

rich *adj*

[people]	rico(a)
[food]	sabroso(a)
[color]	vivo(a)/brillante
to get rich	enriquecerse
the rich	los ricos

ride *n & v*

[on horse]	una cabalgata/un paseo a caballo
[in car, on bicycle]	un paseo en coche/en bicicleta
to go for a ride	pasearse a caballo
to go for a ride in a car	dar un paseo en coche
It's a short ride.	Es poco camino/poca distancia.
He gave me a ride home.	Me llevó a casa en coche.
to ride a horse	montar a caballo
to ride a bicycle	ir en bicicleta
Can you ride a bicycle?	¿Sabes montar en bicicleta?

rider *n*

horse-rider	un jinete/una jineta
[cyclist]	un(a) ciclista
[motor cyclist]	un(a) motociclista

right *adj, adv & n*
appropriate, suitable

	apropiado(a)/propio(a)/indicado(a)/
	conveniente/lo que conviene
the right time	la hora apropiada
the right man for the job	el hombre más indicado para el cargo
to say the right thing	decir lo que conviene
She was wearing the right clothes.	Llevaba la ropa apropiada.
I thought it right to ask him.	Me pareció conveniente preguntarle.

correct

	correcto(a)/exacto(a)/verdadero(a)
the right answer	la respuesta correcta
the right answer [math]	la solución correcta
the right word	la palabra exacta/apropiada
Do you have the right time?	¿Tienes la hora exacta?
Is this the right road for Jalisco?	¿Es ésta el camino de Jalisco?
My watch is right.	Mi reloj va bien.
to be right	tener razón
I'm right.	Tengo razón.
You're quite right.	Estás en lo cierto.
That's right.	Sí, eso es./¡Justo!

opposite of left

	derecho(a)
on/to the right	a la derecha
your right hand	tu mano derecha
the right(-hand) drawer	el cajón de derecha
the right-hand lane	el carril de derecha
to keep to the right	circular por la derecha
the right-hand side	la derecha
right turn	una vuelta a la derecha
to turn right	torcer a la derecha

186

to be on the right [politics]	ser de derechas
a right-winger	un(a) derechista

moral, just

	bueno(a)
right conduct	la buena conducta
to know right from wrong	saber lo que está bien y lo que está mal.
to do the right thing	hacer bien
civil rights	los derechos civiles
equal rights	la igualdad de derechos
women's rights	los derechos de la mujer
You have no right to do that.	No tienes el derecho de hacer eso.

all right

I'm all right.	Estoy bien.
All right? [agreed]	¿De acuerdo?/¿Vale?
[see also okay]	

other

right here	aquí mismo
right now	ahora mismo
to come right	arreglarse/salir bien
It'll all come right in the end.	Todo se arreglará/saldrá bien.
to go right on	seguir adelante
Right on!	¡Vale!/¡Justo!

ring   n

[jewelry]	un anillo/una sortija
engagement ring	una alianza/un anillo de compromiso/ un anillo de pedida/un anillo de comprometida/una sortija de pedida
wedding ring	una alianza/un anillo de boda
boxing ring	un ring/un cuadrilátero
bull ring	una plaza de toros
circus ring	una pista
the rings of Saturn	los anillos de Saturno

ring   v

[to telephone]	telefonear/llamar (por teléfono)
to ring the bell [electric]	tocar el timbre
Ring the bell!	¡Toca el timbre!
[of bells]	sonar
The bells are ringing.	Suenan las campanas.

river   n

river	un río
down/up river	río abajo/río arriba

road   n

[general]	un camino
the road to Mérida	el camino de Mérida
[main road]	una carretera
the road between Lima and the coast	la carretera entre Lima y la costa
[in town]	una calle
road sign	una señal de carretera

robe   n

bathrobe/dressing gown	un batín [man's]/una bata [woman's]

room

[judge's]	una toga/un traje talar
[priest's]	una sotana

room   n
in a house/apartment
un cuarto/una habitación/una
   pieza [LA]/un ambiente [Arg]

bathroom	un cuarto de baño
bedroom	una recámara [LA]/un dormitorio/ una alcoba/un cuarto/una habitación

Julia is working in her room.   Julia está trabajando en su
   cuarto/habitación.

dining room	un comedor
living room	un cuarto de estar/una sala de estar/un salón/un living [Sp]

in hotels
una sala

hotel room	una habitación
double room	una habitación para dos personas
single room	una habitación individual
ladies' room	el lavabo/servicio de señoras
men's room	el lavabo/servicio de caballeros

in public building
una sala

waiting room	una sala de espera
classroom	un aula [fem]
conference/lecture room	una sala de conferencias

space
un espacio/un sitio

Is there room?	¿Hay sitio?
Is there room for this?	¿Cabe esto?
There's room for eight in his car.	Caben ocho en su coche.
Is there room for me?	¿Quepo yo?
There's plenty of room.	Queda mucho espacio libre.

round   [see around]

rubber   n
[material]	el caucho [LA]/la goma [Sp]
It's made of rubber.	Es de goma.

rude   adj
[offensive]
grosero(a)/ descortés(-esa)/ofensivo(a)/
   mal educado(a)

You were very rude to her.	Estuviste muy descortés con ella.
He's a very rude person.	Es una persona muy mal educada.
a rude gesture	un gesto grosero
a rude remark	una grosería
to make rude remarks	decir groserías
a rude word	una palabrota

Ø **rudo(a)** means "rough" or "rude" when referring to wood.

ruin   v
[financial/health/life/reputation]	arruinar
The strike ruined the firm.	La huelga arruinó la empresa.
The climate ruined his health.	El clima arruinó su salud.
[to spoil events, objects]	estropear
The rain ruined the picnic.	La lluvia estropeó la merienda.

My garden was ruined by the storm.	Mi jardín fue estropeado por la tormenta.
His father was ruined.	Su padre fue arruinado.
The city was ruined after the earthquake.	La ciudad quedó en ruinas después del terremoto.

run *v*

[people, animals]	correr
to run downstairs/upstairs	bajar/subir la escalera corriendo
to run in/out	entrar/salir corriendo
[machinery]	marchar/andar/funcionar
The car is running smoothly.	El coche marcha bien.
It runs on gas.	Funciona con gasolina.
The engine was running.	El motor estaba en marcha.
I'll run you to the airport.	Te llevaré al aeropuerto.
The buses do not run on Sundays.	Los autobuses no circulan los domingos./No hay servicio de autobuses los domingos.
The trains run every hour.	Los trenes salen cada hora.
to run a car	tener un coche
to run a temperature	tener una fiebre
to run a business	dirigir una empresa
to run for office	presentarse como/ser candidato(a) para un puesto
to run away	escaparse/huir
to run out of *[commodity]*	agotarse/acabarse
We've run out of money/bread.	Se nos ha acabado el dinero/el pan.
They ran out of gas.	Se quedaron sin gasolina.

189

S

's/s'
[possessive]

[Note: Spanish has no equivalent of the
  English apostrophe s; **de** is used to denote
  possession]

José's house
la casa de José
the boys' father
el padre de los chicos
the dog's owner
el dueño del perro
My car is bigger than my
  boss's.
Mi coche es más grande que el
  de mi jefe.
His tickets are more expensive
  than his friends'.
Sus localidades son más caras que
  las de sus amigos.

sad *adj*
[unhappy]
triste
[deplorable]
lamentable

safe *adj*
from danger
salvo(a)/fuera de peligro/ileso(a)
You'll be safe here.
Aquí estarás fuera de peligro.
safe and sound
sano(a) y salvo(a)
All the passengers were safe.
Todos los pasajeros salieron ilesos.
safely
a buen puerto/sin accidente
We arrived home safely.
Llegamos a casa a buen puerto/sin
  accidente.

secure, not dangerous
seguro(a)/sin peligro/a salvo
a safe beach
una playa sin peligro
This bridge is not very safe.
Este puente no es muy seguro.
These toys are safe.
Estos juguetes no son peligrosos.

sensible
prudente
a safe driver
un conductor prudente
at a safe distance
a una distancia prudente

saint *n*
a saint
un santo/una santa
Saint John
San Juan [Note: **Santo** shortens to
  San before a male saint's name unless it
  begins with **Do** or **To**.]
Saint Dominic/Saint Thomas
Santo Domingo/Santo Tomás
Saint Mary
Santa María

Ø **el santo** also means "saint's day" which in the Spanish-speaking world is often of
greater significance than one's birthday.

sale *n*
sale
una venta
for sale
se vende
House for sale
Se vende (una) casa
to put a house up for sale
ofrecer una casa en venta
on sale
de rebaja
on sale in all book stores
de venta en todas las librerías

annual/summer sale, etc.	un saldo/unas rebajas
clearance sale	una liquidación
public sale/auction	una subasta
Sale! *[in shop windows, etc.]*	¡Grandes rebajas!
sale price *[retail]*	el precio de venta
reduced price	el precio de saldo

salt *n*

salt	la sal

Ø **un salto** means "a jump."

same *adj & pron*

same	mismo(a)/igual
It's the same man.	Es el mismo hombre. *[Note: position of adjective]*
at the same time	al mismo tiempo
It's all the same.	Es lo mismo.
It's all the same to me.	Me es igual.
It's the same old story.	Es lo de siempre.
The same to you!	¡Igualmente!
Same again? *[drinks, etc.]*	¿Igual que antes?/¿Lo de antes?

save *v*

from danger, death, destruction	salvar/rescatar/impedir
to save sb's life	salvar la vida a alguien
The dog saved my life.	El perro me salvó la vida.
The firefighters saved the old mission.	Los bomberos salvaron la misión vieja.
He saved the woman from drowning.	Salvó a la mujer que se estaba ahogando.
They saved me from falling.	Impidieron que cayera yo.
to store	guardar/reservar
We saved some bread and fruit.	Guardamos pan y fruta.
Save me a seat, please.	Guárdame un asiento, por favor.
to collect	coleccionar
Do you save stamps?	¿Coleccionas estampillas/sellos?
money	ahorrar
He has saved a lot of money.	Ha ahorrado mucho dinero.
I am saving up for my vacation.	Ahorro dinero para mis vacaciones.
She's saving up for a car.	Ahorra dinero para comprar un coche.
savings account	una cuenta de ahorros
time	ahorrar
He saved time by buying his ticket in advance.	Ahorró tiempo sacando su boleto con anticipación.
sport	parar
The goalkeeper saved the penalty.	El portero paró el penalty.

say *v*

to say	decir
How do you say "help" in Spanish?	¿Cómo se dice "help" en castellano?
They say it's very popular.	Dicen que es muy popular. *[Note: **que** may not be omitted.]*
It is said to be impossible.	Se dice que es imposible.

No sooner said than done!   ¡Dicho y hecho!

scary adj
[frightening]   espantoso(a)/pavoroso(a)
[easily frightened]   asustadizo(a)
It's a scary place.   Es un sitio espantoso.
a scary movie   una película de miedo

schedule n
[list]   una lista
[of events]   un programa
My schedule includes the cathedral   Mi programa de visitas incluye la catedral.
[work to be done]   un plan
a tight schedule   un plan riguroso
The work is behind schedule.   El trabajo sufre retraso/está atrasado.
The work is on schedule.   El trabajo no sufre retraso.
[timetable]   un horario
The plane is behind schedule.   El avión sufre un retraso.
The train arrived on schedule.   El tren llegó sin retraso.

schedule v
[meeting, visit, etc.]   fijar la hora de
The game is scheduled for five o'clock.   El partido está previsto para las cinco.
[transportation]   establecer el horario de
[work]   proyectar/redactar el plan de
I am scheduled to leave at ten.   Según el programa saldré a las diez./ Se ha fijado mi salida para las diez.

school n
[general]   una escuela
primary school   una escuela primaria
high/secondary school   una escuela secundaria/un instituto (de segunda enseñanza)
junior high school   un colegio de bachillerato elemental
to go to school   ir a la escuela/al colegio [Note: use of definite article]
[college or university]   una universidad
[department of university]   un departamento/una facultad
to finish school   acabar sus estudios

scientist n
scientist   un(a) científico(a)/un(a) cientista [LA]

season n
[of the year]   la estación
[sport, social]   la temporada
soccer season   la temporada de fútbol

seat n
[chair]   un asiento/una silla
[in buses, planes, etc.]   un asiento/una plaza
[in theater, movies, etc.]   una localidad
[ticket for theater, etc.]   una localidad/una entrada
I want two seats for tomorrow.   Quiero dos localidades para mañana.
There are no seats left.   No quedan entradas.

This seat is taken. | Este asiento está ocupado.
Have/Take a seat! | ¡Siéntate!

second *adj*
second-hand | de segunda mano/usado(a)
second-hand clothes | ropa usada
second-hand book/car | un libro/coche de segunda mano

secretary *n*
[in an office] | un(a) secretario(a)
[in government] | un ministro

seed *n*
[for sowing] | una semilla/una simiente
[within fruit] | una pepita
to sow seeds | sembrar de semillas

seem *v*
to seem | parecer
How does it seem to you? | ¿Qué te parece?
He seems very nice. | Parece muy amable.
So it seems. | Así parece.
It seems that they want to stay. | Parece que quieren quedarse.
It does not seem that he is coming. | No parece que venga. *[Note: use of subjunctive]*
It seems to me he's lying. | Me parece que dice mentiras.

self *pron*
in a reflexive verb
myself | me
yourself | te
himself/herself/itself/yourself/oneself | se
ourselves | nos
themselves/yourselves | se
to cut oneself | cortarse
Have you hurt yourself? | ¿Te has hecho daño?
I helped/served myself. | Me serví.

in an imperative
Look at yourself in the mirror! | ¡Mírate en el espejo!
Don't deceive yourself. | ¡No te engañes!

emphatic
I myself | yo mismo(a)
you yourself | tú mismo(a)/usted mismo(a)
he himself/she herself | él mismo/ella misma
we ourselves | nosotros(as) mismos(as)
they themselves | ellos mismos/ellas mismas
you yourselves | ustedes mismos(as)
I'll go myself. | Iré yo mismo(a).
One must do it oneself. | Se debe hacerlo sí mismo.

(all) by oneself
I can't do it by myself. | No puedo hacerlo solo(a).
We went by ourselves. | Fuimos nosotros solos.

self-service *n*
self-service restaurant/store | un autoservicio

senior *adj & n*

senior citizen	un(a) jubilado(a)
a senior [at university]	un(a) estudiante de último año
senior year	el último año de estudios
He is my senior. [age]	Tiene más años que yo./Es más viejo que yo.
He is my senior. [rank]	Tiene categoría superior a la mía.

sense *n*

the five senses	los cinco sentidos
[hearing]	el oído
[sight]	la vista
[smell]	el olfato
[taste]	el gusto
[touch]	el tacto
common sense	el sentido común
sense of humor	el sentido del humor
It doesn't make sense.	No tiene sentido.
[feeling]	una sensación
a sense of grief/pleasure	una sensación de dolor/placer

sensible *adj*

[having good sense]	sensato(a)/prudente
She's a very sensible person.	Es una persona muy sensata.
[reasonable]	razonable/prudente/lógico(a)
The most sensible thing to do would be ...	Lo más razonable sería...
[of clothes]	práctico(a)
He was wearing sensible shoes.	Llevaba zapatos prácticos.

Ø **sensible** means "sensitive."

sensitive *adj*

sensitive	sensible
My sister is very sensitive.	Mi hermana es muy sensible.
He is sensitive to the cold.	Es sensible al frío.
[easily offended]	susceptible
They are sensitive to criticism.	Son susceptibles a la crítica.

Ø **sensitivo(a)** means "sentient" or "aware."

sentence *n*

[grammar]	una frase/una oración
[in law]	una sentencia
to pass sentence	pronunciar sentencia

serious *adj*

[general]	serio(a)
His father is very serious.	Su padre es muy serio.
It was a serious decision.	Fue una decisión seria.
Are you serious (about it)?	¿Lo dices en serio?
I am serious.	Hablo en serio.
[of illness/injury]	grave
Our goalkeeper suffered a serious injury.	Nuestro portero sufrió una lesión grave.
to be seriously ill/injured	estar gravemente enfermo(a)/lesionado(a)

servant n
[domestic]   un(a) criado(a)
civil servant   un(a) funcionario(a)

several adj & pron
several   varios(as)/algunos(as)/diversos(as)
There are several people in   Hay varias personas en la
  the swimming pool.   alberca/piscina.
Several of them attended.   Algunos(as) de ellos/ellas asistieron.
Several of us are going.   Algunos(as) de nosotros(as) vamos.

share n
[of something]   una parte/una porción
in equal shares   por partes iguales
He paid his share of the cost.   Pagó su parte del coste.
[financial]   una acción

share v
[to divide]   partir/dividir
I shared the cake with them.   Dividí el pastel con ellos/ellas.
[to share out]   repartir/distribuir
The money was shared among us.   Repartieron el dinero entre nosotros.
[to have/hold in common]   compartir
We had to share a room.   Tuvimos que compartir una habitación.
I have sth to share with you.   Tengo algo que decirte.

she pron
She's working in Panama.   Trabaja en Panamá.
She will come, but not her   Ella sí vendrá pero su hija no.
  daughter.   [Note: **Ella,** like all the other subject
                                                 pronouns, is usually omitted; it is used for
                                                 emphasis and clarification.]

Ø **ella** can also mean "her" following a preposition, e.g., "It's for her," is translated by **Es
para ella.**

shoot v
[an arrow/bullet/gun]   disparar
to shoot at sb   tirar a alguien/pegar un tiro a
                                                 alguien/disparar contra alguien
They shot at me.   Dispararon contra mí.
Don't shoot!   ¡No dispare! **[usted form]**
[to kill]   pegar un tiro/matar a tiros a alguien
He shot his brother.   Pegó un tiro/Mató a tiros a su hermano.
[to wound]   herir
He shot a motorist.   Hirió a un motorista.
A policeman was shot. [killed]   Un guardia fue matado a tiros.
A policeman was shot. [wounded]   Un guardia fue/quedó herido.
[to execute]   fusilar
He was shot by the soldiers.   Fue fusilado por los soldados.
to shoot a film   rodar una película/filmar

shop n
a store   una tienda
a department store   un almacén
a workshop   un taller

195

shopping n & v

shopping	las compras
to go shopping	hacer las compras/ir de compras/ir de tiendas
shop window	una vidriera/una vitrina [LA]/un escaparate [Sp]

short adj

[length, distance]	corto(a)
a short distance	una distancia corta
shortwave radio	un radio de onda corta
[message]	breve
[person]	bajo(a)
a short man/woman	un hombre bajo/una mujer baja
[time]	corto(a)/breve/de poca duración
a short visit	una visita de poca duración
for a short time	por poco tiempo
to be short of	estar falto(a) de/faltar/no tener

shorts n

shorts	un pantalón corto

should v

	[deber in the conditional or imperfect subjunctive]
You should do it.	Deberías hacerlo.[conditional]
	Debieras hacerlo. [imperfect subjunctive]
I should have helped her.	Debería haberla ayudado./Debiera haberla ayudado/Habría debido ayudarla./ Hubiera debido ayudarla. [Note: alternative forms]

[see also ought]

show n

[exhibition]	una exposición
dog show	una exposición canina
[entertainment]	una función/un espectáculo
The last show starts at 10.	La última función empieza a las diez.
to go to a show	ir al teatro/ir a un espectáculo
TV show	una emisión/un programa

show v

to show sth to sb	enseñar/mostrar algo a alguien
I showed him the letter.	Le enseñé la carta.
to show sb how to do sth	enseñar/mostrar a alguien a hacer algo
to show in	hacer pasar
Show her in.	Que pase./Hágala pasar. [usted form]

shower n

shower	la regadera [LA]/la ducha [Sp]

Ø In Spain la regadera means "watering can."

sick adj

ill	enfermo(a)
to be sick	estar enfermo(a) [Note: estar is used]
to feel sick	sentirse mal
to get sick	caer enfermo(a)/enfermarse

to get seasick/travel sick	marearse

disgusted

to sicken	dar asco a
It makes me sick.	Me da asco./Me repugna.

tired of

to be sick (and tired) of	estar harto(a) de
I'm sick (and tired) of rice.	Estoy harto(a) de arroz.
I'm sick (and tired) of telling you.	Estoy harto(a) de decírtelo.

side n

side	un lado
by the side of	al lado de
by the side of the lake/river	a la orilla del lago/río
by the side of the road	al borde del camino
by/at the seaside	a orillas del mar
on this side	por este lado
on the other side	por otro lado
on both sides	por ambos lados
on one side ... on the other ...	por una parte... por otra...

sidewalk n

sidewalk	una acera/una banqueta [Mex]/ una vereda [Arg]

sign n
with the hand

to make a (rude) sign to sb	hacer una señal (grosera) a alguien

indication

It's a good sign.	una señal/un indicio
It's a sign of rain.	Es buena señal.
There's no sign of it.	Es indicio de lluvia.
	No se lo ve en ninguna parte.

public sign

[notice, placard]	una señal
neon sign	un letrero
road sign	un letrero de neón
shop sign	una señal de carretera
	un rótulo

written symbol

signs of the zodiac	un signo/un símbolo
	los signos del zodiaco

silence n/silent adj

Silence!	¡Silencio!/¡Cállate!
to be silent	callarse/guardar silencio [more polite]
silent	silencioso(a)
silent [people only]	callado(a)
a silent film	una película muda

simple adj

[of things]	simple
It's a simple formality.	Es un trámite simple.
[simple-minded, stupid]	simple
Her brother is simple.	Su hermano es simple.
[uncomplicated, plain]	sencillo(a)
They are simple people.	Son personas sencillas.
to live a simple life	llevar una vida sencilla

since *conj & prep*
time
He's been in London since yesterday.
It hasn't rained since we've been here.
I haven't seen them since they arrived.

desde *[prep]*/desde que *[conj]*
Está en Londres desde ayer. *[Note: present tense]*
No ha llovido desde que estamos aquí. *[Note: present tense]*
No los he visto desde su llegada/ desde que llegaron.

reason
Since they have no money, they cannot go to the concert.

puesto que/ya que
Puesto que no tienen dinero, no pueden ir al concierto.

sincerely *[see yours sincerely]*

single *adj*
[unmarried]
a single man/woman
a single bed/room
a single ticket
a single coat of paint
[only one]
There was a single tree in the square.
There wasn't a single flower in his garden.

soltero(a)
un soltero/una soltera
una cama/habitación individual
un boleto sencillo/de ida
una simple capa de pintura
solo(a)/único(a)
Había un árbol único en la plaza.
No había ni una sola flor en su jardín.

sit/sitting *v*
to sit down
Sit down!
to be sitting down/seated
She's sitting down. *[action]*
She's sitting down. *[state]*
to sit up *[from lying position]*
He sat up in bed.

sentarse
¡Siéntate!/¡Siéntese!/¡Siéntense!
estar sentado(a)
Está sentándose./Se está sentando.
Está sentada.
incorporarse/pararse *[LA]*
Se incorporó en la cama.

size *n*
[general]
What size is it?

It's the size of an egg.
[clothes]
What size do you wear?
What size shirt do you wear?
I wear a size 10.
[shoes, gloves]
What size shoes do you wear?
I wear a size 10.

el tamaño/las dimensiones
¿De qué tamaño es?/¿Cómo es de grande?/¿Qué dimensiones tiene?
Es del tamaño de un huevo.
la talla
¿Cuál es tu/su talla?
¿Qué talla de camisa es la tuya/ la de usted?
Mi talla es el 10.
el número
¿Qué número calzas/calza usted?
Uso/Calzo el número 10.

skirt *n*
skirt

la falda/la pollera *[Arg, Bol, Chi, Uru]*

sleep *v* /asleep *adj* /sleepy *adj*
to sleep
to go to sleep
to be asleep
My wife is asleep.

dormir
dormirse
estar durmiendo/estar dormido(a)
Mi esposa está durmiendo/dormida.

[to spend the night] — pasar la noche/acostarse
He's sleeping at his uncle's. — Pasa la noche en casa de su tío.
to be sleepy — tener sueño
to get sleepy — empezar a tener sueño

slip *n*
[half slip] — una combinación de medio cuerpo
[full slip] — una combinación

Ø **un slip** means "briefs" (men's or women's) in Spain, and in Latin America "swimming trunks."

slow *adj*
slow — lento(a)
It's slow work. — Es un trabajo lento.
They're slow workers. — Trabajan despacio.
a slow train — un tren correo/un ómnibus
Your clock is slow. — Tu reloj se atrasa.
My watch is five minutes slow. — Mi reloj se atrasa cinco minutos./lleva cinco minutos de retraso.

to be slow to do sth/in doing — tardar en hacer algo
They are very slow to reply. — Tardan mucho en contestar.

small *adj*
small — chico(a) *[LA]*/pequeño(a)
a small house — una casa chica/pequeña
una casita *[Note: The suffix **ito** or **ita** is often used to convey the idea of smallness.]*

smart *adj*
elegant — elegante
a smart dress — un vestido elegante
She looks very smart. — Está muy elegante./¡Qué elegante está!

fashionable — de moda
She always wears smart shoes. — Siempre lleva zapatos de moda.
It's a smart restaurant. — Es un restaurante de moda.

bright, intelligent — inteligente/listo(a)/vivo(a)
He's a smart guy. — Es un tío inteligente/listo.

quick, prompt — pronto(a)/rápido(a)
Smart work by the policeman prevented the attack. — Una pronta acción de parte del guardia evitó el atentado.

smell *n & v*
[odor] — un olor
a nice smell — un olor agradable
a bad smell — un mal olor/un hedor
sense of smell — el olfato
to have a keen sense of smell — tener buen olfato
to smell — oler
It smells nice. — Huele bien.
It smelled bad. — Olía mal.
This rose doesn't smell. — Esta rosa no tiene olor.
to smell of — oler a
It smells of garlic. — Huele a ajo.

smoke n & v

smoke	el humo
to smoke (glass, bacon)	ahumar
to smoke (tobacco)	fumar

snack n

to have a snack	tomar un bocadillo/comer algo
snacks [appetizers]	las botanas [Mex]/los antojetos [Per]/ los ingredientes [Arg]/los pasapalos [Ven]/ las tapas [Sp]/los aperitivos [Note: These are the traditional snacks served in bars such as chips, nuts, olives, shrimp, etc.]
snackbar	una cafetería

Ø **un aperitivo** also means a pre-dinner drink.

so adv

so	tan
He is so ill.	Está tan enfermo.
I am so cold/hot.	Tengo tanto frío/calor.
He's so hungry/thirsty.	Tiene tanta hambre/sed.
so much	tanto(a)
They have so much money.	Tienen tanto dinero.
so many	tantos(as)
We have so many friends.	Tenemos tantos(as) amigos(as).
I think so.	Creo que sí./Lo creo.
I don't think so.	Creo que no./No lo creo.
I hope so/not.	Espero que sí/no.
I told you so!	¡Ya te lo dije!
So what?	¿Y qué?
[thus, therefore]	así
and so on	y así sucesivamente

so conj

[as a result]	por (lo) tanto
The box office was closed so I couldn't buy tickets.	La taquilla estaba cerrada y por lo tanto no podía comprar localidades.
so that [purpose]	para que [+ subjunctive]
I gave her the money so that she should pay for the meal.	Le di el dinero para que pagara la comida.
so that [result]	de modo que [+ indicative]
The taxi was late so that we missed the train.	El taxi llegó tarde de modo que perdimos el tren.

solid adj

[general]	sólido(a)
a solid state	un estado sólido
[of gold, silver, oak, etc.]	macizo(a)
The statue is solid silver.	La estatua es de plata maciza.
a solid meal	una comida fuerte/sustanciosa
solid ground	la tierra firme
I have solid grounds for thinking that he is lying.	Tengo buenos motivos para creer que dice mentiras/miente.

some adj

some	algún/alguna [singular] algunos(as) [plural] unos(as)/unos(as) cuantos(as)

Some woman told me.	Alguna mujer me lo dijo.
I'll go to Japan some day.	Algún día iré al Japón.
There were some people in the street.	Había algunas personas en la calle.
I saw them some days ago.	Los vi hace unos días.

a quantity

un poco de/algo de [singular]
algunos(as) [plural]

Do you have some chocolate?	¿Tienes (un poco de) chocolate?
Paco has some rice and flour.	Paco tiene (un poco de) arroz y harina.
There are some cherries on the table.	Hay (algunas) cerezas en la mesa.
	[Note: The Spanish for "some" is frequently omitted when referring to quantity.]

other expressions

some distance away	a cierta distancia
for some reason or other	por alguna que otra razón
some other time	otro día
I spent some three hours there.	Pasé unas tres horas allí.

some *pron*

There's no sugar left. I'll go and buy some.	No queda azúcar. Voy a comprar un poco.
I have some grapes. Do you want some?	Tengo uvas. ¿Quieres unas?
Some of my friends live here.	Algunos de mis amigos viven aquí.

somebody/someone *pron*

somebody	alguien
somebody else	algún otro/otra persona

somehow *adv*

You must do it somehow (or other).	Debes hacerlo de algún modo/de un modo u otro.
Somehow I don't believe you.	Por alguna que otra razón no te creo.

someplace *[see **somewhere**]*

something *pron*

something	algo/alguna cosa
I have something to tell you.	Tengo algo que decirte.
Do you want something to eat?	¿Quieres algo que comer? [Note: use of **que**]
something else	otra cosa

sometimes *adv*

sometimes	algunas veces/a veces/de vez en cuando

somewhere *adv*

somewhere	en alguna parte/a alguna parte
I left my umbrella somewhere.	Dejé mi paraguas en alguna parte.
He's gone somewhere.	Ha ido a alguna parte.
somewhere else	en otra parte/a otra parte
It must be somewhere else.	Debe estar en otra parte.
She went somewhere else.	Fue a otra parte.

201

soon *adv*

soon	pronto/dentro de poco
They'll be back soon.	Volverán pronto/dentro de poco.
See you soon!	¡Hasta pronto!
soon afterwards	poco después
[early]	temprano
too soon	demasiado temprano/pronto
the sooner the better	cuanto antes, mejor
sooner or later	tarde o temprano
as soon as	en cuanto/tan pronto como/así que
He will come as soon as he can.	Vendrá en cuanto pueda. [Note: subjunctive when future time implied]
I came back to New York as soon as I finished school.	Volví a Nueva York en cuanto terminé mis estudios. [Note: indicative where action already completed.]
as soon as possible	cuanto antes/lo antes posible/lo más pronto posible

Ø **pronto** means "ready" in Argentina and Uruguay.

sorry *adj*

[Pardon me?]	¿Perdón?/¿Mande? [Mex]
[Excuse me!]	¡Disculpe!/¡Discúlpeme, por favor! [**usted** forms]
I am very sorry.	Lo siento mucho.
I'm sorry I'm late.	Siento/Lamento llegar tarde.
I'm sorry you're ill.	Siento/Lamento que estés enfermo(a). [Note: subjunctive]
I feel sorry for them.	Les compadezco./Les tengo lástima./Tengo pena por ellos./Me dan lástima.

south *n & adj*

the south	el sur
south(ern)	del sur/meridional
South America	la América del Sur/Sudamérica
South American	sudamericano(a)

space *n*

[general]	el espacio
blank space	un espacio en blanco
outer space	el espacio/el espacio exterior/interplanetario
to clear/leave a space for	hacer/dejar un sitio para
[see also **room**]	

Spanish *adj*

Spanish	español(a) [Note: small 'e']

Spanish *n*

language	el castellano/el español [Note: small 'c' or 'e']
Do you speak Spanish?	¿Hablas castellano/español?
Say it in Spanish, please.	Dilo en castellano/español, por favor.
Spanish is not a difficult language.	El castellano/español no es un idioma difícil. [Note: use of definite article with name of a language except after **hablar** and **en**]

Ø **castellano** means "Castilian" but is used all over the Spanish-speaking world for the Spanish language.

people

the Spanish/Spaniards	los españoles
He's Spanish/a Spaniard.	Es español.
She's Spanish/a Spaniard.	Es española. *[Note: omission of the indefinite article]*

spare *adj*

spare time	el tiempo libre/desocupado
spare parts *[for car, etc.]*	las piezas de recambio/repuesto
spare tire/wheel	un neumático/una llanta/una rueda de repuesto
[left over]	sobrante
I have some spare potatoes.	Tengo unas papas sobrantes.
[available]	disponible
Do you have any spare rooms?	¿Tienen unas habitaciones disponibles?

spare *v*

[do without]	prescindir de
Can you spare her today?	¿Puedes prescindir de ella hoy?
to spare time	conceder/dedicar tiempo
I can spare you five minutes.	Puedo concederte cinco minutos.
Can you spare me a moment?	¿Tienes un momento?
I can't spare the time.	No tengo tiempo.
I can't spare enough time.	No puedo dedicar bastante tiempo.
time to spare	tiempo de sobra
to spare money	dar dinero
I can only spare you 50 pesos.	Puedo darte sólo cincuenta pesos.
to spare sb's life	perdonar la vida a alguien

speak *v*
on telephone

Who's speaking?	¿De parte de quién?/¿Quién habla?
Speaking.	Al habla.
May I speak with ... ?	¿Se puede hablar con... ?

spell *v*/**spelling** *n*

to spell	escribir/deletrear
How do you spell it?	¿Cómo se escribe?
You have spelled it wrong.	Lo has escrito mal.
Can you spell it for me?	¿Quieres deletreármelo?

spend *v*

to spend money	gastar dinero
He spent a lot of money on his car.	Gastó mucho dinero en su coche.
to spend time	pasar tiempo
We spent two years in Chile.	Pasamos dos años en Chile.
to spend time on	dedicar tiempo a
He spends very little time on his garden.	Dedica muy poco tiempo a su jardín.

spoil *[see ruin]*

sport *n*

to play a sport	practicar un deporte *[Note: not jugar]*
sportsman/woman	un/una deportista

stage *n*
[platform]	una plataforma
[in theater]	un escenario/una escena
to go on the stage	hacerse actor/actriz
[of journey]	una etapa
in/by stages	por etapas
at this stage of the journey	en esta etapa del viaje

stair(s) *n*
[a step]	un peldaño/un escalón
staircase	una escalera
to go up/down the stairs	subir/bajar la escalera
moving stairs	una escalera móvil/mecánica
spiral staircase	una escalera de caracol

stamp *n*
postage stamp	una estampilla [LA]/un timbre [Mex]/un sello [Sp]

stand *v*
to stand up	levantarse
[to get to one's feet]	ponerse de pie/pararse [LA]
to be standing	estar
He was standing by the door.	Estaba cerca de la puerta.
[to be on one's feet]	estar de pie/estar parado(a)
My son is the one who is standing.	Mi hijo es el que está de pie.
[to tolerate]	soportar/aguantar
I can't stand it any more!	¡No aguanto más!/¡No puedo más!

starting from *prep*
a partir del lunes	starting from Monday

stay *v*
[to remain]	quedar(se)/permanecer
I stayed in/at home.	Me quedé en casa.
We stayed in bed.	Guardamos cama.
They stayed here for a week.	Se quedaron aquí una semana.
She stayed silent.	Quedó callada.
[to lodge]	hospedarse/alojarse
to stay at a hotel	hospedarse/alojarse en un hotel
to stay with friends	hospedarse/alojarse con amigos
She's staying with friends for a few days.	Pasa unos días con amigos.
Where are you staying?	¿Dónde vives?

other
to stay out	quedarse fuera
She stayed out till midnight.	No volvió a casa hasta medianoche.
to stay up	velar/no acostarse
to stay up late	acostarse tarde
to stay up all night	trasnochar

step *n*
footstep	un paso
step by step	paso a paso
[stair]	un peldaño/un escalón/una grada

to take a step forward/back	dar un paso adelante/hacia atrás

family relations

stepbrother/stepsister	un hermanastro/una hermanastra
stepchild	un hijastro/una hijastra
stepfather/stepmother	un padrastro/una madrastra
stepson/stepdaughter	un hijastro/una hijastra

still *adj*

[motionless]	inmóvil/quieto(a)
Keep/Sit/Stand still!	¡Estáte quieto(a)!
She lay still.	Permaneció inmóvil.
[quiet]	tranquilo(a)/silencioso(a)
Everything was still and quiet.	Todo estaba tranquilo.

still *adv*

still	todavía/aún
They are still in New York.	Están todavía en Nueva York.
He still hasn't arrived.	No ha llegado todavía.
I still remember her.	Todavía la recuerdo./La recuerdo aún.

Ø **aun**, without an accent, means "even."

stomach *n*

the stomach	el estómago/el vientre
I have a stomach ache.	Tengo dolor de estómago.

Ø **estómago** is the general word for "stomach;" **vientre** really means "belly," "bowels," or "womb."

stop *v*

to stop sth/sb	parar/detener algo/ a alguien
He stopped the car.	Paró el coche.
Stop the car!	¡Para el coche!
We stopped a passer-by.	Paramos a un transeúnte.
[to come to a halt]	pararse/detenerse
The car stopped.	El coche se paró.
My watch has stopped.	Mi reloj se ha parado.
to stop doing sth	dejar de hacer algo
The lawyer stopped talking.	El abogado dejó de hablar.
Has it stopped raining?	¿Ha dejado de llover?/¿Ha cesado la lluvia?
[to prevent sb from doing sth]	impedir a alguien hacer algo
He stopped us from working.	Nos impidió trabajar.
[to forbid sb from doing sth]	prohibir a alguien hacer algo
Her mother stopped her from going to the party.	Su madre le prohibió ir a la fiesta.

store *n*

[a shop]	una tienda
a department store	un (gran) almacén
grocery store	una pulpería [LA]/(una tienda de) abarrotes [Mex]/una tienda de ultramarinos [Sp]/una bodega [Car]

storm *n*

a storm	una tormenta/una tempestad

Ø **un tormento** means "torture," "torment."

205

stove n
[for heating]   una estufa
[for cooking]   un hornillo/una cocina
an electric/gas cooker   una cocina eléctrica/de gas

straight adj
straight   derecho(a)/recto(a)
a straight line   una línea recta
straight hair   el pelo lacio/liso

straight adv
Go straight ahead!   ¡Ve todo seguido!/¡Sigue todo derecho!/¡Sigue adelante!
The airport is straight ahead.   El aeropuerto se encuentra todo seguido.

strange adj/stranger n
strange   extraño(a)/raro(a)/curioso(a)
a stranger   un(a) desconocido(a)

Ø **extranjero(a)** means "foreign" or "foreigner."

street n
main street   la calle mayor/principal
down/up the street   calle abajo/arriba

stress n & v
[strain, tension]   la tensión
to be under stress   sufrir una tensión nerviosa
[to emphasize]   subrayar
He stressed its importance.   Subrayó su importancia.
to stress a syllable   acentuar una sílaba

student n
[at elementary or high school]   un(a) alumno(a)
[at college or university]   un(a) estudiante

study v
to study   estudiar
to study for an exam   prepararse para un examen

subject n
[citizen of a country]   un(a) súbdito(a)
[grammar]   un sujeto
[theme, topic]   un tema/una materia/un asunto/una cuestión
[school/university subject]   una asignatura
on the subject of   a propósito de
to change the subject   cambiar de tema/conversación/ volver la hoja

succeed v
[to be successful of a person]   tener éxito
They didn't succeed.   No tuvieron éxito.
to succeed in doing sth   lograr/conseguir hacer algo
I didn't succeed in seeing her.   No logré verla.

[of plans]	salir bien
His plans succeeded.	Sus proyectos salieron bien.
[to a throne, title, etc.]	suceder
He succeeded to the throne of Spain.	Sucedió al trono de España.

success *n*/**successful** *adj*

success	el éxito
successful	exitoso
to be (very) successful	tener (mucho) éxito
a succesful business	una empresa próspera

Ø **éxito** does not mean "exit," which translates as **la salida**.

such *adj & adv*

with a noun	tal
such a house	tal casa
such people	tales personas
with an adjective	tan
such a pretty house	una casa tan linda
such interesting people	unas personas tan interesantes
such a long time ago	hace tanto tiempo

sue *v*

to sue sb for damages	demandar a uno por daños y perjuicios
to sue for divorce	presentar demanda de divorcio/ solicitar el divorcio

suggest *v*/**suggestion** *n*

to suggest	sugerir
to suggest to sb that ...	sugerir/proponer a alguien que...
I suggest you go alone.	Sugiero/Propongo que vayas solo(a). *[Note: use of subjunctive]*
[to advise]	aconsejar/indicar
What are you suggesting?	¿Qué es lo que insinúas/ pretendes?
suggestion	una sugerencia
an immoral suggestion	una idea inmoral
There is no suggestion of treason.	No hay indicio de traición/Nada indica la traición.

suit *n*

[man's]	un traje/un flux *[Ven]*
[woman's]	un conjunto
[cards]	un palo
[legal]	un pleito/un litigio/un proceso
to bring a suit against sb for sth	entablar una demanda contra alguien por algo

suit *v*

to suit *[arrangements, etc.]*	convenir/gustar
Does Friday suit you?	¿Le conviene el viernes?
to suit *[clothes, colors]*	sentar a/ir bien a
That dress suits you.	Ese vestido te sienta/va bien.
Those colors do not suit her.	Esos colores no le sientan bien.

suitable *adj*

suitable	adecuado(a)/apropiado(a)/conveniente

You must wear suitable clothes.
Tomorrow is quite suitable.
This film is not suitable for children.

Debes llevar ropa apropiada.
Mañana me conviene muy bien.
Esta película no es apta para menores.

suitcase n
a suitcase

una maleta/una valija [Arg]

supply v
to supply sth
They supplied us with the
  spare parts/facts/information.

facilitar/proporcionar
Nos facilitaron los repuestos/los
  datos/la información.

support v
physically
Six columns support the roof.

apoyar/sostener
Seis columnas sostienen el tejado./El
  tejado descansa sobre seis columnas.

financially
He has to support two families.
I cannot support myself.

mantener/sustentar
Tiene que mantener dos familias.
No puedo mantenerme.

to favor
Which party/proposal/team do
  you support?
I support [I'm a fan of] the Mets.

apoyar
¿Qué partido/propuesta/equipo
  apoyas?
Soy hincha de los "Mets."

suppose v
to suppose
I suppose so/not.
to be supposed to
He is supposed to meet them at
  the airport.
You're supposed to be in bed.
They're supposed to be in Peru.

suponer
Supongo que sí/no.
deber
Debe recibirlos en el
  aeropuerto.
Deberías estar en la cama.
Dicen que están en el Perú.

suspect v
to suspect
I suspect you of having stolen it.
I suspected as much!

sospechar
Sospecho que lo has robado.
¡Ya me lo figuraba!

suspicious adj
causing suspicion
Her behavior was suspicious.

sospechoso(a)
Su conducta fue sospechosa.

feeling suspicion
I'm suspicious about that.

receloso(a)
Me recelo de eso./Tengo sospechas
  acerca de eso.

swear v/**swearword** n
to swear an oath
to be sworn in
[to curse]
a swearword

prestar juramento/jurar
prestar juramento
jurar/blasfemar
un taco/una palabrota

sweet adj
[naturally sweet]
These grapes are sweet.
[sweetened]

dulce
Estas uvas son dulces.
azucarado(a)

208

a sweetened drink	una bebida azucarada
My coffee is too sweet.	Mi café tiene demasiado azúcar.
[good-natured]	amable/dulce
That's very sweet of you!	¡Eres muy amable!

Ø **el dulce** means "brown sugar" in Central America, Colombia, and Venezuela. Elsewhere **el azúcar negro** is used.

swim *v*

to swim	nadar
to swim across a lake/river	pasar un lago/río a nado
to swim [as a sport]	practicar la natación

swimming pool *n*

una alberca [LA]/una piscina [Sp]

Ø **una alberca** would mean "cistern" to a Spaniard.

to switch off *v*

[electrical apparatus, TV, radio, etc.]	apagar
to switch off the engine	apagar el motor
to switch off the light	apagar la luz

to switch on *v*

[electrical apparatus, TV, radio, etc.]	encender/conectar/poner
to switch on the engine	poner en marcha el motor
to switch on the light	encender la luz

sympathetic *adj*

[showing pity]	compasivo(a)/compadecido(a)
to be sympathetic to sb	compadecerse de alguien/estar compasivo(a) con alguien
[kind]	amable/benévolo(a)

Ø **simpático** means "nice," "good-natured."

sympathize *v*

[in someone's troubles]	compadecerse/condolerse/sentirlo por
I sympathize with the victims.	Me compadezco con las víctimas./ Lo siento por las víctimas.
[on a bereavement]	dar el pésame
I sympathize with you on your son's death.	Te doy el pésame por la muerte de tu hijo.
[to understand]	comprender/entender
I sympathize with your point of view, but ...	Comprendo tu punto de vista, pero...

Ø **simpatizar** means "to get along very well with somebody."

sympathy *n*

[pity, compassion]	la compasión/la condolencia
[kindness]	la amabilidad/la benevolencia
[on a bereavement]	el pésame
to express sympathy	dar el pésame

Ø **la simpatía** means "liking," "affection."

T

table *n*

table   una mesa
table *[Math]*   una tabla
to set the table   poner la mesa

Ø **una tabla** also means "plank," "board."

tablet *n*

[medical]   un comprimido/una tableta

take *v*

in general   tomar/llevar
to take the bus/train, etc.   tomar el tren/el autobús, etc.

to take sb somewhere   llevar a alguien a un sitio/ acompañar
                        a alguien a un sitio

A taxi took me to the station.   Un taxi me llevó a la estación.
He took us to the hospital.   Nos acompañó al hospital.

to take sth somewhere   llevar algo a un sitio
I took my suit to the dry cleaner's.   Llevé el traje a la tintorería.

to take sth from sb   quitar algo a alguien
They took his wallet from him.   Le quitaron su cartera.

other
to take a photograph   sacar una foto(grafía)
to take a walk   dar un paseo
to take a drive/ride   dar un paseo en coche
to take a trip   hacer un viaje
to take an exam   hacer un examen/presentarse a un examen
to take a seat   sentarse
to take after   parecerse a

take in *v*

to take sth in   entrar algo a un sitio
Take the cases in!   ¡Entra las maletas!
to take in a garment   achicar una prenda
[a person]   hacer pasar
I took him into the kitchen.   Le hizo pasar a la cocina.

take off *v*

to take off *[objects]*   quitar/sacar
I took the book off the shelf.   Saqué el libro del estante.
He took off the lid.   Quitó la tapa.
to take off *[clothes]*   quitarse
You must take off your hat.   Debes quitarte el sombrero.
to take off *[aircraft]*   despegar
The plane took off for Havana.   El avión despegó para La Habana.

take out *v*

He took some money out of his   Sacó dinero de su bolsillo.
   pocket.
I took out the garbage.   Boté/Saqué la basura.

They take the children/dog out every day. — Llevan de paseo a los niños/al perro todos los días.

take place *v*
to take place — tener lugar
The game took place yesterday. — El partido tuvo lugar ayer.

take up/down *v*
to take up/down — subir/bajar
I'll take the suitcases up/down. — Voy a subir/bajar las maletas.

take time *v*
Take your time! — ¡No hay prisa!/¡Hazlo con calma!
to take time to do sth — tardar en hacer algo/demorarse en hacer algo *[LA]*
He'll take a long time to do that. — Tardará mucho en hacer eso.

tall
tall — alto(a)
My brother is very tall. — Mi hermano es muy alto.
He's six feet tall. — Mide seis pies.
How tall are you? — ¿Cuánto mides?
How tall is the tower? — ¿Cuántos metros de alto/altura tiene la torre?
The tower is 20 meters tall. — La torre tiene 20 metros de alto/altura.

tape *n & v*
[general, sewing, sport] — una cinta
Scotch tape — la cinta adhesiva
recording tape — una cinta de grabación/una cinta magnetofónica
cassette tape — una casete
tape measure — una cinta métrica
to tape record — grabar en cinta
tape recorder — un magnetofón/un magnetófono
tape recording — una grabación en cinta

taste *v*
to taste — probar
Would you like to taste the wine? — ¿Quieres probar el vino?
It tastes nice. — Está bueno(a)/rico(a)/sabroso(a).
to taste of/like — saber a
It tastes of/like raspberries. — Sabe a frambuesas.

taste *n*
[flavor] — un sabor
a taste of honey — un sabor a miel
[style, manners] — el buen gusto
She has good taste. — Tiene buen gusto.
She has good taste in clothes. — Tiene gusto para vestir.
in good taste — de buen gusto

teach *v*
to teach — enseñar
to teach sb to do sth — enseñar a alguien a hacer algo
He taught me to play the piano. — Me enseñó a tocar el piano.

teacher

I teach English.	Enseño inglés./Soy profesor(a) de inglés.

teacher *n*
[general, high school,
  college, university]   un(a) profesor(a)
[primary school]   un(a) maestro(a)

telephone *[see phone]*

television *n*

to be on television	estar en la televisión
to watch television	mirar/ver la televisión *[Note: use of definite article]*
What's on television?	¿Qué ponen en la televisión?
TV *[familiar]*	la tele
color television	la televisión en colores
TV channel	el canal de televisión
TV program	una emisión
TV remote control	el telemando
TV screen	la pantalla
TV set	un televisor/un aparato de televisión
to switch off the TV	apagar la televisión
to switch on the TV	prender *[LA]*/encender la televisión

tell *v*

[general]	decir
to tell the truth	decir la verdad
to tell sb to do sth	decir a alguien que haga algo/ mandar a alguien hacer algo
Tell him to set the table.	Dile que ponga la mesa./Mándale poner la mesa.
to tell sb a story	contar una historia a alguien

temperature *n*

temperature	la temperatura
The temperature yesterday was 50 degrees.	Registró ayer una temperatura de cincuenta grados.
[medical]	una fiebre/una calentura
to have/run a temperature	tener calentura
I've got a temperature of 102.	Tengo calentura de treinta y nueve grados centígrados.

Ø **tener calentura** means "to be in heat" in Chile, so it is advisable there to use **tener fiebre**.

tend *v*

to tend to	tender a/inclinarse a/tener tendencia a
She tends to travel a lot.	Se inclina a viajar mucho.

test *n*

[scientific]	una prueba/un ensayo
[school, college]	un examen/un test
a driving test	un examen de conducción
[medical]	una prueba/un análisis
a blood test	un análisis de sangre
I had a blood test.	Me hicieron un análisis de sangre.

an eye test   un examen para graduar la vista
*[see also **exam**]*

than   *conj*
He speaks Spanish better than you.   Habla castellano mejor que tú.
They have more money than us.   Tienen más dinero que nosotros.
*[see also **more**]*

thank   *v*
to thank sb for sth   agradecer algo a alguien/ dar
     las gracias a alguien por algo
I thanked her for the present.   Le agradecí el regalo./Le di las
     gracias por el regalo.
I thanked them for coming.   Les agradecí el haber venido./
     Les di las gracias por haber venido.

Thanks/Thank you.   Gracias.
Thank you very much.   Muchas gracias.
Thank goodness!   ¡Menos mal!

that   *conj*
[introducing a clause]   que
He said (that) he would come.   Dijo que vendría.
I think (that) it's raining.   Creo que está lloviendo.
I hope you are right.   Espero que tengas razón.

Ø Although the conjunction "that" is frequently omitted in English, you may not omit **que** in Spanish.

that   *dem pron & adj*
adjective

	masculine	feminine
	ese	esa
	aquel	aquella

I like that picture.   Me gusta ese cuadro.
My wife prefers that picture   Mi esposa prefiere aquel cuadro.
(over there).
He likes that house.   Le gusta esa casa.
We prefer that house (over   Preferimos aquella casa.
there).   *[Note: **aquel/aquella** refer to*
     things that are further away.]

pronoun

	masculine	feminine	neuter
	ése	ésa	eso
	aquél	aquélla	aquello

Which car do you like most?   ¿Qué coche le gusta más? ¿Ése
   That one or that one (over there)?   o aquél?
Which shirt do you prefer?   ¿Qué camisa prefieres? Ésa o
   That one or that one (over   aquélla? *[Note: There is an*
   there)?   *accent on the pronouns.]*
I don't understand that.   No entiendo eso.
     *[Note: The neuter forms **eso** and **aquello***
     refer not to concrete objects or people but
     to whole concepts or ideas.]

Ø **aquél/aquélla** are used to translate "the former," as in **Aquél fue a España, éste fue a México.** "The former went to Spain, the latter went to Mexico."

that   *rel pron*

	que *[subject and object]*
	lo que *[neuter]*
the box that is on the table	la caja que está en la mesa
the film (that) I saw	la película que vi
all (that) I want	todo lo que quiero
[with prepositions]	que/el cual/la cual/los cuales/las cuales/el que/la que/los que/las que
It's the garden (that) there is a palm tree in.	Es el jardín en el cual/en el que hay una palmera.
That's the table (that) I put the money on.	Ésa es la mesa sobre la cual/la que puse el dinero.
Are they the binoculars (that) he was looking through?	¿Son los anteojos por los cuales/los que miraba?
I'm talking about the houses (that) there was a lake behind.	Hablo de las casas detrás de las cuales/las que había un lago.

Ø Although the pronoun "that" is frequently omitted in English, you may not omit **que, el cual, la cual, los cuales, las cuales, el que, la que, los que, las que** in Spanish.

the   *art*

	el *[masc sing]*	la *[fem sing]*
	los *[masc pl]*	las *[fem pl]*
He gave a tip to the waiter.	Dio una propina al mesero. *[Note: **a + el = al**]*	
the months of the year	los meses del año *[Note: **de + el = del**]*	

the one/the ones/those   *dem pron*

	el que/la que/los que/las que
Which book? – The one (that is) on the shelf.	¿Qué libro – El que está en el estante.
Which tie? – The one (that) I bought yesterday.	¿Qué corbata? – La que compré ayer.
Which horses? – The ones (that are) in the corral.	¿Qué caballos? – Los que están en el corral.
Which rings? – The ones (that) she showed us.	¿Qué sortijas? – Las que nos mostró.
It's the one I was talking about.	Es el/la de que hablaba.

their   *adj*

[singular: masc & fem]	su
[plural: masc & fem]	sus
Have you seen their house?	¿Has visto su casa?
They invited their relatives and friends.	Invitaron a sus parientes y a sus amigos. *[Note: adjective repeated.]*

Ø As **su** can also mean "his," "her," "its," and "your," you can add **de ellos/de ellas** after the noun if the meaning is not entirely clear, e.g., **su casa de ellos/ellas** "their house."

theirs   *pron*

[singular]	el suyo/la suya
[plural]	los suyos/las suyas
Is this your car? – No, it's theirs.	¿Es éste su coche? – No, es suyo. *[Note: The definite article is omitted after the verb **ser**.]*
I don't like your house. I prefer theirs.	No me gusta tu casa. Prefiero la suya.

Ø As **suyo/a/os/as** could also mean "his," "hers," or "yours," you can replace them with **de ellos/de ellas** if there is any chance of confusion, e.g., "It's theirs". **Es de ellos/de ellas**.

them pron

[direct object: masculine]	los/les [Note: **Los** is far more common than **les** in Latin America; **les** is frequently used in Spain.]
[direct object: feminine]	las
[indirect object] to them	les
[disjunctive]	ellos/ellas/sí
Do you know them?	¿Los/Les/Las conoces?
Did you lend them the car?	¿Les prestaste el coche?
Yes, I lent it to them.	Sí, se lo presté. [Note: When **les** is followed by **lo, la, los** or **las** it changes to **se**.]
	Sí, se lo presté a ellos/ellas. [Note: As **se** has so many possible meanings you can add **a ellos/a ellas** after the verb to stress that here it means "to them."]
Do you remember them?	¿Te acuerdas de ellos/ellas?
They looked around them.	Miraron alrededor de sí. [Note: **Sí** is used instead of **ellos** or **ellas** as it refers to the same person as the subject of the verb.]
They took the money with them.	Llevaron el dinero consigo. [Note: the special form of **sí** used after **con**.]

themselves [see self]

then adv
at that time

	entonces/por entonces/en ese momento/en aquella época
until then	hasta entonces
since then	desde entonces
I didn't go to bed then.	No me acosté entonces.
He was working in Lima then.	En aquella época trabajaba en Lima.
Then it began to rain.	En ese momento comenzó a llover.

next, afterwards

	luego/después
Then he had lunch and then he went back to the office.	Luego comió y después volvió a la oficina.

then conj

Well then, let's go.	Pues bien, vamos.
Well in that case, I'll stay.	Pues, en ese caso, quedaré.
What do you want then?	Pues, ¿qué quieres?/¿Qué quieres entonces?

there adv

there	allí/allá/ahí
There it is.	Allí está.
They're going there tomorrow.	Van allí mañana.
It's down/over there.	Está allá.
It's there, in front of you.	Está ahí, delante de ti.
right there	allí mismo
there is/are	hay
There is nobody on the beach.	No hay nadie en la playa.
There are no tomatoes.	No hay jitomates.

215

there was/were	había
there will be	habrá

these *dem pron & adj*
adjective

	masculine	feminine
	estos	estas
I like these hats.	Me gustan estos sombreros.	
He's going to buy these ties.	Va a comprar estas corbatas.	

pronoun

	masculine	feminine
	éstos	éstas
Which shoes do you like most?	¿Qué zapatos te gustan más? –	
– I like these (ones).	Me gustan éstos.	
Which boots do you prefer?	¿Qué botas prefieres? – Prefiero	
– I prefer these (ones)	éstas. *[Note: There is an accent on* ***éstos/éstas*** *when they are pronouns.]*	

Ø **éstos/éstas** are used to translate "the latter," as in **Aquéllos fueron a España, éstos fueron a México.** "The former went to Spain, the latter went to Mexico."

they *pron*

they	ellos/ellas
They are strangers.	Son forasteros.
They cannot come, but their friends can.	Ellos no pueden venir, pero sus amigos sí. *[Note:* ***Ellos/Ellas*** *like all the other subject pronouns, are usually omitted; they are used for emphasis and clarification.]*

Ø **Ellos/Ellas** can also mean "them" following a preposition, e.g., "It's for them" is translated by **Es para ellos/ellas**.

thin *adj*

thin	flaco(a) *[LA]*/delgado(a)
to get thin	adelgazar

thing *n*
general

What a strange thing!	¡Qué cosa tan rara!

object

	una cosa/un objeto/un artículo
a thing of value	un objeto de valor
[belongings, possessions]	las cosas
They have some lovely things.	Tienen unas cosas bellas.
Where shall I put my things?	¿Dónde pongo mis cosas?

matter, circumstance

	una cosa/un asunto/lo + adjective
It's quite an important thing.	Es un asunto bastante importante.
the main/most important thing	lo más importante/lo esencial
the best/worst thing	lo mejor/peor
How are things?	¿Qué tal?

think *v*
general

	pensar
He thinks a lot.	Piensa mucho.

to think of doing sth

	pensar hacer algo
I'm thinking of going to Spain.	Pienso ir a España.

to think about sth/sb

	pensar en algo/alguien

What are you thinking about?	¿En qué piensas?
I'm thinking about the vacation.	Pienso en las vacaciones.
She's thinking about her son.	Piensa en su hijo.
to have an opinion about	pensar de/parecer
What did you think of the film?	¿Qué pensaste de la película?/ ¿Qué te pareció la película?
I thought it was very good.	Pensé que fue muy buena./Me pareció muy buena.
to believe	creer
Do you think he'll come?	¿Crees que vendrá?
I think so./I don't think so.	Creo que sí./Creo que no.

third *adj*

the third turning on the right	la tercera bocacalle a la derecha
the third world	el tercer mundo [Note: **Tercero** becomes **tercer** before a noun.]
a third	una tercera parte/un tercio
He only won a third of the votes.	Sólo ganó un tercio de los votos.
third party insurance	el seguro contra tercera persona

thirst *n* /**thirsty** *adj*

thirst	la sed
to be very thirsty	tener mucha sed
to get thirsty	empezar a tener sed

this *dem pron & adj*
adjective

masculine	feminine
este	esta

I like this book.	Me gusta este libro.
He's going to buy this house.	Va a comprar esta casa.

pronoun

masculine	feminine	neuter
éste	ésta	eso

Which car do you like most? – I like this one.	¿Qué coche te gusta más? – Me gusta éste.
Which skirt do you prefer? – I prefer this one.	¿Qué falda prefieres? – Prefiero ésta. [Note: There is an accent on **éste**/**ésta** when they are pronouns.]
I don't understand this.	No entiendo esto. [Note: The neuter form **esto** refers not to concrete objects or people but to whole concepts or ideas.]

Ø **éste/ésta** are used to translate "the latter," as in **Aquél fue a España, éste fue a México.** "The former went to Spain, the latter went to Mexico."

those *dem pron & adj*
adjective

masculine	feminine
esos	esas
aquellos	aquellas

I like those gloves.	Me gustan esos guantes.
My wife prefers those gloves (over there).	Mi esposa prefiere aquellos guantes.
He likes those flowers.	Le gustan esas flores.
We prefer those flowers (over there).	Preferimos aquellas flores. [Note: **aquellos/aquellas** refer to things that are further away.]

pronoun

masculine	feminine
ésos	ésas
aquéllos	aquéllas

Which lemons do you want?   ¿Qué limones quieres? ¿Ésos o
  Those (ones) or those over there?   aquéllos?
Which oranges are you buying?   ¿Qué naranjas compras? ¿Ésas o
  Those (ones) or those over   aquéllas? *[Note: There is an*
there?   *accent on the pronouns.]*

Ø **aquéllos/aquéllas** are used to translate "the former," as in **Aquéllos fueron a España, éstos fueron a México.** "The former went to Spain, the latter went to Mexico."

thousand   *n*
a/one thousand dollars   mil dólares *[Note: no article]*
ten thousand pesos   diez mil pesos

thousands   *n*
There are thousands of them.   Hay miles de ellos.

through   *prep*
place   por/a través de/de un lado a otro de
They ran through the fields.   Corrieron por los campos.
I got in through the front door.   Entré por la puerta principal.

time   hasta/durante
(from) Monday through Friday   desde el lunes hasta el viernes
all through January   durante enero
all through the night   durante la noche entera *[Note:*
     por la noche *means "in the night".]*

means   por/por medio de/debido a/gracias a
Through not knowing the rules,   Por no saber las reglas, perdió
  he lost the game.   el partido.
She got the job through her   Consiguió el puesto debido a/
  sister.   gracias a su hermana.
Through her I learned that you   Por ella supe que iban a casarse.
  were getting married.

other
I'm through. *[finished]*   He terminado.
She's through with him.   Ha roto con él.

throughout   *prep*
place   por todo/por todas partes de
throughout the State   por todo el Estado
throughout Venezuela   por todas partes de Venezuela

time   durante todo/en todo
throughout the year   durante todo el año
throughout my life   durante/en toda mi vida

ticket   *n*
[travel]   un boleto *[LA]*/un billete *[Sp]*
[theater, movies, show, game]   una entrada/una localidad
[plane/boat]   un pasaje *[LA]*/un billete *[Sp]*
a one-way ticket   un boleto/billete de ida
a round-trip ticket   un boleto de ida y regreso/un
     billete de ida y vuelta

season ticket *[rail]*	un boleto de abono
season ticket *[theater, sport]*	un abono de temporada
ticket office/window *[rail]*	una boletería *[LA]*/una taquilla
	[Sp]/un despacho de billetes
complimentary ticket	una entrada de favor
parking ticket	una multa (por aparcamiento indebido)

tidy *adj*

The house is not very tidy.	La casa no está muy ordenada.
He's a very tidy person.	Es una persona muy ordenada.
She has very tidy hair.	Tiene el pelo bien arreglado.
[clean]	limpio(a)

tidy *v*

to tidy sth	arreglar/poner en orden/limpiar algo
to tidy one's hair	arreglarse el pelo
to tidy away one's things	poner sus cosas en su sitio/
	devolver sus cosas a su lugar
to tidy up	arreglar las cosas/ponerlo todo en orden

till *[see until]*

time *n*
in general

	el tiempo
to find/have time for	tener tiempo para
to have plenty of time	tener tiempo de sobra
Time flies.	El tiempo vuela.
on time	a/con tiempo
full-time	de plena dedicación/de jornada completa
part-time	de media jornada/de dedicación parcial
to have a good time	pasarlo bien/divertirse
Have a good time!	¡Que lo pases bien!

by the clock

	la hora
What time is it?/What's the time?	¿Qué hora es?
It's time to leave.	Ya es hora de salir.
at this time of day	a esta hora

occasion

	la vez
this time	esta vez
the first/last/next time	la primera/última/próxima vez
for the first/last time	por primera/última vez
at times	a veces
each/every time	cada vez
many times	muchas veces
several times	varias/algunas veces
sometimes	unas veces
from time to time	de vez en cuando

historical period

	la época/los tiempos
at the time of the Incas	en la época/en los tiempos de los incas
At that time we lived in Italy.	En esta época vivimos en Italia.

period of time

	el período/el plazo/el tiempo/el rato
a long time	mucho tiempo
a long time ago	hace mucho tiempo
a short time	poco tiempo/un rato
a short time ago	hace poco

in a short time	en breve
spare time	ratos libres/horas libres
extra time *[sport]*	la prórroga
point of time	un momento
at the present time	en este momento/en la actualidad/ actualmente
any time	en cualquier momento
at the/that time	por entonces/en aquel entonces
at the same time	al mismo tiempo/a la vez
season	la estación
at this time of the year	en esta estación del año

tin *n*
[metal]	el estaño
It's made of tin.	Es de estaño.
tinplate	la hojalata

tip *n*
[a gratuity]	una propina
[advice]	un consejo/un aviso
[horse racing]	una información/un pronóstico

tire *n*
a tire	una llanta *[LA]*/un caucho *[Ven]*/una goma *[Arg & Uru]*/un neumático *[Sp]*/una cubierta *[Sp]*

tired *adj*
to be tired	estar cansado(a)
to tire/get tired	cansarse
to be tired of *[fed up]*	estar harto(a) de
I'm tired of watching TV.	Estoy harto(a) de mirar la televisión.

to *prep*
direction, destination
	a
He went to Africa/Spain/Lima.	Fue a Africa/España/Lima.
She went to the market/the hairdresser's.	Fue al mercado/a la peluquería.
	[Note: a + el = al]
They went to Marta's.	Fueron a casa de Marta.
the road to Guadalajara	la carretera de Guadalajara
the train to Mérida	el tren de Mérida/con destino Mérida

in order to
	para
I need some money to pay her.	Necesito dinero para pagarle.

with an infinitive
To see is to believe.	Ver es creer.
I want to buy a car.	Quiero comprar un coche.
They went to see her.	Fueron **a** verla.
He forgot to pay the bill.	Se olvidó **de** pagar la cuenta.

other
to be kind to sb	ser amable **con** alguien
How kind of them to take it!	¡Qué amables han sido **en** llevarlo!

today *adv*
today	hoy
[at the present time]	hoy día/hoy en día

a week/fortnight today	de hoy en ocho/quince días

together *adv*

They worked together.	Trabajaban juntos.
All together now!	¡Todos juntos!/¡Todos a la vez!
We were all together in the bar.	Estábamos todos reunidos en el bar.
a get-together	una reunión/una fiesta

toilet *n*

[at home]	el baño/el excusado/el retrete
[public]	los servicios/los baños

tomato *n*

tomato	un jitomate [Mex]/un tomate

too *adv*

also, in addition también

You too? – Yes, me too.	¿Tú también? – Sí, yo también. [Note: The subject pronouns are used.]

too, too much demasiado

This coffee is too cold.	Este café está demasiado frío.
You drink too much.	Bebes demasiado.

top *n*

[of list, table, page]	la cabeza
[of tree]	la copa
[surface]	la superficie
[of bottle]	el tapón/la tapa
at the top of page eight	a la cabeza de la página ocho
at the top of the hill	en la cumbre/cima de la colina
at the top of the stairs/tree	en lo alto de la escalera/del árbol
from top to bottom	de arriba abajo
at top speed	a toda velocidad

topic *n*/**topical** *adj*

topic of conversation	un asunto
essay topic	el tema
a topical issue	un asunto actual/corriente/de interés actual

tour *n & v*

[of country, region]	un viaje/un viaje de turismo/una excursión
[of building, exhibition]	una visita
conducted tour	una excursión con guía/una visita en grupo
package tour	un viaje con todo incluido
[by actors, musicians, sports teams]	una gira
to tour/make a tour of	viajar por/recorrer/visitar
They are touring Costa Rica.	Viajan por/Recorren Costa Rica.
We toured the factory/palace.	Visitamos la fábrica/el palacio.
The team is on a tour of Mexico.	El equipo está de gira en México.
My friends are on tour.	Mis amigos están de viaje.
We're touring.	Hacemos viajes de turismo.
The Tour of France [cycling]	La Vuelta a Francia
a tour of duty	un turno de servicio

toward(s) *prep*
place, time — hacia
towards Toledo — hacia Toledo
towards three o'clock — hacia las tres

feelings — con/para con
My feelings towards her have changed. — Mis sentimientos para con ella han cambiado.

town *n*
[large town, city] — una ciudad
[small, country town] — un pueblo/una población
to go to town — ir a la ciudad
I live in town. — Vivo en la ciudad.
She's out of town. — Está fuera/de viaje.
Let's go downtown. — Vamos al centro.

trade *n*
[calling, occupation] — el oficio
He's a plumber by trade. — Es de oficio plomero/fontanero.
[business] — el negocio
[industry] — la industria
foreign trade — el comercio exterior
[craft] — la artesanía

traffic *n*
[transportation] — el tráfico/la circulación/el tránsito [LA]
The traffic is heavy/light. — Hay muchos/pocos coches.
rush-hour traffic — la circulación de la hora punta
two-way traffic — la doble circulación
one-way traffic — la dirección única/el sentido único/una mano [Arg]/el tránsito [Chi]/una vía [Col]
traffic circle — una glorieta/un cruce giratorio/un redondel
traffic jam — un embotellamiento/un atasco
traffic lights — las luces de tráfico/el semáforo
traffic sign — una señal de tráfico
[drugs] — el tráfico
drug traffic — el tráfico de narcóticos

train *v intrans*
to train for *[sport]* — entrenarse para
I'm training for the Olympics. — Me entreno para los Juegos Olímpicos.
to train for a profession — seguir un curso de formación profesional/cursar sus estudios

train *v trans*
to train an athlete — entrenar a un(a) atleta
to train an animal — amaestrar un animal
to train sb for a job/profession — preparar a alguien para un puesto/una profesión

training *n*
[sports] — el entrenamiento/la preparación
physical training — la gimnasia/la cultura física
to be in training — estar entrenado(a)/en forma
[professional] — la formación

transfer *v*
[to a new position/place]   trasladarse
The company transferred to Bogotá.   La empresa se trasladó a Bogotá.
I was transferred to Quito.   Me trasladaron a Quito.
[to a new course]   cambiar a otra asignatura
[transportation]   transbordar/hacer transbordo
The passengers must transfer   Los pasajeros deben transbordar/
   in Córdoba.   hacer transbordo en Córdoba.
Martín has been transferred to   Martín se ha traspasado al Real
   Real Madrid.   Madrid.

Ø **trasladarse** is used in many parts of Latin America to mean "to move house."

translate *v*
to translate from Spanish to   traducir del castellano al inglés
   English
Translate into German.   Traduce al alemán.

transportation *n*
[in general]   el transporte
public transportation   los transportes colectivos/públicos
means of transportation   el medio de transporte

Ø **la transportación** exists but is not used a great deal.

trash *[see garbage]*

tray *n*
a tray   un charol *[Mex]*/una bandeja *[Sp]*

treat *n & v*
to pay for sb   convidar/invitar
He's treating us to dinner.   Nos ha convidado a cenar.
It's my treat.   Invito yo.

medical
to treat patients   atender/tratar a enfermos(as)
He is being treated for 'flu.   Le tratan para la gripe.

personal relations
They treated me very well.   tratar a alguien
    Me trataron muy bien.

Ø **tratar de** means "to try to."

trip *n*
a business trip   un viaje de negocios
to take a trip   hacer un viaje
[see also tour]

trouble *n*
difficulty, problem   la dificultad/el inconveniente
What's the trouble?   ¿Qué pasa?/¿Pasa algo?
to get into trouble   meterse en un lío
to be in trouble with the police.   tener dificultades con la policía.
The plane has engine trouble.   El avión tiene una avería del motor.

bother   la molestia/ladificultad/el esfuerzo
It's no trouble.   No es molestia./No cuesta nada.
It's not worth the trouble.   No vale la pena.

trouble

to take the trouble to do sth	tomarse/darse la molestia de hacer algo

medical

to have heart trouble	tener una enfermedad cardíaca

trouble *v*

I'm sorry to have to trouble you.	Lamento tener que molestarte.
Please don't trouble yourself!	¡No te molestes!/¡No se moleste!
	¡No te preocupes!/¡No se preocupe!

trunk *n*

[case]	un baúl [Col]/una cajuela [Mex]/ una maletera [Per]/ una maleta
[of car]	un portaequipaje(s)/un maletero
[of tree]	un tronco
[of elephant]	una trompa

try *v*

[make an effort]	esforzarse/hacer un esfuerzo
She tried very hard.	Hizo grandes esfuerzos.
[to attempt]	tratar/intentar
to try to do sth	tratar de/intentar/probar hacer algo
He'll try to help us.	Tratará de/Intentará ayudarnos.
[to taste]	probar
Would you like to try the wine?	¿Quiere usted probar el vino?
to try on [clothes]	probarse
I would like to try on the jacket.	Quisiera probarme la chaqueta.

tuition *n*

tuition fees	la matrícula

turn *n*

a turn to the left/right	una vuelta a la izquierda/derecha
Turn to the left.	Da una vuelta a la izquierda.
No right turn!	¡Prohibido girar a la derecha!
Whose turn is it?	¿A quién le toca?
It's my turn.	Me toca a mí.
by/in turns	por turnos/sucesivamente

Ø **el turno** means "turn of duty," "shift," e.g., **el turno de noche** means "the night shift."

turn on/off *v*

to turn on [electrical apparatus, TV, radio, etc.]	encender/conectar/poner
to turn on the engine	arrancar el motor/poner en marcha el motor
to turn on the light	encender la luz

turn round *v*

[car]	dar la vuelta (a un coche)
You must turn (the car) round here.	Tienes que dar la vuelta (al coche) aquí.
[person]	darse vuelta [LA]/voltearse [LA]/ volverse [Sp]
I turned round to see what was happening.	Me di la vuelta para ver lo que pasaba.

turnpike *n*

turnpike	una autopista de peaje

twenty one *adj*

twenty one   veintiun(o)/veintiuna
He's twenty one.   Tiene veintiún años. *[Note:*
                                        ***Veintiuno** becomes **veintiún**, with an*
                                        *accent added on the **u**, before a masculine*
                                        noun.]

How many girls are there? –   ¿Cuántas chicas hay? – Veintiuna.
  Twenty one.

twice *adv*

twice   dos veces
twice a day/week/month/year   dos veces el día/la semana/el mes
                                          /el año

type *n*

[kind]   un tipo
people of that type   gente de ese tipo
[character]   un tipo/un sujeto/un tío
What a strange type he is!   ¡Qué tío tan raro es!
[in printing]   un tipo/una letra/un carácter
bold/italic type   las letras negritas/cursivas

type *v*

to type   escribir a máquina/mecanografiar
typing   la mecanografía
typist   un(a) mecanógrafo(a)

typo *n*

[printing error]   una errata/un error de imprenta/
                                          un gazapo *[fam]*
[spelling error]   un error de ortografía
[typing error]   un error de mecanografía

U

U-boat *n*
a U-boat

un submarino alemán

ugly *adj*
[physical]
[figurative]
[dangerous]
an ugly situation
[unpleasant]
an ugly guy
to be in an ugly mood

feo(a)
peligroso(a)/feo(a)
peligroso(a)
una situación peligrosa
lamentable
un tipo de cuidado
estar de un humor de perros

un-
[negative prefix]

unable
unoccupied
unnatural
unkind
unambitious
unaccompanied
un-American

*[There are several different equivalents
in Spanish for the prefix **un-**.]*

incapaz
desocupado(a)
no natural
nada amistoso(a)
poco ambicioso(a)
sin compañía
antiamericano(a)

uncomfortable *adj*
[physical discomfort]
These clothes are
  uncomfortable.
I was very uncomfortable in
  that bed.
[ill at ease]
He looked very uncomfortable
  during the interview.
They made life uncomfortable
  for her.

incómodo(a)
Esta ropa es incómoda.

Me encontré muy incómodo(a) en
  esa cama.
inquieto(a)/molesto(a)
Pareció muy inquieto durante la
  entrevista.
Le crearon dificultades a ella.

under *prep*
[stationary]
He was sitting under the tree.
[involving motion]
We went under a bridge.
[under the rule of]
under the Aztecs
[less than]
the numbers under thirty
I finished it in under two
  hours
[according to]
under Article 5 of the
  Constitution
under my contract

bajo/debajo de
Estaba sentado debajo del árbol.
por debajo de
Pasamos por debajo de un puente.
bajo
bajo los aztecas
menos de/inferior a
los números menos de/inferior a treinta
Tardé menos de dos horas en
  acabarlo.
conforme a/según
conforme al Artículo 5 de la
  Constitución
según mi contrato

226

underneath *adv*

underneath	debajo
It's underneath.	Está debajo.
They went underneath.	Fueron por debajo.

unfortunate *adj*

person

	desgraciado(a)/desdichado(a)
They are most unfortunate.	Son muy desgraciados(as).
How unfortunate you were!	¡Qué mala suerte tuviste!

event

an unfortunate event	funesto(a)/desgraciado(a)
	un suceso desgraciado

regrettable

It's unfortunate that he cannot pay them.	Es de lamentar que no pueda pagarles. *[Note: subjunctive]*

comment, manner

I made an unfortunate remark.	infeliz/inoportuno(a)
	Hice una observación inoportuna.

unfortunately *adv*

unfortunately	por desgracia

unless *conj*

unless	a menos que *[+ subjunctive]*
	si no *[+ indicative]*
We will play tennis tonight unless it rains.	Jugaremos al tenis esta noche a menos que llueva.
Unless you tell him, he won't know anything.	Si no se lo dices, no sabrá nada.

unlike *prep*

unlike	a diferencia de
Unlike the others she's going to the theater.	A diferencia de los otros ella va al teatro.

until *conj*

until	hasta que *[+ subjunctive with future time; + indicative with past time]*
	hasta *[+ infinitive]*
I'll wait until she arrives.	Esperaré hasta que llegue.
I waited until she arrived.	Esperé hasta que llegó.
I walked for ten miles until I reached the river.	Caminé diez millas hasta llegar al río. *[Note: **Hasta** and the infinitive are used because the subject of both clauses is the same.]*

until *prep*

until	hasta
She waited until five o'clock.	Esperó hasta las cinco.

up *adv & prep*

up	arriba/por arriba
What was he doing up there?	¿Qué estaba haciendo allá arriba?
His house is further up the street.	Su casa está más allá en la calle.

verb + **up**

to be up	estar levantado(a)
to come/go up	subir

upset

to get up [from bed, a seat]	levantarse (de)/pararse [LA]
to get up [to stand]	ponerse de pie
to lift sb/sth up	levantar a alguien/algo
I went up the street.	Subí la calle.
He ran up the street.	Corrió calle arriba.
She ran up the stairs.	Subió las escaleras corriendo.
to run up bills	contraer deudas
to take/bring sth up	subir
Bring the suitcases up, please.	Haga el favor de subir las maletas.
It's up to you.	Te toca a ti.

upset adj
[physically]	trastornado(a)
She has an upset stomach.	Tiene el estómago trastornado.
He's feeling a little upset.	Siente indispuesto.
[mentally]	trastornado(a)/apurado(a)
Her mother was very upset.	Su madre estaba muy apurada.
He is easily upset.	Se apura por cualquier cosa.
[angry at]	enfadado(a)/disgustado(a) por
I was upset at his behavior.	Estaba enfadado(a) por su conducta.

upstairs adv
to go upstairs	ir arriba/subir la escalera
We sleep upstairs.	Dormimos en el piso superior.
the apartment upstairs	el apartamento de arriba

us pron
[direct object]	nos
[indirect object] to us	nos
[disjunctive, object of prepositions]	nosotros/nosotras
He saw us on the beach.	Nos vio en la playa.
They gave the clothes to us.	Nos dieron la ropa.
Give it to us!	¡Dánoslo!
Don't give them to us!	¡No nos los des!
These are for us.	Éstos son para nosotros/nosotras.

U.S. [United States] n
| the United States (US) | (los) Estados Unidos ([los] EE. UU.) |

use n
directions for use	el modo de empleo
to make use of sth	servirse de/utilizar algo
What use is that machine?	¿De qué sirve ese aparato?
Is that any use?	¿Sirve para algo?
It's no use.	No sirve para nada./Es inútil.
What's the use?	¿Para qué?
What's the use of doing that?	¿De qué sirve hacer eso?
Can I be of use?	¿Puedo ayudar?/¿Puedo servirle en algo?

use v
to use	usar/emplear/servirse de/utilizar
I used a knife to open it.	Empleé un cuchillo para abrirlo.
What word do you use in Greek?	¿Qué palabra usas en griego?
What's it used for?	¿Para qué sirve?
It's used for building.	Sirve para construir.

I could use a drink!	¡Qué sed tengo!/¡Me gustaría tomar algo!
I could use a holiday!	¡Qué bien me vendrían unas vacaciones!
A handkerchief was used as a bandage.	Se utilizó un pañuelo como venda. /Un pañuelo sirvió de venda.

used *v*
[to express regular actions in the past]

*[Use either the imperfect tense or the imperfect of the verb **soler** followed by the infinitive.]*

When I lived in Madrid I used to spend Sundays in the country.	Cuando vivía en Madrid, pasaba/ solía pasar los domingos en el campo.
They never used to arrive before ten.	Nunca llegaban/solían llegar antes de las diez.

used *adj*
accustomed to

acostumbrado(a) a

She's still not used to this climate.	Todavía no está acostumbrado(a) a este clima.
to get used to sth	acostumbrarse a algo
You must get used to his way of doing it.	Debes acostumbrarte a su modo de hacerlo.

second-hand

de segunda mano/de ocasión/ usado(a)

He sells used cars.	Vende coches de segunda mano.

Ø **usado(a)** often means "worn" or "worn out."

used up

agotado(a)

Their provisions are used up.	Sus provisiones están agotadas.

usual *adj*
usual

acostumbrado(a)/habitual

He went out at the usual time.	Salió a la hora acostumbrada.
as usual	como siempre/como de costumbre
What will you have? The usual? *[a drink, food]*	¿Qué vas a tomar? ¿Lo de siempre?

usually *adv*
usually

por lo general

He usually has a beer.	Por lo general toma una cerveza./ Suele tomar una cerveza. *[Note: the verb **soler** can also be used.]*

utility *n*
a public utility

una empresa de servicio público

V

vacancy n
[in hotel]
Do you have any vacancies?

"No vacancies"
We have no vacancies for May.

[see also **openings.**]

un cuarto/una habitación vacante
¿Hay algún cuarto vacante?/¿Tiene
  algo disponible?
"Completo"
Para mayo no hay nada disponible.
  /En mayo todo está lleno.

vacation n
vacation
to be on vacation
to take a vacation
to spend the summer vacation

las vacaciones [Note: usually plural]
estar de vacaciones/pasar las vacaciones
tomarse unas vacaciones
veranear

vain adj
[useless, fruitless]
in vain
My efforts were in vain.
[conceited]
Her sister is so vain.

vano(a)/inútil
en vano
Mis esfuerzos resultaron inútiles.
vanidoso(a)/presumido(a)
Su hermana es tan vanidosa.

valid adj
valid
It is a valid argument.
I have a valid ticket.
Your ticket is no longer valid.
[of laws]
That law is still valid.

válido(a)/valedero(a)
Es un argumento válido.
Tengo un boleto valedero.
Tu boleto ha caducado ya/ya no vale.
vigente
Esa ley es todavía vigente.

valuable adj
Is it valuable?
valuables

¿Vale mucho?/¿Tiene valor?
los objetos de valor

various adj
[different]
for various reasons
in various ways
[several]
Various prisoners have escaped.

diferentes/distintos(as)/diversos(as)
por diversas razones
de diversos modos
algunos(as)/varios(as)
Varios presos se han escapado.

verge n & v
[border, edge]
on the verge of
to be on the verge of doing sth
She was on the verge of tears.
to verge
He is verging to the left.

el borde/el margen
al borde de
estar a punto de hacer algo
Estaba a punto de echarse a llorar.
orientarse/inclinarse
Se orienta/inclina a la izquierda.

verse n
[poetry]

las poesías/los versos

230

He writes verse.	Escribe versos.
a verse of a poem	una estrofa
a line of verse	un verso

very *adv*

[with an adjective]	muy
very pleasant	muy agradable
[with a noun]	mucho(a)
It's very hot.	Hace mucho calor.
very much	muchísimo(a)
very many	muchísimos(as) *[Note: Do not use* ***muy*** *with* ***mucho.]***

vessel *n*

[ship]	una nave
[receptacle]	una vasija/un recipiente
blood vessel	un vaso sanguíneo

vested *adj*

vested	concedido(a)
a vested interest	un derecho adquirido/un interés personal
to have vested interests in a company	tener intereses en una empresa

video *n & v*

a video camera	una videocámara
a videocassette	un casete de vídeo/un videocasete
a videorecorder (VCR)	un vídeo/una videograbadora
a videorecording *[act]*	una videograbación
a videorecording *[object]*	un videograma
a videotape	una cinta de vídeo/una videocinta

visitor *n*

a visitor	un(a) visitante/una visita
[tourist, excursionist]	un(a) turista/un(a) excursionista
[see also ***guest]***	

vivid *adj*

[color, light]	intenso(a)
[imagination,impression, memory]	vivo(a)
[description]	gráfico(a)/enérgico(a)/pintoresco(a)

vulgar *adj*

[common]	común/corriente
[lacking refinement]	vulgar/ordinario(a)
[rude]	grosero(a)
a vulgar joke	un chiste verde
Don't be vulgar!	¡No seas grosero(a)!

W

wage   *n*
[*of worker*]
[*of employee*]
wage earner

el salario
el sueldo
un asalariado

wage   *v*
to wage a campaign
to wage war

emprender/proseguir una campaña
hacer guerra

wait   *v*
to wait
Wait a moment!
to wait for

esperar/aguardar
¡Espera un momento!
esperar [*Note: no preposition to
   translate "for"*]

I am waiting for the bus.
I've been waiting for my wife
   for ten minutes.
We'll wait until she returns.

Estoy esperando el autobús.
Hace diez minutos que espero a
   mi esposa.
Esperaremos hasta que vuelva.
   [*Note: subjunctive*]

to wait up
to wait at table
to wait on sb

velar/no acostarse
servir a la mesa
servir a alguien

waiter/waitress   *n*
a waiter

un garzón [*Arg & Uru*]/un mesero
   [*Col & Mex*]/un mesonero [*Ven*]/un mozo
   [*Bol & Per*]/un camarero[*Sp*]

a waitress

una garzona [*Arg & Uru*]/una
   mesera [*Col & Mex*]/una mesonera [*Ven*]/
   una moza [*Bol & Per*]/una camarera [*Sp*]

walk   *n & v*
in general
I was walking by the river.
She walks very slowly.
Can your child walk?
He has had an accident and
   cannot walk yet.

caminar/andar
Caminaba a orillas del río.
Camina muy despacio.
¿Sabe andar tu niño?
Ha sufrido un accidente y ya no
   puede andar.

to go for a walk
I went for a walk through the park.
Do you want to take a walk?

ir de paseo/dar un paseo
Fui de paseo por el parque.
¿Quieres dar un paseo/una vuelta?

as opposed to driving or riding
I prefer to walk to the office.
Let's walk.

ir a pie/andar
Prefiero ir a pie a la oficina.
Vamos a pie.

wall   *n*
[*exterior wall*]
the walls of the house
[*inside wall*]

un muro
los muros de la casa
una pared

There are pictures on the wall.	Hay cuadros en la pared.
[garden wall]	una tapia
[city wall]	una muralla
the old walls of Valencia	las antiguas murallas de Valencia

want υ

to want	querer/desear
I want two seats.	Quiero dos plazas.
He wants to go to Madrid.	Quiere ir a Madrid.
He wants us to go to Madrid.	Quiere que vayamos a Madrid.
	[Note: use of subjunctive]

Ø **querer** also means "to love," e.g., **Quiere a su esposa.** "He loves his wife."

warm adj

liquids, things

	caliente
The water is quite warm.	El agua está bastante caliente.
They need warm clothes.	Necesitan ropa caliente.
[lukewarm]	tibio(a)

climate

	cálido(a)
a warm climate	un clima cálido
[season, day]	caluroso(a)/de calor
a warm day/summer	un día/verano caluroso

of people

to be warm	tener calor
I'm very warm.	Tengo mucho calor.
to give sb a warm welcome	dispensar a alguien un recibimiento/
	una bienvenida caluroso(a)
warm-hearted	afectuoso(a)

of weather

to be warm	hacer calor
It's very warm here in the summer.	Hace mucho calor aquí en el verano.

warmly adv

[affectionately]	afectuosamente/cariñosamente
[cordially]	calurosamente
[enthusiastically]	con entusiasmo

wash υ

to wash sb/sth	lavar algo/a alguien
I must wash this shirt.	Debo lavar esta camisa.
She was washing the child's face.	Lavaba la cara al niño.
to wash (oneself)/have a wash	lavarse
I wash before breakfast.	Me lavo antes del desayuno.
She was washing her face.	Se lavaba la cara.
to wash the dishes	fregar los platos/lavar los platos [Arg & Uru]
the washing [dirty clothes]	la ropa sucia/la ropa para lavar
the washing [clean]	el tendido/la colada
a washing machine	una lavadora
a dishwasher	un lavaplatos

Ø **fregar** has obscene connotations in Argentina and Uruguay, so in those countries use **lavar** with **los platos.**

washbasin n

washbasin	un lavabo/un lavamanos [Bol, Ecu, Per]

233

waste

waste n & v

It's a waste of effort.

It's a waste of time.
[litter]
Waste! [sign on garbage cans]
to waste food
to waste money [to spend on
  unnecessary things]
[to squander money]
to waste time
a wastebasket

watch v

to watch a film/TV program
I didn't watch that program.
to watch closely
He doesn't play; he prefers to
  watch.
to watch over [look after]
I have to watch over the children.
to watch over [sick person]
Watch out!

way n
road, route
You will have to ask the way.
Which is the way to the
  station, please?
I showed them the way to the
  church.
on the way to Santiago
to go out of one's way
the way in/out
"No way through"
to go the wrong way
to make one's way to
She made her way to the hotel.

distance
a long way off
a short way off
Mérida is a long way from here.

direction
This way, please.
Which way are you going?
one-way [street, road]

manner
in this/that way

Do it this way!
way of life
You can do it any way you like.

Es un esfuerzo inútil/una pérdida
  de energía.
Es tiempo perdido/una pérdida de tiempo.
los desperdicios
¡Desperdicios!
desperdiciar la comida
gastar dinero

desperdiciar/malgastar dinero
perder/desperdiciar el tiempo
un cesto de los papeles/una papelera

ver una película/un programa
No vi ese programa.
mirar/observar/contemplar
No juega; prefiere mirar.

cuidar/vigilar
Tengo que cuidar a los niños.
velar
¡Cuidado!/¡Ojo!

un camino/una carretera
Tendrás que preguntar por el camino.
¿Por favor, qué camino tomo para
  ir a la estación?
Les indiqué el camino a la
  iglesia.
camino de Santiago
desviarse del camino
la entrada/salida
"Cerrado el paso"
equivocarse de camino
dirigirse a
Se dirigió al hotel.

a gran distancia/a lo lejos/muy lejos
a poca distancia/no muy lejos
Mérida está muy lejos de aquí.

Por aquí, por favor.
¿Por dónde vas?
dirección única/sentido único/una
  mano [Arg]/tránsito [Chi]/una vía [Col]

la manera/el modo
de esta/esa manera
de este/ese modo
¡Hazlo de esta manera/de este modo!
el estilo de vida
Puedes hacerlo de cualquier modo
  que te guste. [Note: subjunctive]

other
by the way

a propósito

we *pron*
we
we men
we women
They have no money; we have
plenty.

nosotros [masc]/nosotras [fem]
nosotros los hombres
nosotras las mujeres
Ellos no tienen dinero; nosotros
tenemos mucho. [Note: **nosotros/
nosotras,** like all the other subject
pronouns, are usually omitted; they are
used for emphasis and clarification.]

weather *n*
What's the weather like?
The weather is fine/bad.
The weather is hot/cold.
a weather forecast

a weather report

¿Qué tiempo hace?
Hace buen/mal tiempo.
Hace calor/frío.
un parte/boletín/pronóstico
meteorológico
un boletín meteorológico

wedding *n*
a wedding
silver/golden wedding
a wedding cake
the wedding day
a wedding dress
a wedding present
a wedding ring
to have a church/civil wedding
to have a quiet wedding

una boda/un casamiento/unas bodas
las bodas de plata/oro
una tarta/un pastel de boda
el día de boda
un traje de novia
un regalo de boda
un anillo de boda
casarse por la iglesia/por lo civil
casarse en la intimidad/en privado

week *n*
a week
two weeks
a week today
the weekend

una semana/ocho días
dos semanas/quince días
de hoy en ocho días
el fin de semana

weigh *v* /**weight** *n*
to weigh
What/How much do you weigh?
It weighs 100 kilos.
to lose weight
to put on weight

pesar
¿Cuánto pesas?
Pesa cien kilos.
adelgazar
engordar/hacerse más gordo(a)

welcome *adj*
Welcome on board! [plane]
Welcome to Chile!
You're always welcome here.
You're welcome. [response to
"thank you"]
You're welcome to use my car.
He's welcome to come with us.

¡Bienvenidos a bordo!
¡Bienvenido(a)(os)(as) a Chile!
Estás en tu casa./Está en su casa.
De nada./No hay de qué.

Mi coche está a tu disposición.
Puede acompañarnos.

welcome *n & v*
a welcome

una bienvenida

well

Welcome to Tijuana [sign]	Bienvenida a Tijuana
to welcome sb	dar la bienvenida a alguien
[to meet]	recibir
He welcomed us at the airport.	Nos recibió en el aeropuerto.
They gave me a warm welcome.	Me dispensaron una calurosa acogida.

well adv

successfully

	bien
They did it very well.	Lo hicieron muy bien.
He was always well dressed.	Siempre iba bien vestido.

concessive

Well, I'm not sure.	Pues, no estoy seguro(a).
well now	ahora bien
well then	pues bien
Well?	¿Y entonces?
Well then?	¿Y qué?
Well, I'll explain.	Bueno, te lo explicaré.

health

to be well	estar bien
to feel well	sentirse bien
I'm very well.	Estoy muy bien.
to get well	reponerse

what inter adj

What time is it?	¿Qué hora es?
What's the weather like?	¿Qué tiempo hace?
What records did you buy?	¿Qué discos compraste?
[see also which]	

what exclam

What/What a(n) ... !	¡Qué...!
What a character he is!	¡Qué tipo es!
What a fool you are!	¡Qué tonto(a) eres!
What a pity!	¡Qué lástima!
What!	¡Cómo!

what inter pron

What happened?	¿Qué pasó/sucedió?
What do you want?	¿Qué quieres?
What are you thinking about?	¿En qué piensas?
What did you dream about?	¿Con qué soñaste?
What are you afraid of?	¿De qué tienes miedo?
What else?	¿Qué más?
What is it?/What's this?	¿Qué es?/¿Qué es esto?
What are they?	¿Qué son?
What's it made of?	¿De qué es?
What is it like?	¿Cómo es?
What is your name?	¿Cómo te llamas?/¿Cómo se llama?
What? [I beg your pardon.]	¿Cómo?
Do you know what happened?	¿Sabes qué/lo que pasó?
Don't you know what he said?	¿No sabes qué/lo que dijo?

What is/are ... ?

What is your address?	¿Cuál es tu/su dirección?/¿Cuáles son tus/sus señas?

236

What is your address here in Quito?	¿Cuál es tu/su domicilio aquí en Quito?
What is your phone number?	¿Cuál es tu/su número de teléfono?
What is your first name?	¿Cuál es tu/su nombre de pila?
What is your surname?	¿Cuál es tu/su apellido?
What are your favorite films?	¿Cuáles son tus/sus películas preferidas?

what *rel pron*
[that which]

	lo que
That's not what I want.	Eso no es lo que quiero.
What I like most is chess.	Lo que me gusta más es el ajedrez.

whatever *adj*

whatever	cualquier *[sing]*/cualesquier *[pl]*
I'll wear whatever clothes I like.	Voy a ponerme cualquier ropa que me guste. *[Note: subjunctive]*
He'll pay for whatever books I need.	Pagará cualesquier libros que necesite. *[Note: subjunctive]*

whatever *pron*

Do whatever you like!	¡Haz todo lo que quieras!
Whatever it may be.	Sea lo que sea.
Whatever happens.	Pase lo que pase.
Whatever he says.	Diga lo que diga.
Whatever you see.	Cualquier cosa que veas. *[Note: subjunctive in the above examples]*
Whatever I have is yours.	Todo lo que tengo es tuyo.

when *adv & conj*

when	cuando
When it's sunny I go to the beach.	Cuando hace sol voy a la playa.
I'll go to bed when I'm tired.	Me acostaré cuando tenga sueño. *[Note: use of subjunctive when future time is referred to]*
When will you buy a new car?	¿Cuándo comprarás un coche nuevo? *[Note: accent on **cuándo** when it is a question]*
I asked him when he would go.	Le pregunté cuándo iría.

whenever *adv & conj*

Come whenever you like.	Ven cuando quieras. *[Note: subjunctive]*
Whenever that may be.	Cuando quiera que sea. *[Note: subjunctive]*
I visit them whenever I can.	Les visito cuando puedo.
Whenever he visited us he used to give me candy.	Cuando nos visitaba me daba caramelos.

where *adv*
interrogative

	¿dónde?
Where are you?	¿Dónde estás?
Where are you going?	¿Adónde vas?
Where are you from?	¿De dónde eres?
Where does the bus leave from?	¿De dónde sale el autobús?

wherever

relative

I go where I like.	Voy donde quiera. *[Note: subjunctive]*
That's the house where my father was born.	Ésa es la casa donde nació mi padre.

Ø Note the accent on **dónde** as an interrogative.

wherever   *adv*

Wherever I go my dog comes with me.	Dondequiera que vaya mi perro me acompaña. *[Note: subjunctive]*
Wherever they are you must find them.	Dondequiera que estén debes encontrarlos. *[Note: subjunctive]*

whether   *conj*

I asked him whether he could help us.	Le pregunté si podría ayudarnos.
Do you know whether the bus has left yet?	¿Sabes si el autobús ya ha salido?
I doubt whether she speaks Russian.	Dudo que hable ruso. *[Note: subjunctive after **dudar que**]*

which   *inter adj*

Which newspaper do you want?	¿Qué periódico quieres?
Which shoes did you buy?	¿Qué zapatos compraste?
*[see also **what**]*	

which (one)   *inter pron*

which one/which ones	cuál/cuáles
Which one do you prefer?	¿Cuál prefieres?
Which ones did you sell?	¿Cuáles vendiste?

which   *rel pron*

	que *[subject and object]*
	lo que *[neuter]*
The cat which killed the bird is mine.	El gato que mató al pájaro es mío.
The car (which) he drives is Italian.	El coche que conduce es italiano.
He went to visit his aunt, which pleased her greatly.	Fue a visitar a su tía, lo que le gustó muchísimo.
[with prepositions]	que/el cual/la cual/los cuales/las cuales/el que/la que/los que/las que
Those are the shops I was thinking about.	Ésas son las tiendas en las que pensaba.

Ø Although the pronoun "which" is frequently omitted in English, you may not omit **que, el cual, la cual, los cuales, las cuales, el que, la que, los que, las que** in Spanish.

Ø Most English speakers make little or no distinction between "that" and "which." Fortunately the Spanish forms cover both.

See also **that** *[rel pron]*.

whichever   *adj & pron*

You can have whichever hat you like.	Puedes tener cualquier sombrero que te guste. *[Note: subjunctive]*
Give her whichever of the books she wants.	Dale cualquier de los libros que quiera. *[Note: subjunctive]*

while *conj*
time

While I was in Spain, my dog died.

I'll do it while you are at the office.

mientras

Mientras estaba en España, murió el perro.

Lo haré mientras estés en la oficina. *[Note: subjunctive when future is referred to]*

whereas

She is studying French while her brother is studying physics.

mientras (que)

Ella estudia el francés mientras (que) su hermano estudia física.

concessive
[although]

While I think it is difficult I insist you do it.

aunque

Aunque pienso que es difícil, insisto en que lo hagas.

who/whom *inter pron*

Who?

Whom?

Who told you that?

Who are coming to the party?

Who(m) did you see?

Who(m) was he talking about?

¿Quién? *[sing]* ¿Quiénes? *[pl]*

¿A quién *[sing]* ¿A quiénes? *[pl]*

¿Quién te lo dijo eso?

¿Quiénes vienen a la fiesta?

¿A quién(es) viste?

¿De quién(es) hablaba?

who/whom *rel pron*

que *[subject]*
a quien/a quienes *[object]*

the man who was here yesterday

the man (whom) I saw

the women (whom) she met

[after a preposition]

the man (whom) you were afraid of

the actress (whom) I was thinking of

el hombre que estaba aquí ayer

el hombre a quien vi

las mujeres a quienes encontró

quien/quienes

el hombre de quien tenías miedo

la actriz en quien pensaba

Ø Although "whom" may be omitted in English, the Spanish equivalent cannot be.

he/she/those who

he/she who

He/she who wants to can go in.

el que/la que

El/la que quiera puede entrar.
[Note: Subjunctive is used if the reference is to an indefinite person or persons.]

those who

Those who have arrived early will receive a prize.

los que/las que

Los/las que han llegado temprano recibirán un premio.

whoever/whomever *pron*

Whoever he/she is

Whoever finds them can keep them.

Quienquiera que sea *[Note: subjunctive]*

Quienquiera que los encuentre puede quedarse con ellos.
[Note: subjunctive]

You can tell who(m)ever you like.

Whoever told you is lying.

Puedes decírtelo a cualquiera.

Quien/El que te lo dijo dice mentiras.

whole *adj & pron*

the whole world

Tell me the whole truth.

el mundo entero

Dime toda la verdad.

whose

I toured the whole of Caracas.	Recorrí todo Caracas.
They heard the whole thing.	Lo oyeron todo.
We bought the whole lot.	Compramos todo.

Ø **todo el mundo** means "everybody."

whose   *inter adj & pron*

Whose ... ?	¿De quién/quiénes... ?
Whose is this knife?	¿De quién es este cuchillo?
Whose money is this?	¿De quién es este dinero?

whose   *rel pron*

whose	cuyo(a)/cuyos(as)
the man whose son is in prison	el hombre cuyo hijo está en la cárcel
the man whose wife is ill	el hombre cuya esposa está enferma
the tourists whose cases were lost	los turistas cuyas maletas se perdieron
the ladies whose husbands are away	las señoras cuyos esposos están fuera

why   *adv & conj*

Why did you do that?	¿Por qué lo hiciste?
I don't know why she left.	No sé por qué se marchó.
That's why I cannot pay you.	Por eso no puedo pagarte./Ésa es la razón por la que no puedo pagarte. [Note: not **por qué**]

wife   *n*

wife	la esposa/la mujer [Sp]

willing   *adj*

to be willing	querer/querer hacerlo/estar dispuesto(a)
Are they willing to help her?	¿Quieren ayudarla?/¿Están dispuestos(as) a ayudarla?
No, they're not willing.	No, no quieren.

window   *n*

a window	una ventana
a shop window	una vidriera [LA]/una luna [Per] /un escaparate [Sp]
[of a car]	una ventanilla

wish   *n & v*

a wish	un deseo
to make a wish	pensar un deseo
to wish sb a happy birthday/ a happy Christmas/a happy new year/a good journey	desear a alguien un feliz cumpleaños/ unas felices Pascuas/un feliz año nuevo/un buen viaje

to want

I wish to see the manager.	Deseo/Quiero ver al gerente.
I wish I were there.	Ojalá estuviera allí.
I wish you could come.	Ojalá pudieras venir. [Note: use of imperfect subjunctive after **ojalá**]

with   *prep*
in general   con

with me/you	conmigo/contigo
with him(self)/her(self)	consigo
*[see under **him** and **her**]*	
with you(rself)/you(rselves)	consigo
*[see under **you**]*	
[with "no"]	sin
with no difficulty	sin dificultad

other

the man with the beard	el hombre de la barba
You cannot enter the mosque with your shoes on.	No puedes entrar en la mezquita llevando puestos los zapatos.
with all speed	a toda prisa
with a single blow	de un solo golpe
to be covered with mud/snow	estar cubierto(a) de lodo/nieve
to be filled with water	estar lleno(a) de agua
to be in love with sb	estar enamorado(a) de alguien
to be pleased/satisfied with sth	estar contento(a)/satisfecho(a) de
It's pouring with rain.	Está lloviendo a cántaros.
to jump with joy	saltar de alegría
to tremble with fear	temblar de miedo
to be "with it"	estar al tanto/estar al día
to be "with it" *[clothes]*	estar de moda

within *prep*

within the city	dentro de la ciudad
within a radius of five miles	en un radio de ocho kilómetros
within 20 meters of the camp	a unos veinte metros del campamento
within a week	dentro de una semana/antes de terminar la semana

without *prep*

without	sin
without a car/any money	sin coche/dinero *[Note: no article]*
without any problems	sin problema

word *n*

[in general]	la palabra
word for word	palabra por palabra
words of a song	la letra
in other words	en otros términos/es decir
without a word	sin decir palabra
What is the word for ... in Spanish?	¿Cómo se dice... en castellano?

work *n*

[task to be done]	el trabajo
I have a lot of work to do.	Tengo mucho trabajo que hacer.
[employment, job]	el trabajo/el empleo/la ocupación
I don't like my work.	No me gusta mi trabajo.
to be at work	estar en la oficina/la fábrica/la tienda, etc.
to have work	tener trabajo/un empleo
to be out of work	estar desempleado(a)/estar parado(a)/no tener trabajo
a work permit	un permiso de trabajo
[art/literary/music]	una obra

work

the works of Cervantes	las obras de Cervantes
roadworks	las obras de carretera
[see also **job**]	

work v

people

	trabajar
My brother works nights.	Mi hermano trabaja de noche.
to work the land	cultivar la tierra

things

The elevator doesn't work.	El ascensor no funciona.

worker n

[general]

	un(a) trabajador(a)
He's a hard worker.	Es muy trabajador.
the workers [political]	los obreros
manual/blue-collar worker	un(a) obrero(a)
a skilled worker	un(a) obrero(a) cualificado(a)
clerical/white-collar/shop worker	un(a) empleado(a)

worn out adj

[things]	gastado(a)/estropeado(a)
His boots are worn out.	Sus botas están estropeadas.
[people]	agotado(a)/rendido(a)
I'm worn out.	Estoy rendido(a)./No puedo más.

worry v

to worry	preocuparse por/inquietarse por
Don't worry about that!	¡No te preocupes por eso!
She is very worried about her exams.	Está muy preocupada por sus exámenes.
This problem is worrying me.	Este problema me inquieta.

worse/worst adj

worse	peor
the worst	el/la peor
The red one is worse than the white.	El rojo es peor que el blanco.
The green is the worst.	El verde es el peor.
This is the worst film I've seen.	Ésta es la peor película que haya visto. [Note: subjunctive]
the worst thing is	lo peor es

worse/worst adv

I play worse than my sister.	Juego peor que mi hermana.
My brother plays the worst.	Mi hermano juega peor./Es mi hermano que juega peor.
How do you feel now? – Worse.	¿Cómo te sientes ahora? – Peor.

worth adj

to be worth	valer
How much is it worth?	¿Cuánto vale?
It isn't worth anything.	No vale nada.
Is it worth studying Latin?	¿Vale la pena estudiar el latín?
It isn't worth it/the trouble.	No vale la pena.

would v

conditional

[conditional and imperfect subjunctive tenses]

My father said he would do it.	Mi padre dijo que lo haría.

I would like to go to the
   Philippines.

Querría/Quisiera ir a las
   Filipinas. *[Note: The imperfect
   subjunctive can be used instead of the
   conditional tense; this is especially the case
   with* **querer**.*]*

I would do it if I could.

Lo haría si pudiera. *[Note: Imperfect
   subjunctive is used after* **si** *in unfulfilled
   conditions.]*

I would have done it if I could.

Lo habría hecho si hubiera podido.

habitual action in the past
[imperfect tense]
When I was in New York I would
   go to the theater every week.

Cuando estaba en Nueva York iba
   al teatro todas las semanas.

polite requests
I would like to reserve a
   table, please.
I would like a coffee, please.

Quisiera reservar una mesa, por
   favor.
Me gustaría tomar un café, por favor.

wrong   *adj & adv*
morally wrong
It's wrong to kill.
He was wrong to do that.
[unfair]

malo(a)
Matar es un crimen.
Hizo mal en hacer eso.
injusto(a)

incorrect or mistaken
to be wrong

equivocarse/estar equivocado(a)/
   no tener razón

You're wrong. *[making a mistake]*
You're wrong. *[made a mistake]*

Te equivocas.
Te has equivocado./Estás
   equivocado(a).

to get sth wrong
I took the wrong way.
She went to the wrong office.
You're doing it wrong.
The answer is wrong.

equivocarse de algo
Me equivoqué de camino.
Se equivocó de oficina.
No se hace así.
La respuesta es incorrecta/inexacta.

trouble
Is something wrong?
What's wrong with you?
to be wrong *[machinery]*
Something's wrong with my
   watch.
to go wrong *[machinery]*
It's been going wrong for days.

¿Pasa algo?
¿Qué te pasa?
no andar bien
Mi reloj no anda bien.

andar fallando
Hace unos días que anda fallando.

X

x-ray *n*

X-rays   los rayos X
an X-ray   una radiografía
to X-ray   radiografiar

Y

year *n*

a year	un año
twice a year	dos veces al año
last year	el año pasado
next year [in present time]	el año que viene
next year [in past time]	el año siguiente
He's five years old.	Tiene cinco años.
for (many) years	durante (muchos) años
Happy New Year!	¡Feliz Año Nuevo!
New Year's Day	el día del Año Nuevo
New Year's Eve	la noche vieja
the fiscal/school year	el año económico/escolar

yellow *adj*

[color]	amarillo(a)
[coward]	(un) cobarde

yet *adv & conj*

time

	todavía/aún
not yet	todavía no
It hasn't started yet.	Todavía no ha comenzado.
yet again	otra vez más

however

	sin embargo
He was tired, yet he couldn't sleep.	Estaba cansado; sin embargo no podía dormir.

you *pron*

subject

[familiar singular]	tú
	vos [mainly Argentina & Uruguay]
[familiar plural]	vosotros/vosotras [Spain only]
	ustedes (Uds.)
[formal singular]	usted (Ud.)
[formal plural]	ustedes (Uds.)
	[Note: like the other subject pronouns, all the above are usually omitted; they are used for emphasis and clarification.]
Is that you?	¿Eres tú?/¿Sos vos?/¿Es usted?/ ¿Son ustedes?/¿Sois vosotros(as)?

object

[familiar singular]	te [direct & indirect; also used in Argentina, Uruguay and Costa Rica for people addressed as *vos*.]
[familiar plural]	os [Spain only]
	los/las [direct] les [indirect]
[formal singular]	lo/la [direct]
	le [indirect]

your

[formal plural]	los/las [direct]
	les [indirect]
I can't hear you.	No te/lo/la/los/las/os oigo.

disjunctive

[familiar singular]	ti
	vos [mainly Argentina & Uruguay]
[familiar plural]	vosotros/vosotras [Spain only]
	ustedes (Uds.)
[formal singular]	usted (Ud.)
[formal plural]	ustedes (Uds.)
This is for you.	Esto es para ti/vos/usted/ustedes /vosotros(as).

reflexive

[familiar singular]	te
	vos [mainly Argentina & Uruguay]
[familiar plural]	os [Spain only]
	se
[formal singular & plural]	se
At what time do you get up?	¿A qué hora te levantas/se levanta(n)/os levantáis?

your adj

[familiar singular]	tu/tus [also used when addressing people with **vos**.]
[familiar plural]	vuestro/s, vuestra/s [Spain only]
	su/sus
[formal singular & plural]	su/sus
your house	tu/su/vuestra casa
your parents	tus/sus/vuestros padres

yours pron

[familiar singular]	el tuyo/la tuya
	los tuyos/las tuyas
[familiar plural]	el vuestro/la vuestra
	los vuestros/las vuestras [Spain only]
	el suyo/la suya
	los suyos/las suyas
[formal singular & plural]	el suyo/la suya
	los suyos/las suyas
Is that his luggage? – it's yours.	No, ¿Es ése su equipaje? – No, es tuyo/suyo/vuestro. [Note: The definite article is omitted after the verb **ser**.]
I can't find my keys. Will you lend me yours?	No encuentro mis llaves. ¿Quieres prestarme las tuyas?/¿Quiere(n) prestarme las suyas?

Ø As **suyo/a/os/as** could also mean "his," "hers," or "theirs," you can replace them with **de usted/de ustedes** if there is any chance of confusion: e.g., "It's yours". **Es de usted/de ustedes**.

yours sincerely
in a business letter

Le saluda atentamente/Atentamente /Su seguro servidor

246

in a personal letter	Cordialmente/Con un cordial saludo/Un abrazo

youth   *n*
[stage of one's life]   la juventud
[young person]   el/la joven
youth hostel   un albergue de juventud

yucky   *adj*
yucky   asqueroso(a)

Z

zip *n*
zip code

el código postal

zipper *n*
a zipper

un cierre/una cremallera

zoom *n & v*
[noise]
[lens]
to zoom by

un zumbido
un objetivo zoom
pasar volando

NTC SPANISH TEXTS AND MATERIALS

Computer Software
Basic Vocabulary Builder on Computer
Amigo: Vocabulary Software

**Videocassette, Activity Book,
and Instructor's Manual**
VideoPasaporte Español

Graded Readers
Diálogos simpáticos
Cuentitos simpáticos
Cuentos simpáticos
Beginner's Spanish Reader
Easy Spanish Reader

Workbooks
Así escribimos
Ya escribimos
¡A escribir!
Composiciones ilustradas
Spanish Verb Drills

Exploratory Language Books
Spanish for Beginners
Let's Learn Spanish Picture Dictionary
Spanish Picture Dictionary
Getting Started in Spanish
Just Enough Spanish

Conversation Books
¡Empecemos a charlar!
Basic Spanish Conversation
Everyday Conversations in Spanish

Manual and Audiocassette
How to Pronounce Spanish Correctly

**Text and Audiocassette Learning
Packages**
Just Listen 'n Learn Spanish
Just Listen 'n Learn Spanish Plus
Practice and Improve Your Spanish
Practice and Improve Your Spanish
Plus

High-Interest Readers
Sr. Pepino Series
La momia desaparece
La casa embrujada
El secuestro

Journeys to Adventure Series
Un verano misterioso
La herencia
El ojo de agua
El enredo
El jaguar curioso

Humor in Spanish and English
Spanish à la Cartoon

Puzzle and Word Game Books
Easy Spanish Crossword Puzzles
Easy Spanish Word Games & Puzzles
Easy Spanish Vocabulary Puzzles

Transparencies
Everyday Situations in Spanish

Black-line Masters
Spanish Verbs and Vocabulary Bingo Games
Spanish Crossword Puzzles
Spanish Culture Puzzles
Spanish Word Games
Spanish Vocabulary Puzzles

Handbooks and Reference Books
Complete Handbook of Spanish Verbs
Spanish Verbs and Essentials of Grammar
Nice 'n Easy Spanish Grammar
Tratado de ortografía razonada
Redacte mejor comercialmente
Guide to Correspondence in Spanish
Guide to Spanish Idioms

Dictionaries
Vox Modern Spanish and English Dictionary
Vox New College Spanish and English Dictionary
Vox Compact Spanish and English Dictionary
Vox Everyday Spanish and English Dictionary
Vox Traveler's Spanish and English Dictionary
Vox Super-Mini Spanish and English Dictionary
Cervantes-Walls Spanish and English Dictionary

For further information or a current catalog, write:
National Textbook Company
a division of *NTC Publishing Group*
4255 West Touhy Avenue
Lincolnwood, Illinois 60646-1975 U.S.A.